KIMONO

KIMONO

A MODERN HISTORY

TERRY

SATSUKI

MILHAUPT

REAKTION BOOKS

To Chie, Tsuru, Grace, Joyce and Karen

Published by Reaktion Books Ltd
Unit 32, Waterside
44–48 Wharf Road
London N1 7UX, UK
www.reaktionbooks.co.uk

First published 2014, reprinted 2016
Copyright © Terry Satsuki Milhaupt 2014

The publishers would like to thank The Great Britain Sasakawa Foundation
for its support in the publication of this work

Printed and bound in China

A catalogue record for this book is available from the British Library

ISBN 978 1 78023 278 2

CONTENTS

INTRODUCTION

Recognizable by its T-shaped outline, fluttering sleeves and flowing vertical panels draped from the wearer's shoulders, the kimono embodies Japan, real and romanticized, familiar and foreign. In the popular imagination, the kimono often represents an unchanging, tradition-oriented, eternal Japan. But how and when did the identification of the kimono as Japan's national costume occur? Why is the kimono more closely associated with the female than the male body? What processes led to the transformation of the kimono from an everyday garment to an icon of Japan?

A review of the clothing worn by models on the covers of 'Ladies' Companion' (*Fujin no Tomo*), one of Japan's leading twentieth-century women's magazines, provides a visual barometer of shifting post-Second World War attitudes towards the kimono. Of the women featured on the covers from 1949 to 1956, more are shown wearing Western-style clothing than Japanese. From 1957 to 1962, the models themselves appear more cosmopolitan, their hair colour becoming lighter and lighter until it is rendered almost blonde and their facial characteristics more closely resembling Caucasian rather than Asian features. From 1967 to 1992, only one or two covers per year feature a woman wearing a kimono. However, without exception, the first issue of every year depicts a woman wearing a formal kimono ensemble. Thus, from the late 1960s until the early 1990s, the kimono was primarily promoted as a costume suitable for special occasions such as New Year's celebrations or Adult Day ceremonies held in January, linking the kimono more closely with 'tradition' rather than 'fashion'.[1]

Visual artefacts such as the covers of 'Ladies' Companion' reveal how the T-shaped silk kimono came to take on a symbolic meaning in the second half of the twentieth century. Valued as a ceremonial garment and national costume, it continues to be worn in its traditional form for special occasions. However, since the beginning of the twenty-first century, women from a new generation have started to be drawn to it for less formal, more fashion-oriented reasons. To this younger generation of women, the clothing that their grandmothers and even their mothers might refer to as *yōfuku*, or

'Western-style' clothing, is as familiar as it is to their American and European contemporaries. To a select group within this younger generation, the kimono is an appealing alternative to the clothing they grew up with. In contrast to their mothers and grandmothers, who favoured newly manufactured, classic kimono fashions, some of today's younger generation prefer vintage, second-hand kimonos. Aware of the generational differences among kimono consumers, magazine publishers now cater to particular market segments. In 2003, 50 years after the publisher Fujin Gahō released the first issue of 'Beautiful Kimono' (*Utsukushii Kimono*), a new magazine called 'Kimono Princess' (*Kimono Hime*) hit the news-stands. Whereas 'Beautiful Kimono' had emphasized classical and high-end kimonos worn primarily by women in their forties, fifties and sixties, the new publication focused on a younger market (illus. 1, 2). The title *Kimono Hime*, written with the word 'kimono' in romanized letters (which are usually reserved for foreign words), followed by the Chinese character for 'princess' (*hime*) targeted the newly emerging, kimono-buying women in their twenties and thirties. *Kimono Hime* emphasized a new 'kimono look' that often featured the brightly coloured, bold patterns popular in the 1920s and '30s, styled in edgy, unconventional combinations.

Reflecting contemporary trends, the kimonos featured on the pages of *Kimono Hime* are not exclusively promoted as ceremonial wear, but rather are

1 Cover of *Utsukushii Kimono* (Spring 2003), published by Hachette Fujin Gahō.

2 Cover of *Kimono Hime* (April 2003), published by Shotensha.

showcased as a variant form of the subculture phenomenon generally referred to as *kawaii* or 'cute'. The *kawaii* style originated in the mid-1970s among young women. Many contemporary publications targeting this younger generation of kimono wearers portray this 'cute' style with comic-like illustrations and staged scenes incorporating fanciful backdrops. The magazine *Kimono Hime* subscribes to this 'playful attitude' (*asobi gokoro*), showcasing kimono and obi combinations that are accessorized with matching handbags and jewellery, which asserts a less ceremonial, more light-hearted way of wearing kimonos. The magazine, capturing both local and global elements of the kimono in order to appeal to young people around the world, is only one of many manifestations of the reinvention of the kimono 'tradition' within Japan today.

In recent years, enthusiasm for conventional and unconventional modes of kimono dress has spread via social networks and other electronic media to like-minded women around the world. Regardless of nationality, these young women view the kimono as simply another form of dress. They freely reimagine the kimono's use, not unlike their grandmothers' adaptations of kimonos into tea or dressing gowns a century earlier. The profusion of media images on the Internet enables kimono enthusiasts to transcend geographical and social borders to create new styles and settings for kimono wearers around the world.

Wearing kimonos has become another way for younger generations to form their own fashion 'tribes' and identify with a particular social group. These non-traditional kimono wearers have codified their styles in order to conform to recognizable group identities. In Japan, the relationship between social identity and dress dates back to the sumptuary edicts of the Edo period (1600–1868). To this day, social groups in Japan devise strict rules mandating certain 'looks' that indicate, through clothing choices, one's affiliation with the group. Even rebel subculture groups, more commonly referred to as 'tribes' or *zoku*, dress in styles such as Gothic Lolita that employ prescribed rules for each type of 'look'.[2]

Whether young or old, rural or urban, wealthy or middle class, kimono wearers convey multiple messages to viewers. Similar to past hierarchies of membership based on regulated codes of dress, nuanced rules of dress are once again in place. But today, those rules are recognizable only to informed members who participate in the group's shared code of conduct. Those outside the 'tribe' only see that the wearer is engaging in an unconventional form of 'traditional' dress.

Publications on how to wear kimonos remain a staple of many Japanese bookstores. The differentiated target audiences of these publications even reflect the classical kimono's increasing multiplicity of symbolic meanings.

For example, in 2006, Fujin Gahō, the publisher
of 'Beautiful Kimono', released a special issue
entitled 'The Fundamentals of Kimono' (*Kimono
no kihon*).[3] It includes a brief history of the
kimono; descriptions of the various types of
kimono for women, men and children; the proper
season or occasion for wearing specific types; a
section on how to coordinate the ensemble of
kimono, obi and other accoutrements; and a
section on how to care for kimonos. Similarly, the
May 2009 cover of the magazine *An An* (illus. 3),
which targets the general populace of young
Japanese women rather than the more specific
group of young women interested in vintage
kimonos, features a young model posed in a
conventional, ceremonial long-sleeved kimono.
The issue emphasizes the 'etiquette appropriate
for a young Japanese woman' (*Nihon joshi
no tashinami*) and includes an article titled
'Rediscovering Japan's Traditional Culture'.

3 Cover of *An An* (May
2009).

Another type of kimono book serves to encourage Japanese women,
who are often viewed as the bearers of 'tradition', to consider the kimono as
a clothing item for everyday wear rather than limiting its use to ceremonial
occasions. In 2005, Domyō Mihoko, chief curator of the Bunka Gakuen
Fashion Museum and a professor at Bunka Joshi Daigaku, authored a book
entitled 'The Beauty of the Kimono Quickly Understood: From Hairdressing
to Footwear' (*Sugu wakaru kimono no bi: kamikazari kara hakimono made*).[4]
The same year, the Tokyo-based Parisian designer Maïa Maniglier published
a book encouraging women (presumably Japanese women since the book was
written in Japanese) to enjoy the experience of wearing kimonos – a pleasure
the author had recently discovered.[5] The essayist and illustrator Hirano Eriko
published 'Let's Wear Kimono!' (*Kimono, Kiyō, yo!*) in 2008.[6] Written in a
simple, engaging style coupled with her own illustrations, this small-format
paperback offered an appealing entry into a world some Japanese view as
foreign. Also in 2008, the publisher of *Momi*, playfully written with the
Chinese characters for 'safflower' and 'silk', began to issue a series of small-
format magazines targeting women in their twenties and thirties. An article
in the second issue of *Momi* instructed readers on how to coordinate kimonos
and accessories, and how to neatly pack them into a small suitcase for a one-
week trip to the French fashion capital, Paris.[7] One cannot help but wonder if
the would-be traveller in the article is modelled, albeit in contemporary guise,

on the iconic figure of Uno Chiyo who, as described in chapter Five, designed kimonos suited for the streets of Paris. Pop culture figures such as the actress and singer Aida Shōko use their celebrity status to promote the kimono to a Japanese audience.[8] Even *manga* (Japanese-style comics) and *anime* (animation) artists such as the CLAMP illustrator Mokona have got in on the act. Her book *CLAMP Mokona's Okimono Kimono* includes some of her original kimono designs, her kimono ensembles styled for specific outings, and her interview about kimonos with pop star Ami Onuki of Puffy AmiYumi. Initially released in Japanese in 2007, the book was translated into English in 2010 in order to reach a global audience.[9]

As this brief review of recent publications reveals, the design, function and meaning of this garment have shifted dramatically in the last 50 years.

The mutability of the kimono is part of a much longer pattern that began at the end of the seventeenth century and accelerated in the second half of the nineteenth century. The kimono has long served as a tableau on which to inscribe, describe and absorb the effects of modernization, a record of Japan's efforts to shape its national identity on the world stage.

The history of the kimono in the period covered by this book – roughly from 1850 to the present day – is relatively under-researched, occupying an expansive, uncharted territory. Major gaps in our knowledge exist between the end of the Edo period, when the kimono was an everyday garment worn by many in Japan, to today, when it is primarily reserved for extraordinary occasions. Moreover, although canonical works have been identified and comprehensive studies have been published on clothing and the textile history of the pre-modern Momoyama (1573–1600) and Edo eras, certain subjects – the significance of pattern design books, for example – have only garnered scholarly attention in the last decade. Yet these pattern books document the existence of an organized and interdependent organization of clothing production in Japan from as early as the seventeenth century that provided the underpinnings of what I will refer to as the modern kimono fashion system (more on this below). In addition, they chronicle the motifs, dye colours and design compositions popular during each particular year. For example, within the pages of the earliest published pattern book is a design with six large cricket cages covering the back of a garment (illus. 5). When compared with a turn-of-the-century kimono, with its more naturalistic rendering of crickets amidst grasses and cages concentrated around the lower hem and sleeve areas, there is no denying that kimono fashions shifted to match the times (illus. 4). Kimono pattern books of the later Meiji (1868–1912), Taishō (1912–26) and Shōwa (1926–89) eras, made of thick, heavy paper lavishly embossed and embellished

5 Page with design of cricket cages, from *On-Hiinagata* ('Kosode Pattern Book', 1667), vol. 1, woodblock-printed book, ink on paper.

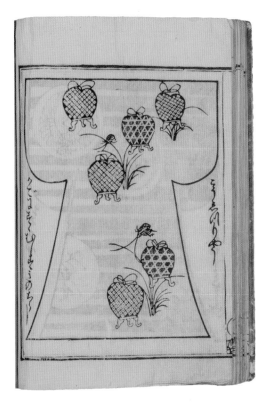

4 Woman's summer kimono (*hitoe*) with design of crickets and cricket cages, late 19th–early 20th century, resist-dyeing, hand painting and silk embroidery on gauze silk ground.

with gold and silver paint, provide datable benchmarks for identifiable kimono design trends. The composition, motif and palette of each design illustrated in these books can, in turn, be compared with extant kimonos, serving as a basis to establish a general chronology of styles (illus. 6, 7).[10]

Extant kimonos provide another source for exploring the kimono's material history – and assessing how and why the kimono came to be a cultural icon. These garments are snapshots of a specific time and place – a frozen moment of history visible in the material from which they are woven and decorated, the designs that adorn them, the form in which they are constructed and their mode of presentation. Imagine examining an individual kimono through an optical device that permits viewing on micro- and macroscopic scales. By zooming in, the details of the kimono's material and weave structure are apparent, allowing the viewer to make conjectures about the garment's production and the techniques and tools employed by the people involved in its making. Moving from this central focus outward to gain a slightly broader perspective, sellers of kimonos – wholesalers, department stores and, later, antique and second-hand market dealers – come into focus. Zooming out even further, the primary consumer and, later, private collectors and museum curators, appear. Considered in this way, the borders between an object, its maker, its marketer and ultimately its consumer are relational and reflexive.

6 Page from 'Collection of Shōun's Patterns' (*Shōun moyō shū*), a book of modern kimono designs (1901), polychrome woodblock-printed book, embossing, ink, colour and metallic paint on paper.

7 Woman's long-sleeved kimono (*furisode*) with design of hydrangeas and cherry blossoms, late 19th–early 20th century, resist-dyeing and hand painting on satin silk ground.

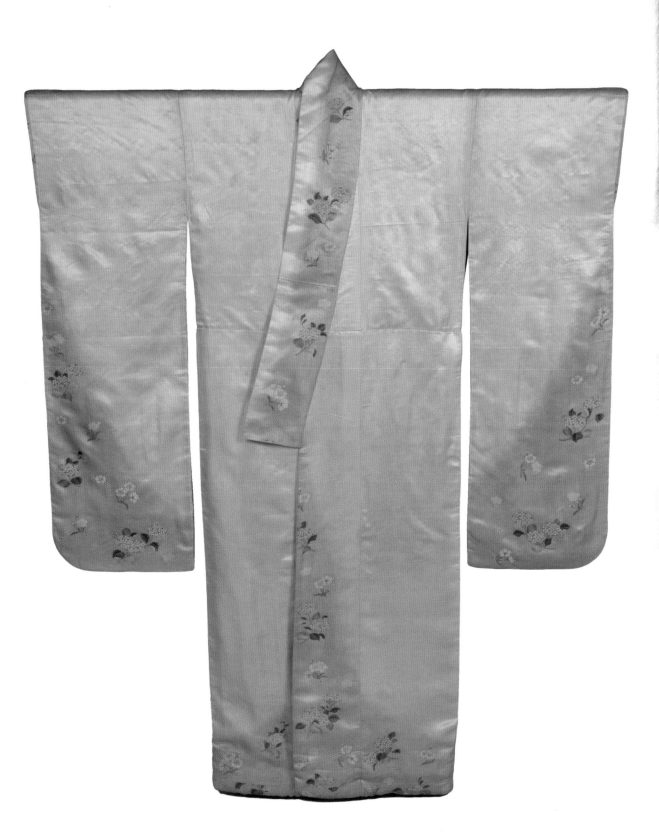

When subjected to an individual viewer's gaze, the interpretation of a kimono's values – historical, aesthetic, economic, social, cultural, symbolic – and meanings, at the time of its initial production and through its use and re-use, are filtered through that specific viewer's lens. Collectively, these individualized ways of consuming and viewing kimonos become suggestive clues that can be gathered and recounted in more general patterns. This perspective offers a more comprehensive understanding of who controls, at various moments in time, the making, marketing and wearing of kimonos, and concurrently, whose identities get displayed on whose bodies. As will become apparent when viewed historically, after the 1870s the story of the kimono is focused on kimono fashions for women.

Recounting the story of an individual kimono's initial production, sale, ownership, use and later adaptations reveals much about Japan's history. Objects of known provenance and date, such as the wedding robe produced for the bride who married into the prominent Itō family in 1897, offer glimpses into the past (illus. 8). For the occasion, this wealthy merchant family selected a figured silk patterned with tortoiseshell designs, sumptuously decorated with imperial carriage wheels amidst cherry blossoms floating on waves, embroidered with gold and silver threads. Carefully preserved in the Marubeni Collection for over 100 years and displayed today as an object of art, this wedding robe is one landmark in the timeline of kimono design history.

Images of people wearing kimonos convey the context for understanding who wore them, for which occasions and how they were worn. Prints, paintings and pattern books – and later, magazine ads, posters and photographs – pictorialize shifts in the relationship between the kimono and the body and illustrate how the widening obi sash altered the distribution of designs on the kimono.

Measurements of extant Momoyama-era garments reveal that the body panels were approximately twice the width of the sleeve panels (illus. 9, 10). Given the extra girth, the garment hung more loosely around the body, and it was held in place with a narrow sash or cord wrapped around the hip area. Paintings of this period depict figures that appear fleshier than those of the following Edo era. While this may be due to the style of a particular artist or his school, it might also result from the illusion created by the style of wearing the actual garment loosely tied around the body.

By the mid-seventeenth century, the width of the body panel equals that of the sleeve panel on extant garments. In essence, the circumference of the body section of the garment became narrower than on its Momoyama-era counterpart, with the obi still tied low, around the hips. The obi remained relatively narrow, allowing for relatively uninterrupted decoration on garments from the mid- to late seventeenth century. Often referred to as the Kanbun-style

8 Woman's wedding over-robe (*uchikake*) with design of cartwheels floating amid a stream of cherry blossoms, 1897, resist-dyeing with gold and silver-leaf painting and embroidery on patterned silk.

and named for the Kanbun era (1661–73) during which it flourished, designs of this time boldly sweep across the upper back and shoulder area, and down towards the hem.

By the mid-eighteenth century, the obi had widened considerably, and was tied in elaborate configurations popularized by Kabuki actors and courtesans. This wider obi essentially bifurcated the garment into upper and lower design spaces. Kimono designers responded by concentrating their efforts on patterns that allowed for a visual disruption around the wearer's mid-section and wasted little effort on areas that would be covered by the elaborately tied, wider obi.

In the late eighteenth and early nineteenth centuries, the obi covered much of a woman's torso. Again, kimono designers responded by balancing

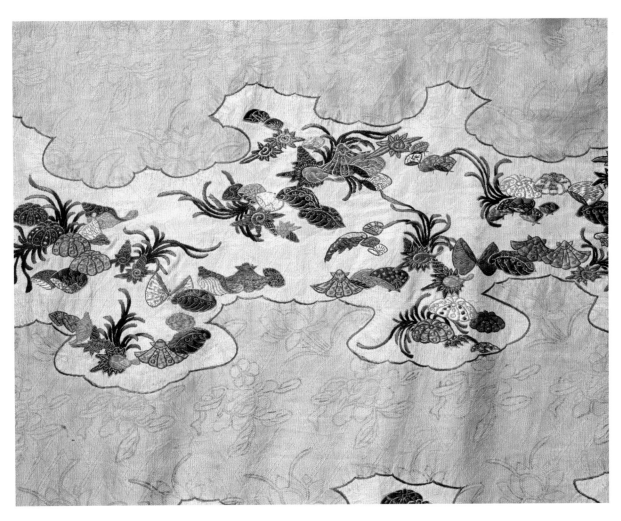

9, 10 Garment with small-sleeve openings (*kosode*) with design of shells and sea grasses, and detail, early 17th century, silk embroidery and gold leaf imprinting patterned with warp floats on plain-weave silk ground.

the visual emphasis on the obi with designs concentrated around the lower half of the kimono, with most pattern elements eventually pooling around the hem. Visual imagery reminds us of the integral relationship between the kimono and the obi, and how the way the garment was wrapped and tied around the body contributed to ideals about fashionable silhouettes, ranging from stout to svelte at different historical moments.

An actual kimono, and the constellation of images and texts used to interpret a particular kimono's meaning, remains relatively unchanged. What changes is the viewer's frame of reference, as over time new material comes to light, or as perspectives shift. Ultimately these refracted impressions can never be entirely comprehensive or definitive. But when integrated, they do present a montage of history susceptible to interpretation, permitting the extrapolation of trends over time and across geographical borders. Based on an analysis of select objects, images and records – both historical and contemporary – this book examines the kimono in both microscopic and macroscopic perspectives, revealing patterns in the evolution of the modern kimono.

This is a book about the modern kimono. As a garment, the kimono is, of course, an element of fashion. Yet the terms 'modern', 'kimono' and 'fashion' present a conundrum. Each of these terms is highly contested, their meanings hotly debated among specialists. But in more general usage – as in the phrase 'modern kimono fashion system' which will be used to describe important relationships among designers, makers and promoters of kimonos – these terms demarcate a period of time when a particular type of garment (the kimono) operated within a larger sociological system (fashion).[11]

In this book 'modern' refers to the period from 1850, just before the American fleet under the command of Commodore Perry arrived in Japan to force open its ports to expanded international trade, to the present day.[12] During this period, Japan evolved from a relatively secluded confederation of domains administered by the Tokugawa military government (shogunate) into a national polity under a centralized government, extensively engaged in international commerce and geopolitics. Massive reformation of the government, the rise of empire, and military defeat were experienced in turn. These monumental shifts in political ideology and global stature infiltrated every aspect of Japanese life, including daily decisions such as what to wear. As the cultural critic and art historian Okakura Kakuzō (also known as Tenshin, 1862–1913) observed in his book *The Ideals of the East* (1904), changes in Japan's national identity also influenced the attire of its people:

> The advent of the American Commodore Perry finally opened the flood-gates of Western knowledge, which burst over the country so as almost to sweep away the landmarks of its history. At this moment Japan, in the re-awakened consciousness of her new national life, was eager to clothe herself in new garb, discarding the raiment of her ancient past.[13]

One 'raiment of her ancient past' that survived the rush to 'clothe herself in new garb' was the kimono. Increasingly, however, the kimono came to be associated with women's bodies, not men's, with attendant changes in its symbolism.

In 1868, the Tokugawa military regime collapsed and the professional bureaucrats of the new Meiji government called for a more 'civilized and enlightened' society. In their attempt to place Japan on equal footing with

Western nations, officials began to appear in what was then termed 'Western-style clothing' or *yōfuku*, as distinguished from *wafuku*, or Japanese-style clothing (illus. 11). The Meiji emperor first appeared in public in a Western-style uniform in 1872, only four years after the official shift to a centralized government with the emperor as its titular head (illus. 12). Around this time, the kimono became less recognizable as a distinguishing mark of social status or occupation, and was increasingly identified as Japan's national dress. Japanese people, who until this time identified themselves principally with a particular socio-economic stratum (aristocrat, samurai, farmer, artisan or merchant), increasingly saw themselves as members of a larger social group with an emergent national identity, rather than one based on social status and feudal domain.

On 17 January 1887, an imperial proclamation encouraged women of Japan to adopt Western modes of dress as the empress herself had done the previous year.[14] Despite the opportunity for women to jettison the kimono, neither women nor men did so altogether. In public, and in official appearances, men donned Western-style suits and uniforms. In the privacy of their homes and for informal occasions, however, the kimono remained the garment of choice. The velocity of change witnessed in men's clothing habits was quite palpable, as evidenced in woodblock prints from that era of men predominantly wearing Western-style clothing. Women, however, were slower to adopt the bustles and corsets popular in Europe and America. The kimono retained its currency among Japanese women, albeit with significant changes in its attendant and intended meanings, as will be explored below.

Current interpretations of the word 'kimono', now part of the international lexicon and defined in the *Oxford English Dictionary* as a 'long, loose Japanese robe worn with a sash', or 'similar dressing gown', were shaped during the modern era beginning in the Meiji period. The term 'kimono', an abbreviation of *kirumono* (literally 'thing to wear') derives its current definition from this time. For centuries, a variant of the T-shaped kimono was commonly worn in Japan, but it was referred to as a *kosode,* a garment with small-sleeve openings.[15] Prior to the increasing awareness of Western-style clothing in Japan from the 1850s onwards, most Japanese referred to individual garments by specific terms, as discussed in chapter One.

These garments were cut from a single roll of cloth, commonly referred to as a *tan*, which measures approximately 34–40 cm in width and 11–12 m in length. Loom widths varied slightly over time, as did the cutting layout, which is based on simple, straight-edged construction techniques, and which minimizes the waste of fabric. Generally, the roll of cloth was cut into seven pieces – two body panels, two sleeve panels, two front overlaps and a collar –

11 Utagawa Hiroshige III, 'Cherry Blossom Viewing in Ueno Park' (from the 'Famous Places of Tokyo' series), 1881, triptych of polychrome woodblock prints, ink and colour on paper.

12 Utagawa Kuniyasu, 'Mirror of High Officials of the Empire' (*Kokoku kōkan kagami*), 1887, triptych of polychrome woodblock prints, ink and colour on paper.

and their straight edges were sewn together by hand to form the garment. Variations in the construction of the garment's details, for example the shape of the sleeve or the way the sleeve was attached to the body panel, indicated if it was made for a man or a woman. Status was indicated by the materials used to weave the fabric, whether silk, ramie, hemp or cotton, or by the labour-intensity of its decorative patterning. Commoners often wove and decorated their own cloth, sewed their own kimonos, unstitched them for laundering and re-sewed them for further use. When parts of an adult kimono became worn, the garment could be unstitched and re-sized for a child, or the fabric re-used to make other household items. The more lavish kimonos, like the ones illustrated in this chapter, were created by a group of loosely affiliated artisans working under the direction of a producer. The client would select the roll of cloth, often white silk that was available in various grades and could be a plain, patterned or textured fabric. In consultation with the producer, the client would then select the design and the preferred colours, using a kimono pattern book as a guide. The producer would take the roll of silk to the workshops of the various artisans whose skills were required for the multiple stages in the production process – pattern designer, dyer, embroiderer, seamstress – and deliver the finished garment to the client.

Each garment type bore its own name, depending on its sleeve length, function and the materials selected for its design. Today, most of these garments are subsumed under the single term 'kimono'. In response to the influx of Western-style clothing beginning in the mid-nineteenth century, the Japanese became aware of their distinctive mode of dress. It was from this time that the distinct categories of Western-style clothing (*yōfuku*) and Japanese-style clothing (*wafuku*) gained prominence. Within the *wafuku* category, the term 'kimono' gained currency, particularly outside Japan. In the Japanese lexicon, the word *kimono* continues to circulate, even today, in variant writing styles with inherited connotations: in *kanji* (Chinese characters), *hiragana* (the phonetic syllabary usually reserved for Japanese words), *katakana* (generally the phonetic syllabary used for words of foreign origin) and in its romanized form. Extant kimonos, as well as the shifting meanings of the word itself, chronicle cultural developments, reflect shifts in aesthetic tastes and denote social identities. As such, the kimono and its meaning have changed with the times – it is anything but 'traditional'.[16]

This brings us to the term 'fashion'. As with most words, the term 'fashion' is historically and contextually determined.[17] Fashion is often defined and described in relation to European clothing, while Japanese-style clothing – and the kimono in particular – stands apart from this limited category.[18]

Recent scholarship on fashion, however, questions the exclusivity of this mode of thinking and calls for an expanded definition of fashion that 'must encompass the basic process of style change, without the requirement that it be the continuous process evident in recent Western industrial societies'.[19] In his discussion of fashion in the Western context, the philosopher Lars Svendsen notes that 'fashion in its modern sense – with quick changes and a constant challenge to the individual to keep abreast of the age – did not become a real force until the eighteenth century'.[20] Fashion is often defined as a phenomenon that targets change for the sake of change.[21] The *Oxford English Dictionary* defines fashion as a 'current popular custom or style, esp. in dress', and secondarily as a 'manner or style of doing something'. Clearly, the terms 'fashion' and 'clothing' are not interchangeable. Fashion is intangible; clothing is tangible.[22] But, as the OED's definition implies, the two are closely associated.

In Japan, the term *ryūkō*, comprising the characters for 'to flow' and 'to conduct oneself or to proceed' has been used to express the concept of 'styles' or 'trends'. Other Japanese terms for similar concepts, such as *imamekashii* or 'up-to-date' and *tōfū* or 'current style', had been in use for centuries before the introduction of the foreign word *fuasshon* into Japan. The term *fuasshon*, the Japanese pronunciation of the English term 'fashion', and written in *katakana* characters, has also come into common usage to refer to changes in styles. As with the kimono garment itself, the many terms for fashion connote nuanced meanings that are often misinterpreted in cultural translations.

As fashion statements, modern kimono designers incorporated novel materials, techniques, motifs and compositions into their repertoire in order to create the most up-to-the-minute designs. For example, yachts and European-style architecture, surprising to the Japanese eye in the first half of the twentieth century, appeared on kimonos (illus. 13). The rendering of the landscape and the shading effects on this particular kimono, reminiscent of Western-style oil painting techniques, were adapted to Japanese dyeing techniques. It would be simplistic to argue that Japan was 'borrowing' these motifs or painting techniques from the West in their efforts to impart a 'modern' feel to the kimono.[23] Rather than copying or imitating the West – which actually adopted the kimono format from Japan – kimono designers in Japan sought to employ the latest materials and techniques to create new designs that were distinctive to the Japanese context. Other examples that on the surface may appear 'traditional' to our twenty-first century eyes are innovative in more subtle ways. A kimono decorated with the conventional combination of plum, pine and bamboo motifs, commonly referred to as *shōchikubai*, might at first glance appear 'traditional' (illus. 14). Yet its playful expression of hand-painted pines, woven bamboo and embroidered and stylized plum blossoms, and its unusual composition that breaks the design space into a broad upper band of deep purple and a narrower band of lavender at the hem, would likely have surprised and delighted a Japanese customer. In other words, this kimono was likely considered new and up-to-date at the time of its production by anyone who recognized how the composition and techniques disguised and transformed conventional motifs.

Throughout history, changes in the kimono's design, use and meaning have reflected transformations in Japanese society, politics, economics and international status. Within Japan, the kimono evolved from an item of daily wear to become an iconic marker of Japaneseness. In Japan's early twentieth-century colonial territories, the kimono was worn both by the colonizer and the colonized, sending complex signals depending on whose body it adorned.[24] Exported to and embraced by consumers in Europe, Britain and America, the kimono functioned as costume as well as clothing. Drawing upon broader discussions of gender, cosmopolitanism, consumerism and fashion theory, the following chapters consider how one Asian nation embraced modernity on its own terms – how Japan manipulated the kimono in its quest to establish a recognizable national identity in an increasingly cosmopolitan world.

Situating the kimono within its early nexus of production, marketing and consumption, the first chapter, 'The Foundations of a Kimono Fashion Industry', discusses the fabrication of the kimono within a pre-modern integrated fashion system. This historical overview focuses on kimono pattern books, which have been published continuously since as early as 1666. These pattern books provide evidence of a sophisticated system of production, distribution and consumption of fashionable attire in Japan in the late seventeenth century, which forms the core of the modern kimono industry. The chapter examines how kimono makers, marketers, consumers and leaders of fashion collaborated in their efforts to perpetuate an 'economy of desire' and stimulate demand for fashionable clothing. For the Japanese, elements of changing fashions were manifest not in the silhouette of a garment (as in European, British and American fashion), but within the confines of the kimono's outline. Documents reveal how kimono producers of the Edo era constantly pressured weavers and dyers to develop new patterns, colours, decorative techniques and compositions to satisfy their fashion-hungry customers.

Chapter Two, 'Modernizing the Kimono', focuses on the selective incorporation of foreign materials and technology imported to Japan during the second half of the nineteenth century and their combined effect on kimono design trends. The chapter indicates that, rather than adopting or copying

Overleaf
13 Woman's long-sleeved kimono (*furisode*) with design of yachts in a landscape setting, 1920s–30s, paste-resist dyeing on silk crepe ground.

14 Woman's kimono with design of pines, plum and bamboo, second quarter of the 20th century, ink and gold, silk embroidery on figured silk ground.

imported tools and concepts whole cloth, as is commonly assumed, Japan's approach to modernizing the kimono industry was adaptive and innovative. This chapter also describes the increasing integration of Japan's domestic textile industry into world textile markets and surveys the shifting symbolic and economic values of silk, cotton and other types of fabrics utilized in kimono production.

The third chapter, 'Shopping for Kimonos, Shaping Identities', discusses the effects of the emergence of Japanese department stores in the first few decades of the twentieth century, new advertising techniques, the rise of a largely female consumer base and the wide distribution of magazines targeting a female readership through domestic marketing strategies and distribution channels. The politics of display, promotion of branded goods and changing aesthetics of taste all had an impact on consumers' demands for specific modes of dress that reflected distinct social identities.

Chapter Four, 'The Kimono Ideal Migrates West', chronicles the kimono's journey to Britain, Europe and America from the 1850s and through the first half of the twentieth century. This chapter describes how the kimono's appropriation by artists and designers active within and outside Japan has contributed to the construction of the 'kimono ideal'. To the British, Europeans and Americans, the kimono personified an exotic and often erotic Japan. Recognizing outsiders' interest in kimonos, the Japanese – from institutions to private individuals – manipulated and promoted the 'kimono ideal', modifying perceptions of this form of dress.

Chapter Five, 'Kimono Designers', examines how the role of kimono makers evolved from nameless artisans to designated Living National Treasures, and analyses how the shifting status of the maker paralleled the kimono's transformation from an item of everyday clothing to an exclusively ceremonial garment. The broad chronological sweep of this chapter, from the eighteenth century to the period after the Second World War, provides the perspective needed to understand this transformation.

The final chapter, 'Everyday and Extraordinary, Then and Now', offers reflections on how the kimono's use and meaning in contemporary society relates to its past. Recent Japanese publications and observers of street fashion suggest that Japan experienced a 'kimono boom' in the decades around the turn of the twenty-first century. Nostalgia for the Taishō era appeared in the form of vintage kimonos paired with jeans or cut and re-sewn into chic garments. Perhaps stimulated by popular interest in the modern kimono, private collectors have begun exhibiting their treasures, publishers have devoted entire issues of magazines to the topic, scholars have expanded their historical horizons to incorporate the study of nineteenth- and twentieth-century kimonos, and vintage and newly produced kimonos are available for sale globally through the Internet. Whether incorporating old kimonos into new looks or simply collecting them as objects to be viewed and appreciated, kimonos of myriad styles remain in fashion among disparate groups both within and outside Japan's borders.

ONE

THE FOUNDATIONS OF A KIMONO FASHION INDUSTRY

Fashions have changed from those of the past and have become increasingly ostentatious. In everything people have a liking for finery above their station. Women's clothes in particular go to extremes. Because they forget their proper place, extravagant women should be in fear of divine punishment. Even the robes of the awesome high-ranking families used to be of nothing finer than Kyoto *habutae*. Black clothing with five crests cannot be called inappropriate to anyone from *daimyo* down to commoner. But in recent years, certain shrewd Kyoto people have started to lavish every manner of magnificence on men's and women's clothes and to put out design books in color.

Ihara Saikaku[1]

The modern kimono fashion system arose from institutional foundations shaped at the turn of the seventeenth century. During that time, the Tokugawa family came to power, establishing a military government with its capital in Edo (modern-day Tokyo), and organizing the feudal domains into a semblance of the nation state now recognized as Japan.[2] During the Edo period, the four-tiered social ranking system positioned the governing samurai at the top, supported by farmers who tilled the land and provided daily staples. Artisans who crafted material goods ranked third in the social hierarchy, while the merchants who traded in those products occupied the lowest recognized social status. Together the artisans and merchants were classified as 'townspeople', or *chōnin*, and constituted the basis of the urban economy. A Kanbun-style *kosode* of the type favoured by *chōnin* is shown opposite (illus. 15). The outward appearance of a clearly defined hierarchy, however, camouflaged significant economic disparities and contradictions. Some samurai were quite poor and engaged in menial tasks, while some merchants, ostensibly occupying the bottom social stratum, attained economic success on a par with elite samurai. Moreover, the elite constituted only a small percentage of Edo-period society; the peasantry constituted more than 80 per cent of the population. Clothing visually distinguished classes, but did not coincide with the official social ranking system. For example, farmers,

15 Woman's garment with small-sleeve openings (*kosode*) with design of fishing net and characters ('*uguisu*', warbler), probably 1660s, silk, metallic threads, silk embroidery, tied resist-dyeing (*shibori*).

who ranked second in the social hierarchy, wore clothing made of durable, inexpensive materials with sleeves that afforded ease of movement (illus. 16, 17). Peasants could rarely afford the luxurious silks worn by some of the wealthier, but socially inferior, townspeople. The main social cleavage existed between the ruling samurai and the commoners. This situation was aggravated by the fact that, although political power was held by the shogunate, economic power was slowly filtering from the samurai class into the hands of the merchants. The merchant class became the patrons of the arts and fashion-makers of the day, displaying their material wealth to the chagrin and envy of the samurai elite.

Conspicuous consumption displayed through clothing choices exposed the entangled relationship between social and economic status in seventeenth-century Japan. In his book 'Japanese Family Storehouse' (*Nihon Eitaigura*, 1688), the social satirist Ihara Saikaku (1642–1693) lamented the large amounts of money spent on lavish clothing in pursuit of the desire to live above one's station in life. He admonished women for their extravagance and for disregarding proper deportment. Implicated in fuelling the desire for 'finery above their station' were 'shrewd' producers of pattern design books. These pattern books, or 'design books' as Saikaku referred to them, reveal the existence of an integrated fashion system among the three major cities of Kyoto, Osaka and Edo from at least the third quarter of the seventeenth century. This genre of books, commonly referred to as kimono pattern books (*kosode moyō hinagatabon*), appear to have served three interrelated functions as kimono makers' manuals, consumer catalogues and fashion plates or adver-tisements. All three functions were crucial to the promotion and development of the textile industry, and the existence of these books is strong evidence of a sophisticated fashion system in seventeenth-century Japan. By facilitating a steady demand for new garments and emphasizing the rapidly changing styles of the time, textile purveyors and textile producers, in tandem with the publishing industry, all derived benefits from changing fashions.

Trends in clothing design were documented in *ukiyo-e* woodblock prints of the fashion leaders of the day: namely, women of the pleasure quarters and Kabuki actors. The woodblock prints, coupled with the pattern books, not only provide a wealth of information about prevailing styles of that era, but also reveal possible collaboration between the textile and publishing industries in their mutual efforts to stimulate consumers' desire for fashionable attire.[3] Based on his study of Isoda Koryūsai's 'Pattern Book of the Year's First Designs, Fresh as Spring Herbs' (*Hinagata wakana no hatsumoyō, c.* 1775) print series, Allen Hockley suggests the existence of a 'relationship between the brothel owners, the *Hinagata* prints, and fabric or kimono merchants' (illus. 18).[4] Although conclusive evidence documenting who underwrote the cost of such print series

16, 17 Farmer's jacket, and detail, first half of 20th century, recycled strips of woven cotton for wefts and wisteria for warps.

continues to elude scholars, many agree that publishers selected the print designers and featured subject-matter based on their assessment of what would sell. In other words, the prints were commercial products.

Woodblock-printed images showcased fashionable clothing available to consumers in Edo-period society. Prints from such series as 'Contemporary Beauties in Summer Garments' (*Natsu ishō tōsei bijin*, *c.* 1804–06) by Kitagawa Utamaro (1753–1806) served as a form of visual communication between the kimono producer, the kimono seller and the consumer, and may be viewed as a form of advertising.[5] Single-sheet print designers like Utamaro participated in the promotion of textile makers and kimono sellers. In Utamaro's 'Contemporary Beauties' series, conspicuous logos of actual kimono purveyors emblazon shop curtains that flutter behind female models promoting the latest summer garments (illus. 19).[6] In each print, a woman models a summer garment made from a particular type of fabric. The upper left or

18 Isoda Koryūsai, 'Courtesan Takamura of the Komatsuya with her Two Young Attendants', from the series 'Pattern Book of the Year's First Designs, Fresh as Spring Herbs' (*Hinagata wakana no hatsumoyō*), *c.* 1775, polychrome woodblock print, ink and colour on paper.

right corner of the print features an actual logo from shops such as Echigoya, Matsuzakaya, Daimaru and Shirokiya, along with a brief description of the featured textile. This series of nine prints promoted the textile products, the shops and quite possibly even the print designer's virtuosity in the handling of textile subject matter.[7] Thus the textile maker, the kimono seller and the print designer, as well as the publisher, all benefited from the sale and circulation of the 'Contemporary Beauties' series.[8]

Prints, pattern books, works of fiction and shopping guides produced by the publishing industry stimulated an awareness of the types of goods that were available, what was considered fashionable and where the goods could be purchased.[9] The publication of pattern books, like that of woodblock prints,

19 Kitagawa Utamaro, 'Suited to Tie-dyed Fabrics Stocked by Matsuzakaya' (*Matsuzakaya shi-ire no shibori muki*), from the series 'Contemporary Beauties in Summer Garments' (*Natsu ishō tōsei bijin*), *c.* 1804–06, polychrome woodblock print, ink and colour on paper.

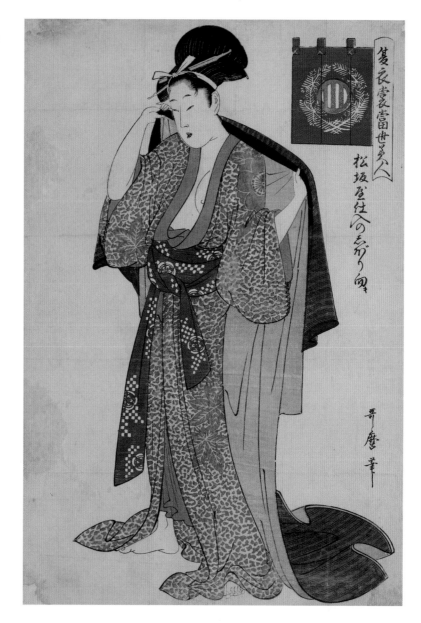

was a collaborative effort requiring input from several participants: publisher, designer, carver and printer.[10] The publisher was central to the effort. His responsibilities entailed commissioning and marketing the prints, as well as overseeing the various stages of a print or book's production.[11] In fact, designers, block carvers and printers worked under the direction of the publishers, and were sometimes employed by them. Kimono pattern books are thus firmly fixed at the crossroads of the publishing and textile industries.

The pre-modern advertising tactic of using celebrities to model and market clothing is, of course, still evident today. As the literary and cultural historian David Pollack has observed:

20, 21 Woman's garment
with small-sleeve openings
(*kosode*) with design of
willow tree and Chinese
characters (and detail:
character '*hige*', whiskers),
18th century, paste-resist
dyeing and stencil dyeing
with silk embroidery and
couched gold thread on silk.

It was not enough that actors and courtesans, in their important function as human billboards, should be seen wearing the latest designs and fashions, and that artists, like paparazzi, should seek to depict them that way for devoted fans avid for every last shred of information about them. Actors, courtesans, sumo wrestlers, shop girls, restaurants, and teahouses worked together with the artists who depicted them in much the same lucrative constellations of advertising practices that have been used by Japanese media and department stores in recent decades, continuing the old practice of using popular [celebrities] to sell all manner of goods.[12]

By linking textile manufacturers, kimono makers and kimono purveyors in these 'lucrative constellations of advertising practices', pattern books open a window onto the origins of the kimono fashion world.

Styled for Status

Edo-period pattern books focused primarily on designs for variant types of the T-shaped garment known today as the kimono. The *kosode*, the prototype of the modern kimono, was only one among many sartorial choices. In the early eighteenth century, some women of the merchant class favoured *yūzen* (paste resist)-dyed robes with designs of flowing calligraphic characters embedded in the foliage of a single standing tree (illus. 20, 21). Reflective of its wearer's sensibility, taste and knowledge of classical poetry, these garments challenged the viewer to decipher and identify the poetic allusion presented. Young, unmarried women wore *furisode*, a garment of similar construction to the *kosode* but distinguished by long, fluttering sleeves. An *uchikake*, often more heavily padded at the hem to enhance the drape of the garment, was worn as an outer garment or overrobe. An early nineteenth-century bride's *uchikake*, embellished with auspicious symbols such as ornamental paper decorations folded to resemble dried abalone strips (*noshi*, traditionally associated with the ceremonial exchange of betrothal gifts) as well as cranes and tortoises (symbols of longevity), can be seen opposite (illus. 22). Clothing revealed a person's wealth; the materials and exquisite workmanship invested in this wedding garment asserted the economic status of its owner and her merchant-class family.

A light summer garment, or *katabira*, resembles the *kosode*'s form, but is unlined and made of bast fibres derived from plants rather than silk.[13] A lightweight, unlined summer garment made of silk was referred to as a *hitoe*. A family crest prominently featured along the shoulder area of a robe – such as the highly recognizable Tokugawa crest – served to identify the garment as a

22 Woman's wedding over-robe (*uchikake*) with design of auspicious imagery, early 19th century, shaped-resist dyeing with silk embroidery and couched gold thread on silk.

23, 24 Woman's summer
garment (*hitoe*) with design of
cormorant fishing and Tokugawa
crest (detail), early 19th century,
paste-resist dyeing with silk
embroidery and couched gold
thread on silk.

25 Woman's summer kimono (*hitoe*) with design of cormorant fishing, second quarter of the 20th century, paste-resist dyeing and hand painting with silk embroidery and supplementary weft lacquered threads on silk.

family treasure for which no expense was spared (illus. 23, 24). During the Edo era, some women of the military class favoured imagery of cormorants and fishing boats for their summer wardrobe. This combination of elements retained its popularity as a summer motif well into the twentieth century, although it was no longer reserved for members of the elite. In its updated iteration, vividly coloured cormorants and floral patterns made with chemical dyes explode against a subdued backdrop of stylized swirling water patterns, a syncopated re-envisioning of the native Rinpa and exotic Art Nouveau styles (illus. 25).

Many other styles of garments existed in Japan during the Edo era. Different types of garments reflected the wearers' economic and social status, gender, age and occupation. Certain articles of clothing visibly differentiated people of diverse social classes, and simultaneously distinguished an individual within a specific group.[14] The materials, motifs and construction of military campaign coats (*jinbaori*), for example, marked their wearers as men belonging to the military class (illus. 26). Modelled after European tailoring techniques popularized by Dutch and Portuguese traders active in Japan from the late sixteenth to the early seventeenth century, the *jinbaori* identified its wearer as a member of an elite group familiar with the world outside of Japan's borders. The *jinbaori* accentuated an individual's personal taste in a number of ways. Rare materials such as imported Persian carpets, feathers of exotic birds or animal pelts were used in their construction. Bold, striking designs emblazoned on the garment's back heightened the wearer's visibility on the battlefield.

Members of the military class, who ostensibly occupied the top rung of the four-tiered social ladder of the Edo period, found themselves increasingly constrained economically. Battlefield prowess became less essential in relatively peaceful, increasingly mercantilist Edo-era society. For members of the merchant class, the tension generated by the disparity between their subordinate social position and their burgeoning wealth found expression in their penchant for elaborate and conspicuous clothing. The Tokugawa government responded by issuing sumptuary laws to regulate the types of dress suitable for specific classes of society.[15] These laws, promulgated from the seventeenth to the nineteenth century, reflect the government's attempt to maintain rigid social distinctions by prohibiting individuals from transgressing class boundaries and thereby upsetting the prevailing social hierarchy.[16] An edict issued in the Mito domain in 1829, for example, allowed 'those above the rank of samurai [to] wear undergarments made of silk or pongee as may their wives and daughters', and ordered 'all those of a rank below that of samurai [to] use only cotton clothing'.[17]

Edo-period society was stratified based on neo-Confucianism, the guiding philosophy of the ruling Tokugawa shogunate. Confucian ideology not only

26 Man's military campaign surcoat (*jinbaori*) with design of a torn fan, late 18th–early 19th century, metallic threads, silver and bone on wool and silk.

legitimized the ordering of society and the preservation of the status quo, it also emphasized the importance of frugality. Thus, the sumptuary edicts were also designed to discourage the flaunting of material wealth by the merchant class, and perhaps to thereby conceal underlying economic realities. As early as 1617, a law was issued in Edo prohibiting gold and silver leaf appliqué on the clothing of prostitutes.[18] An order in 1656 threatened the arrest of anyone dressed in splendid clothes or bearing a presumptuous appearance.[19] After the great Edo fire of 1657, strict regulations were issued concerning the colour and style of decoration that merchants were allowed to wear. One of the amusements of the merchant class was finding ways to circumvent these regulations. In 1663, the shogunate issued an order limiting the amount of money that could be spent on clothing worn by the empress dowager, the imperial princesses, the shogun's consorts and attendant ladies of the castle; a similar order issued in 1713 regulated the dress of *daimyōs'* (feudal lords') wives as well.[20] The order of 1713 stated that 'clothing which has become usual is permitted. But you should not frequently replace your garments with fine ones. Articles bestowed upon you are exceptions.'[21] The exemption for 'articles bestowed' may have contributed to the practice of wealthy merchants requesting that artists make fine, one-of-a-kind, painted kimonos to be given as gifts.

Kimono fashion competitions among the wives of merchants, each vying for recognition in their circumscribed world, demonstrate how a garment's value was influenced not only by the existence of labour-intensive decorative techniques, but also by the name of the garment's maker. An oft-repeated bit of Japanese fashion lore tells the story of a fashion competition among women from the three urban metropolises: Kyoto, Edo and Osaka.[22] According to this story, the wife of Naniwaya Jūemon, a wealthy trader from Osaka, wore an 'exquisite scarlet satin kimono, embroidered with scenes of Kyoto in silver and gold'. The Edo representative, purportedly the wife of Ishikawa Rokubei, appeared wearing a simple black kimono embroidered with sprays of *nanten*, a slender evergreen shrub with small red berries. The ladies of Kyoto thought that the rather dull black kimono from Edo was no match for the brilliant robe of the Osaka contender, until further information convinced them otherwise. Apparently, the black kimono worn by the Edo representative was 'designed by the great [Ogata] Kōrin [1658–1716] and . . . the nanten berries had not been embroidered but were made of rare red coral. The obi was antique Chinese gold brocade. The kimono was not only dignified but also worth a fortune.'[23]

In another version of the story that appeared in the late eighteenth-century gazetteer 'An Old Man's Weeds' (*Okinagusa*), the contestant from Edo wears a simple black kimono, again designed by Kōrin, surrounded by her attendants, who are all dressed in colourful garments.[24] In this version, the juxtaposition of a single figure wearing a black robe designed by Kōrin against a bevy of colourful garments allowed the Edo contestant to stand out in her refined simplicity.

Thus in eighteenth-century Japan, savvy consumers already recognized designer-brand garments. So popular were Kōrin-inspired motifs that pattern books invoked his name long after his death.

Pattern Books

The first kimono pattern books were published in 1666 (illus. 27).[25] Approximately 170 to 180 were published between 1666 and 1820.[26] Most images appearing in kimono pattern books followed a standardized format with a woodblock-printed illustration featuring a kimono-shaped outline decorated with various motifs. Within some publications, textual commentary further specified the dye colours, dyeing methods and other decorative techniques for a particular design. Within a 'large-scale market economy' that was 'abetted by the publishing industry', kimono producers pressured weavers and dyers to develop new colours, decorative techniques, patterning and compositions to satisfy their fashion-hungry customers.[27]

The pattern books appear to have emerged as desirable commodities in themselves around the late 1680s, as evidenced by the appearance of *hinagatabon* titles in catalogues and at the end of books of other genres.[28] For example, the end page of 'Picture Book of the Pond's Heart' (*Ehon ike no kokoro*, 1740), illustrated by Nishikawa Sukenobu (1671–1750) and published by Kikuya Kihei, lists other titles by Sukenobu as well as kimono pattern books illustrated by a man named Nonomura.[29] As textile and clothing historian Maruyama Nobuhiko notes, pattern books associated with the names of specific designers began to proliferate in the Genroku era (1688–1704), suggesting a stable market for *hinagatabon* that allowed designers to specialize in this genre of illustration.[30]

Pattern books served as a kimono maker's design source and as a kimono seller's catalogue of available merchandise. Illustrations from woodblock-printed pattern books, which often bear publication dates, can be matched with extant garments. An early-eighteenth-century *kosode* with designs of hanging scrolls dangling from willow trees executed in the *yūzen*-dyeing technique, for example, is plainly related to the illustration in the pattern book entitled 'Patterns of the Well of the Chrysanthemum' (*Kiku no i*, 1719).[31] A slightly later example pairs an eighteenth-century kimono bearing a scene of fishermen pulling a boat through a marsh of reeds with a similar design from the pattern book 'Sleeves' Peak' (*Hinagata sode no yama*, 1757) (illus. 28, 29).

The evolving relationship between kimono makers and sellers throughout the Edo period ultimately affected

27 Page with design of plovers over waves from *On-hiinagata* ('Kosode Pattern Book', 1667), vol. 1, woodblock-printed book, ink on paper.

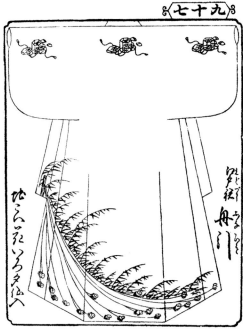

28 Woman's garment with small-sleeve openings (*kosode*) with design of men pulling fishing boats through reeds, 1775–1800, paste-resist dyeing with silk embroidery and ink painting on silk.

29 Sasaki Seibei, design no. 97 with men pulling boats through reeds, from pattern book 'Sleeves' Peak' (*Hinagata sode no yama*, 1757), woodblock-printed book, ink on paper.

the function and production of pattern books. The establishment of the Tokugawa shogunate in the city of Edo in the early seventeenth century required that producers in Kyoto service customers in the distant region of Edo, at least until a textile industry could be established closer to that region. The pattern books, therefore, were no longer just a tool to be used by dyers and clothing designers, but became a medium for suppliers to communicate with consumers. ('Consumers' in this case had the resources to order custom-made clothing from pattern books, unlike the majority of the population, who wove and dyed their own clothing. As such, pattern books obviously catered to a narrow audience concerned with the fashionable, not necessarily the practical.) Garments illustrated in pattern books were available to a woman of means, regardless of her position within the formal social hierarchy.[32]

The publication 'Compendium of Patterns of Our Country' (*Wakoku hiinagata taizen*, 1698) provides one example of the marketing of Kyoto designs to the Edo populace. This became possible as the woodblock-printing industry extended its initial base in Kyoto to Osaka, and eventually to Edo.[33] Analysis of this publication reveals several connections between the textile and publishing industries. The designer of the kimono patterns featured in the book was a Kyoto dyer–painter named Imura Katsukichi. One of the earliest named designers – a practice unknown in the world of single-sheet woodblock prints – Imura designed at least four different pattern books.[34] In each book, the designer's work is identified as 'picture by the Kyoto dyer–painter Imura Katsukichi', implying that he was engaged in the textile industry. But he also interacted with the publishing industry, producing kimono designs for pattern books.[35] Moreover, the publication information on the end sheet of one book suggests that, by the late seventeenth century, publishers from Edo and Kyoto cooperated in the distribution of pattern books. 'Compendium of Patterns of our Country' was initially distributed in Edo by the publisher Nishimura Rizaemon and in Kyoto by Muta Jizaemon. The distribution of the book in Edo implies that the publishers believed people in Edo would be interested in designs created by a Kyoto-based dyer, and that fashions had migrated beyond regional boundaries.

An illustration attributed to Hishikawa Moronobu (*d. c.* 1694) from a pattern book known as 'Kosode Patterns: Crests Inserted' (*Mon-iri Kosode no hinagata, c.* 1680) provides an early example of the use of a pattern book. The illustration depicts a man with a pattern book laid open in front of him and two garments on racks beside him, listening to the instructions of his female customer. Obviously set within the customer's home, this illustration depicts the textile merchant at work.[36] Hishikawa Moronobu is a figure who could be said to stand at the intersection of the textile and publishing worlds. Moronobu's biography is vague, though many claim he was the grandson of an indigo dyer (Hishikawa Shichiemon) and the son of an embroiderer from Hoda in Awa province (part of present-day Chiba prefecture).[37] Moronobu's textile background may have provided him with a particular appreciation for fabrics and designs, which he conveyed through his paintings. In addition to paintings and illustrations for books, Moronobu is also credited with producing a number of kimono pattern books (illus. 30).[38] The preface to a pattern book attributed to Moronobu proclaims the illustrator's desire to present novel designs.[39]

Other illustrations provide examples of the use of pattern books and single-sheet illustrations of kimono designs by consumers and merchants. In a manual of proper female conduct known as the 'Picture Book of Purple Edo' (*Ehon Edo murasaki,* 1765), an illustration by Ishikawa Toyonobu shows a mother instructing her two daughters in the selection of an *uchikake*. At the mother's right lies a pattern book and to her left are bolts of fabric. In this example, the actual function of the pattern book is ambiguous. The pattern

30 Attributed to Hishikawa Moronobu, page with book and handscroll design from 'Newly Published Kosode Pattern Book' (*Shinpan kosode on-hinagata,* 1677), woodblock-printed book, ink on paper.

31 Katsukawa Shunshō, 'The Echigoya Kimono Shop' (print no. 12) from the series 'The Cultivation of Silkworms' (*Kaiko yashinai gusa*), *c.* 1772, polychrome woodblock print, ink and colour on paper.

book's illustrations may have been provided to the customer, together with the bolts of silk, in order to help the customer visualize the finished product. Or perhaps the book is also functioning as a fashion magazine, representing the most up-to-date designs and influencing the fashion choices of customers.

In another example, 'The Echigoya Kimono Shop' from the series 'The Cultivation of Silkworms' (*Kaiko yashinai gusa*), illustrated jointly by Katsukawa Shunshō and Kitao Shigemasa, a clerk from the Echigoya kimono shop (later to become the Mitsukoshi department store in the early twentieth century) visits two women in their home (illus. 31). He is about to present a bolt of crepe-silk

(*chirimen*), and has already spread a
single-sheet illustration or drawing
of a *kosode* design on the floor in
front of the customer. Here the
illustration serves the quite practical
function of helping the customer
visualize the finished kimono.

Nishikawa Sukenobu, a Kyoto-
based *ukiyo-e* painter and book
illustrator of such titles as the previously mentioned 'Picture Book of
the Pond's Heart', is another well-
known figure in the book publishing
and painting worlds.[40] In the first
volume of a set of five kimono pattern books designed by Nishikawa
entitled 'Nishikawa's Book of
Patterns' (*Nishikawa hinagata*,
1718), the frontispiece depicts
women perusing a pattern book
with a bolt of cloth nearby (illus.
32). One woman declares 'Such an
unusual design', while her compan-
ions provide affirmations such as
'Select one that pleases you' and
'This one should do'.[41] The two-
page frontispiece from the fourth
volume portrays a male figure,
possibly the artist himself, drawing
a kimono design with a brush (illus.
33).[42] To the right of the artist is a

colophon that can be roughly translated as 'Just as you prefer', with a woman
beside him responding, 'Be sure to brush in all the detail'. In the illustration,
the entire kimono design is produced on a single sheet of paper. This suggests
that the designer was commissioned to create a design that could be circulated
either as a single-sheet woodblock print or an illustrated page in a kimono
pattern book, because in the conventional binding method for Japanese books,
two kimono designs would have been drawn on the same sheet, which was
then folded for insertion into the book. The inclusion of what may be a self-
portrait of the designer suggests that the status of pattern-book designers was
equal to that of designers of other types of published material.

32 Nishikawa Sukenobu, women looking at *kosode* pattern books, frontispiece of 'Nishikawa's Book of Patterns' (*Nishikawa hinagata*, 1718), vol. I, woodblock-printed book, ink and colour on paper.

33 Nishikawa Sukenobu, couple designing *kosode* patterns, two-page frontispiece from 'Nishikawa's Book of Patterns', vol. IV, woodblock-printed book, ink and colour on paper.

A detailed illustration revealing the multiple functions of kimono pattern books appears in the frontispiece of the book entitled 'Pattern Book for Order Selections' (*Chūmon no hinagata*, 1716) (illus. 34).[43] In this image, a merchant seated on a veranda presents a selection of fabrics to his client. The merchant's assistant, anticipating a long wait, relaxes near his box of goods in the lower right corner. Within the room attached to the veranda, women excitedly copy designs from the pattern book, seeming to obsess over the latest products. In a detail of the women, one remarks, 'The dyed items from Kyoto are fabulous', while another observes, 'The patterns in these order books are wonderful.'[44] The woman perusing the pattern book exclaims, 'I agree. Let's choose designs from this book', while the woman seated in the position of prominence states, 'Be sure to tell them to be careful.'

From this one scene, it is clear that kimono pattern books functioned as sellers' catalogues for use by customers. Less clear is the purpose of copying designs. Were designs from pattern books copied and disseminated to friends in the way we might tear an ad from a *Vogue* magazine to get a friend's opinion? Or was the copy taken to a kimono maker who might produce a knock-off at a cheaper price? Did the merchant have a proprietary interest in or copyright to the images, or did he benefit in some way from their reproduction and circulation? The fact that the preface to this 'Pattern Book for Order Selections' was written by Imura Katsukichi, possibly the same man who illustrated the previously described 'Compendium of Patterns of Our Country', suggests that kimono patterns created or endorsed by noteworthy designers such as Imura

34 Interior of a dye house or kimono shop, two-page frontispiece from 'Book of Custom-made Kimono Designs' or 'Pattern Book for Order Selections' (*Chūmon no hinagata*, 1716), preface by Imura Katsukichi ('dyer artist', *somemono eshi*), vol. I, woodblock-printed book, ink on paper.

or by established painters such as Hishikawa Moronobu or Nishikawa Sukenobu enhanced the cultural and social value of the kimonos made from those patterns beyond that of their original function.

Designing and Desiring Fashionable Attire

Information about the latest trends in colours, designs and obi-tying styles was disseminated through woodblock prints and kimono pattern books that also served as fashion magazines.[45] This raises the question of the relationship, if any, between the publishers of kimono pattern books and publishers of single-sheet prints depicting the leading actors and courtesans of the day, who many argue were the trendsetters of their time. The textile and dye specialist Monica Bethe theorized that fashion leaders, woodblock prints, kimono pattern books and the textile industry might have interacted in the following way:

> [A] well-known actor would commission from one of the dye houses a new shade or hue. (New designs were often taken up as well.) His appearance in the new color would create a stir among theatergoers of Edo and Osaka (where the Kabuki houses were located). *Ukiyo-e* print makers would further popularize the color by their faithful representations of the theatrical idol in costume. With luck, the color would catch on, to become not only the actor's trademark but also a fad among the general public. Fad status assured the color a place in the *hiinagata* design books, and this, of course, would popularize it even further. Young women, particularly of the merchant class, were the most avid imitators of theatrical fashions, including fashions in color, but the military class and imperial court followed their lead . . .[46]

The most celebrated illustration of Bethe's thesis is the popularization of a tea-brown colour with undertones of black and red that became all the rage after the *onnagata* actor (female impersonator) Segawa Kikunojō II (1741–1772) wore it on the Kabuki stage (illus. 35).[47] Segawa Kikunojō II, also known as Rokō, was a particularly popular eighteenth-century *onnagata*, and the name Rokō came to be used as a brand name for various products.[48] The dye colour came to be called *Rokō-cha*, *Rokō* being the pen name adopted by Segawa Kikunojō for the publication of his haikus and *cha* designating a tea-brown colour.[49] This colour was so popular that a sample was included in the 'Reference Manual of Model Designs' (*Tekagami moyō setsuyō*, 1793).[50]

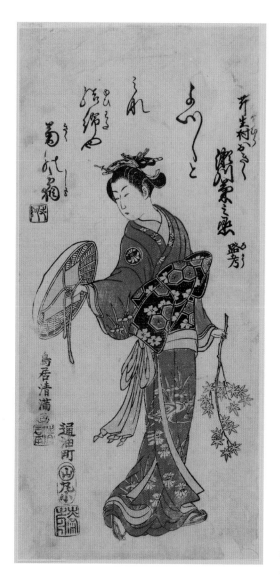

35 Torii Kiyomitsu I, 'The Actor Segawa Kikunojō II as Okiku', 1759, polychrome woodblock print, ink and colour on paper.

At least one pattern book appears to have served the dual function of promoting the various actors themselves and advertising the garments they wore. Textile dyers, pattern book publishers, actors and Kabuki houses may have collaborated in their efforts to establish and stimulate fashionable trends. The kimono pattern book 'Blossoms of the Year' (*Toshi no hana*, 1691) depicts an actor of the Kamigata region on one page, while the facing page features the back view of the garment worn by the actor, information on its dyeing techniques and colours, and the actor's crests.[51] This pattern book functioned as a form of advertising for the Kabuki theatres as well as the textile and publishing industries. It is not clear, however, who underwrote the cost of producing the books or their impact on fashion trends.

Kimono pattern books are often evaluated in conjunction with another genre of publication targeted at a female audience: women's etiquette manuals. These publications often address two separate components: dress and behaviour. However, kimono pattern books and women's etiquette manuals worked in tandem to explain the role of clothing in women's deportment. The women's manual 'Collection of Rules of Etiquette for Women' (*Onna shorei shū*) was published around the time of the earliest pattern books. Pattern books served the dual function of illustrating the latest styles and instructing people on how to select garments appropriate to their status.[52] When the 'Pattern Book of a Collection of Ten Thousand Women' (*O-hiinagata man'nyoshū*, circa 1673–84) was issued, the publisher deliberately included models wearing kimonos. The preface states:

> Since the time *kosode* designs were first produced as small-scale drawings called *hinagata*, *kosode moyō hinagatabon* have spread throughout society. In recent years, however, there have been many *kosode* made from these design books that were not flattering or suitable to the people who were to wear them, because of their age or appearance. Accordingly, in this publication we have included a drawing of a particular woman wearing *kosode*, so that the customer can choose one that suits her own appearance.[53]

The gradual shift in economic power from the samurai class to the newly affluent merchant class resulted in major changes in the relationship between producer and consumer.[54] Within the textile industry, there was a shift towards the production of standard types of kimonos for the general populace, rather than one-of-a-kind garments for elite clientele in Kyoto and Edo. The pattern books conveyed information to the customer about prevailing fashion trends, from which the customer could choose a favourite pattern. The excerpt quoted above from the 'Collection of Ten Thousand Women' suggests that one potential drawback of ordering directly from a pattern book was the risk that a garment might not be appropriate for the wearer.

By the late seventeenth century, pattern books also conveyed information about the styles suitable for a customer's age and status. The pattern book 'Patterns of the Shōtoku Era' (*Shōtoku hinagata*, 1713) is divided into sections based on styles appropriate to particular types of clientele (illus 36).[55] Designs were labelled with such descriptions as 'palace style', 'mansion style', 'castle-toppler style' (a euphemism for a high-class courtesan), 'bathhouse maiden style', 'young male (*wakashu*) style' and 'actor's style', followed by fitting designs for each of these types. A garment's construction, colours, composition and applied decorative motifs signalled the gender, occupation and status of the wearer, at least to viewers cognizant of sartorial codes.

Pattern books then, like fashion magazines today, functioned as barometers by which to gauge shifts among the fashion leaders of the time. The use of clothing to blur or camouflage social distinctions caused one writer to lament:

> The vogue for crested, plain, or striped *kosode* imitates the dress of prostitutes. In the past, women of society wore glittering *kosode*, such as those decorated with embroidery and thin gold leaf, and prostitutes [*yūjo*] wore plain or striped garments in order to distinguish them from other women. The same was true of obi – ordinary women of fashionable society wore narrow obi, and prostitutes' obi were very wide, so that one

36 Nishikawa Sukenobu, 'courtesan style' (*keisei-fū*) *kosode*, page from 'Patterns of the Shōtoku Era' pattern book (*Shōtoku hinagata*, 1713), woodblock-printed book, ink on paper.

could tell which was which. But today women of the world imitate prostitutes and put on plain or striped *kosode* with wide obi. This is mere imitation and indicates no discernment whatsoever.[56]

By increasing their visibility, the reproduction and circulation of images of people wearing a particular design popularized the most desirable clothes available in the urban centres. By conflating consumption and desire, kimono pattern books enhanced product visibility and allowed consumers with disposable income to entertain the idea of owning a garment that others might covet.

Kimono pattern books might be viewed as mere records of garments available in the market at a given moment in history. If, however, kimono pattern books are considered a 'representation employed for the purpose of stimulating desire', as David Pollack suggests, it is possible to envision how the textile and publishing industries collaborated to set and stimulate fashion trends, thereby increasing the desire for new kimonos, pattern books and single-sheet prints depicting popular courtesans and actors modelling the most novel designs, colours and fabrics.[57] (While it is unclear if textile sellers underwrote the production costs of prints that featured their establishments, or if the textile makers whose products were promoted contributed to the production of prints such as Utamaro's 'Contemporary Beauties' series, everyone potentially benefited from the promotion.[58]) The cult of celebrity and the proclivity for cross-promotion initiated in the Edo period through product endorsements by entertainers established precedents for modern marketing strategies widely used to this day. Pattern books link the textile and publishing industries in the larger matrix of the sophisticated fashion system already operating in late seventeenth-century Japan.

TWO

MODERNIZING THE KIMONO

If we look at contemporary Western women's wear, we find that it combines a top or jacket and a skirt in the manner of our ancient Japanese system of dress. This is not only suitable for the formal standing bow but is also convenient for action and movement and makes it only natural to adopt the Western method of sewing. In carrying out this improvement, however, be especially careful to use materials made in our own country. If we make good use of our domestic products, we will assist in the improvement of techniques of manufacture on the one hand, and will also aid the advancement of art and cause business to flourish. Thus the benefits of this project will reach beyond the limits of the clothing industry. In changing from the old to the new, it is very difficult to avoid wasteful expenditures, but we can certainly achieve our goal if everyone, according to their abilities, makes a special effort to lead a frugal life. These are my aspirations for the reform of women's costume.

Chōya shinbun (17 January 1887)[1]

From the opening of Japan's ports to expanded international trade in the mid-1850s through to the 1890s, a wave of imported materials, technologies and designs infiltrated Japan's shores. Empress Shōken's imperial memorandum of 1887, quoted above and circulated in the *Chōya* newspaper, exhorted her female compatriots to adopt Western-style fashion, with the caveat that they support domestic manufacturers.[2] This reveals the rising tensions faced daily by women of means who were able to choose from the myriad Western and Japanese modes of dress available to them (illus. 37).[3] The empress's exhortation implies that many Japanese women continued to favour their native dress over imported bustles, corsets and boots. But her sentiment also reflects recognition of the importance of the domestic textile industry and the value of its products as a means to raise the foreign capital necessary to fuel Japan's efforts to modernize.

As documented by woodblock-printed images and photographs, the empress tended to wear Japanese dress in the first few decades of her husband's reign from 1868 to 1886. She continued to wear Japanese-style clothing

37 Yōshū (Toyohara) Chikanobu, sewing of Western clothes for high-ranking ladies (Empress Shōken promoting Western modes of dress), 1887, triptych of polychrome woodblock prints, ink and colour on paper.

even after the Emperor Meiji appeared in Western-style uniforms in 1872.[4] From about 1887, however, the empress favoured Western-style dresses over kimonos, even when her subjects continued to wear their native dress (illus. 38, 39, 40).[5] While it is unclear what impact the empress may have had as a trendsetter for the average Japanese woman, her circle of influence certainly extended to female members of the imperial family, her attendants and the wives of government officials, particularly those who made public appearances with their husbands at government-sponsored events.[6] An early twentieth-century kimono owned by a daughter of Prince Arisugawa, who married into the Tokugawa family, provides evidence of the continued appreciation of the kimono, even among elite women who had been encouraged to adopt Western-style dress (illus. 41). As continues to be true today, the selection of appropriate garments in Japan was dictated by time, place and occasion.

The epoch from 1884 to 1889, commonly referred to as the Rokumeikan ('Deer Cry Pavilion') era, represents the nadir of Japanese dress among the elite (illus. 42). Proving Japan to be equal to Western nations became a priority for the country in its efforts to revise the 'unequal treaties'. These had been negotiated by the United States Consul to Japan Townsend Harris (1804–1878) as a result of Commodore Perry's visit. The Rokumeikan building, designed by the British architect Josiah Conder (1852–1920), symbolized the aspirations of the Japanese elite to be seen as equal to their British, European and American counterparts. The two-storey brick building – a pastiche of Western-style architectural elements ranging from Italian Renaissance

38, 39 Empress Shōken's ceremonial dress, and detail, late 19th–early 20th century, roses woven and embroidered with various grades of wrapped gold thread and sequins on silk satin.

40 Nakajima Ishimatsu, 'Likenesses of their Imperial Highnesses' (*Teikoku shison no on-kage*), 1896, colour lithograph, ink and colour with gold on paper.

to American Victorian – was the site of gala celebrations.[7] Japanese men appeared in Western-style regalia and Japanese women wore luxurious ball gowns, although women continued to wear kimonos for less formal events. While woodblock prints and photographs record some of the most visible personages of the period in Western-style dress, much of the Japanese population not featured in prints and photographs still wore kimonos.

When the Meiji government was formed in 1868, the social hierarchy based on the four-tiered class system of samurai, farmer, artisan and merchant

42 Yōshū Chikanobu, 'Illustration of the Ladies' Charity Bazaar at the Rokumeikan' (*Rokumeikan ni oite kifujin jizenkai no zu*), 1887, triptych of polychrome woodblock prints, ink and colour on paper.

41 Woman's long-sleeved kimono (*furisode*) with flowing water and Western autumn flowers and plants design, previously owned by Mieko, second daughter of Prince Takehito Arisugawa, *c.* 1908, paste-resist dyeing on silk.

of the previous Edo era gave way to a comparatively more egalitarian social system. The new government aimed to abolish class distinctions. In reality, distinctions between elite and commoner persisted through the nineteenth century, and dress was the most visible manifestation of the new social hierarchy. When Emperor Meiji, revered as the physical embodiment of the Japanese nation, first donned Western-style clothing for formal occasions, his act publicly symbolized Japan's willingness to shed traditional modes of dress in favour of Western fashions and its desire to take its place as an equal on the world stage. Considering that only a decade earlier Japanese government personnel sent to Washington to ratify the Harris Treaty wore full Japanese-style regalia, the change must have startled the average Japanese subject.

Japan's encounter with Western powers was coupled with the donning of Western dress in the highest echelons of Japanese society. Government and military officials followed the emperor's lead and adopted Western-style suits and uniforms in 1872. For the proclamation of the Constitution of the Great Empire of Japan in 1889, the emperor and his entourage appeared in Western-style uniforms or formal regalia, and the empress, too, wore a Western-style gown with a long train (illus. 43). By contrast, the emperor had appeared on an earlier occasion in the inner sanctuaries of the palace to perform a ceremony promulgating new laws in ancient Japanese-style court dress.[8] Western-style uniforms were the dress of choice for the military, police and students at select schools. Members of the imperial court and bureaucrats

opted for Western-style suits and accessories as civilian clothing. Men engaged in commerce or working as labourers still wore Japanese-style dress. In the comfort of their homes, most men opted for Japanese-style dress, usually a simple under-kimono, or *nagajuban* (illus. 44, 45).

The genesis of ideals associating Western clothing with a modernized West and the kimono with a traditional Japan are rooted in this era. At the time of their initial exposure to Western-style dress, the Japanese felt they were in an inferior position. Accordingly, the major incentive for the Japanese to adopt Western-style dress was to appear more like members of other nations – nations they feared would try to dominate them. While there were documented cases of 'the conscious rejection of outright imitation [of Western models] and the pursuit of indigenous rationality', cosmopolitan fashions incorporating Western and Japanese clothing items and elements are heavily documented in a range of visual media from this era.[9] Individuals attempted to appear simultaneously 'modern' and 'Japanese'. As time progressed, however, the perception of Western-as-modern versus Japanese-as-traditional was further fragmented into gendered spheres in which males, as agents of progress, generally wore modern, Western-style dress in public appearances.[10] Kimono-clad females emerged as symbols of cultural continuity and the preservers of the nation's sartorial heritage.[11] This phenomenon supports the long-standing observation that women in many rapidly changing societies often 'become the repositories of "traditional" values imputed to them by men'.[12] Within Japan, a separate mythologizing process associated modernity with the urban sphere and positioned the rural countryside as 'traditional'.

43 Yōshū Chikanobu, 'Ceremony of the Issuance of the Constitution', 1889, triptych of polychrome woodblock prints, ink and colour on paper.

In 1872, the Japanese nation itself received new garb for its growing national psyche in the form of a national flag bearing the gold chrysanthemum emblazoned on a red background.[13] The flag symbolized the coalition of a confederation of feudal domains into a single political entity. The increased speed of communication and transportation of the modern era facilitated the government's ability to cultivate an extensive cultural awareness of new trends on a national scale. Although Japan was unified under the Tokugawa rulers in the early seventeenth century, it was not until the early Meiji era that Japan perceived itself as a nation state on the order of Western countries.[14] Existing in relative isolation for almost two and a half centuries, Japan emerged on the international stage in the late nineteenth century. Like the new flag, the kimono was one of the nation's most visible symbols.

Fibres, Filaments and Fabrics

The materials and technology available at the moment of production dictate the weaving, dyeing and decorative techniques available to the textile artisan. Japan's encounter with the West beginning in the mid-nineteenth century deeply affected the materials, production techniques and value of worn objects.

A list of gifts presented by Japanese officials to the government of the United States and Commodore Perry's entourage in March 1854 reveals that textiles were one of Japan's prized products.[15] Various types of fabrics, in addition to lacquer, bamboo and porcelain objects, were included in this diplomatic exchange. Perry, however, regarded the lot as 'of little value'.[16] Perhaps the 'value' to which Perry referred was conceived in strictly material, rather than symbolic terms.[17] The only textile objects among the Americans' gifts to the Japanese, consisting principally of books, arms, libations, perfume, clocks and tools, were a 'flowered silk embroidered dress' for the empress, and bolts of 'scarlet broadcloth' and 'scarlet velvet' for the emperor.[18]

Woollens and velvet brought as gifts by Perry's expedition or obtained cheaply in the United States by the Japanese mission were valued commodities in 1860s Japan. When the Japanese mission visited Washington in 1860, one of the chroniclers lamented that

> most officers are wasting their days in the city trying to buy watches and woolen material and velvet, and none are interested in discovering the institutions and conditions of America. People are purchasing things by twos and threes, even by fours and fives, so that they can sell them upon return home. They dash around looking for the cheapest store. How disgraceful it is![19]

44, 45 Man's informal garment or under-kimono (*nagajuban*) with design of the Thirty-six Immortal Poets, and detail, early 20th century, stencilled paste-resist dyeing on silk.

While woollen materials and velvets were prized in Japan for their novelty at this early stage of Japan's exposure to Western material goods, Japan's sericulture and silk-reeling industries quickly attained international acclaim. The pébrine disease that attacked the silkworms of France and Italy and devastated their silk-producing industries in the mid-1850s put inordinate pressure on Japanese and Chinese silk producers to fill the increased demand from Europe.[20] Silkworm breeding practices, and later silk-reeling technology in Japan, contributed to a robust domestic industry. Supported by both the government and private sector, Japanese silk exports skyrocketed, and Japan became the world's leading exporter of silk by 1912 (illus. 46).[21] Foreign capital obtained from silk and cotton exports supplied much-needed funds to finance the modernization of Japan. Much of the labour that produced these textile exports was performed by women.

Prior to the establishment of a thriving domestic sericulture industry, Japan was once dependent on superior raw and finished silk imports from China. Many of the extant sixteenth-century silk garments of the elite were fabricated from imported Chinese silk that was ranked as being of the highest quality available at the time (see illus. 9). In 1685, however, the Tokugawa government restricted imports of raw silk from China. Kyoto weavers turned to domestic silk producers for import substitutes, stimulating the development of Japan's independent sericulture industry. By the mid-eighteenth century, the Nishijin area of Kyoto, the established centre of the silk-weaving industry, relinquished some of its dominance to regional areas such as Gifu, Hachiōji, Isezaki, Kiryū, Nagahama and Tango.[22] Japan's import-substitute strategy for Chinese raw and woven silk over the course of the seventeenth century proved prescient. Some of these regional areas – in particular, Hachiōji near Tokyo, Isezaki and Kiryū in present-day Gunma prefecture, and towns such as Suwa, Okaya and Nagano in present-day Nagano prefecture to the west of Gunma – continued to provide silks for the burgeoning domestic and international markets during the Meiji era.[23]

46 Yōshū Chikanobu, beautiful woman with a towel, calendar print for April 1910 targeted at the export market, 1909, polychrome woodblock print, ink and colour on paper.

International demand for healthy silkworm eggs and reeled silk caused some regions, such as the lower Ina valley (Shimoina, in present-day Nagano prefecture), to shift from producing by-products such as silk and lacquerware for local and domestic consumption to sericulture, reeled silk and related enterprises for overseas markets made accessible through ports newly opened to foreign trade, such as Yokohama in 1859.[24] In some cases, land previously designated for rice cultivation was converted to production of the more lucrative crop of mulberry leaves, needed to feed silkworms. The previously diverse Shimoina economy became more and more dependent on a single industry, silk, servicing distant markets. This economy suffered as the international (particularly American) demand for silk subsided by the 1930s.[25]

Japanese-bred silkworms proved relatively resistant to the pébrine disease that plagued the French and Italian sericulture industries, and led to the export of Japanese silkworms to the European market.[26] For a time, French and Italian silk manufacturers relied on Chinese exports re-exported via England, but the French in particular found it more lucrative and less threatening to circumvent England and deal directly with China and Japan.[27]

During the period of greatest European demand for Japanese raw silk, Japan's silk-reeling industry depended on hand-reeling, producing an irregular, uneven product when compared to French and Italian silk. To remedy this situation, silk weavers in Lyon experimented with combining silk with other fibres, such as cotton and wool, in order to stretch their dwindling silk supplies. The Europeans, however, quickly recognized the need to modernize silk-reeling techniques in Japan to meet their need for a uniform standard. Technology transfer and direct foreign investment in Japan's sericulture and silk-reeling industries in turn benefited Europe's silk industries.[28]

In the United States from the 1850s to the 1900s, silk manufacturing technologies, particularly the widespread use of the power loom, created additional markets for Japan's raw silk exports. Moreover, an increased market demand in the United States for inexpensive, lightweight, finished silk goods, woven on hand looms in Japan, expanded the market for finished Japanese silk goods. From 1870 to 1900, u.s. raw silk imports increased tenfold, much of it supplied by China and Japan. Japan would become one of the largest exporters of raw silk to the United States, supplying more than 70 per cent of the raw silk imported into the United States in 1916.[29]

Japan's dominance of the raw silk industry in the early twentieth century was aided by coupling 'modern genetic science with Japan's strong indigenous tradition of biological innovation in sericulture [that] resulted in the discovery of the F1 hybrid silkworm'.[30] The F1 hybrid silkworm not only standardized the variety, thereby ensuring uniform output contributing to ease of reeling, but also increased productivity allowing Japanese farmers to offer high-quality cocoons at a lower cost than their Italian and Chinese competitors. 'By the 1920s and 1930s, the apex of kimono production in Japan, the domestic silk-reeling industry was among the most technologically advanced in the world.'[31] With the invention of rayon, chemical advances in synthetic fibre production would eventually triumph over Japan's dominant position in silk manufacturing.

While the Japanese silk industry captivated the European and American markets, the Japanese cotton industry exported to its Asian neighbours: Korea and China.[32] This was a marked reversal of previous trends. At the beginning of the sixteenth century, cotton was still a rare commodity in Japan, and as such was highly prized. Prior to domestic cultivation in Japan, cotton was imported from China, probably from as early as the thirteenth century, and from Korea in the fifteenth century. As a novelty cloth, cotton initially ranked as a luxury item. Many of the cloth bags (*shifuku*) prized by tea connoisseurs to protect their treasured tea caddies were made from imported cotton. Colourful cotton Indian calicoes and chintz fabrics captivated the Japanese imagination, and were transformed into tobacco pouches (illus. 47). But as Japan's nascent cotton industry took root and expanded throughout the seventeenth century, cotton shed its elite status and eventually found its way onto the backs of commoners. Warmer, cheaper and more flexible than the rougher bast fibre cloth in use at the time, cotton became the fibre of choice for supplying local needs, and eventually demand increased outside the regions where temperate climates and longer growing seasons provided conditions conducive to cotton cultivation.

Cotton in its variant forms – as seed cotton, yarn and woven cloth – became an important commodity during the Edo period. As William Hauser points out in his study of the cotton trade, 'marketing patterns shifted from small-scale local marketing units to a focus on major urban centres and finally to a national system of commodity distribution with both urban and rural foci of marketing activity.'[33] Cotton cultivation in Japan began around the second

47 Pouch with design of birds and flowers, 18th century, printed colours and gold on cotton.

quarter of the sixteenth century, and by the early seventeenth century knowledge of cultivation practices had spread to regions conducive to producing
this crop. A survey of 1679 lists eight cotton cloth traders and seventeen seed
cotton traders active in the Osaka region. By the early eighteenth century,
cotton cloth was ranked according to quality, with the Ise Matsuzaka area
earning top honours, followed by Settsu and Kawachi, and middle-grade
cloth produced in Mikawa, Owari, Kii and Izumi.[34] Climatic differences,
soil conditions and phases of technology transfer contributed to recognizable
gradations in the products of particular regions.

By the early nineteenth century, cotton merchants in the city of Edo
pressured city officials to inhibit competition from 'outsiders'.[35] The nascent
industry grew to become a small-scale secondary crop for regional farmers and
village households engaged in the weaving of cotton cloth not only to meet
personal needs, but as a form of side employment, producing cotton goods
for the domestic market.[36] For example, Chōshū domain imported raw cotton
from other parts of the country and wove it into cloth for home use, and by
the 1730s began to trans-ship to the Osaka market, prompting nearby regions
to engage in cotton cultivation, ginning, spinning and weaving.[37] Cotton
exports from Japan took two major forms – as cotton yarn and as woven cloth.
Assorted types of cloth, made possible by the selective breeding of cotton, led
to an increased variety of available raw material. Technical developments in
weaving and dyeing contributed to regional differentiations and specialities.[38]
By the early 1880s, regional communities, such as Shimoina, spun and wove
cotton not only for local consumption but also for distant markets. By 1914,
Japan dominated the cotton export industry.[39]

Japan's textile production activities expanded to overseas markets, not
only in the form of domestically produced goods for export, but also in the
form of privately owned mills based on Chinese soil. American and European
enterprises preceded Japan's entry into the cotton-spinning mills in China,
and initial attempts by the Japanese to gain a foothold in China failed. The
Tōyō Spinning and Weaving Company entered China in 1896 and Mitsui
entered in 1895, in the guise of the Shanghai Spinning Company. But both
closed their Chinese enterprises within a few years. Disincentives and taxes
imposed by the Chinese Qing dynasty government (1644–1911) influenced
the Japanese mill owners' decision to concentrate their cotton-spinning
operations in Japan and export finished yarn to the Chinese. In the first
decade of the twentieth century, Japanese businesses would return to China
in the form of joint ventures or, in the case of the Naigai Wata Company,
wholly owned mills in order to deflect the predicted competitive threat that
China would pose in the coming years.[40] Eventually, Japanese-owned mills,
such as the Naigai Wata Company in Shanghai, would outpace British mills,

and by the 1930s, Japanese mills established in China produced 'nearly 40 percent of all China's machine-spun yarn and about 57 percent of all its machine-woven cloth'.[41]

Domestic shifts in the perceived and actual value of certain fibres is chronicled through a study of fibres derived from various trees or grass plants, generally referred to as bast fibres. The ability to cultivate and weave hemp (*taima*) and ramie (*chōma* or 'China grass') generically known as *asa* ('leaf and plant fibres') in Japanese, into cloth was likely introduced from the Korean peninsula in late Neolithic times. Fibres from wild trees and vines, or tree-bast fibres, were cultivated and processed in Japan to produce baskets, nets, mats and other utilitarian articles. With the introduction of *asa* cultivation and processing techniques to Japan, the desirability of grass-bast fibres for woven cloth replaced the more time-consuming, labour-intensive production of cloth from tree-bast fibres. In urban areas and in regions where cotton was readily accessible via established trading routes, cotton would displace *asa* as the clothing material of choice for commoners. Inhabitants of mountainous areas were slower to trade their 'thick-cloth' (cloth woven from mulberry tree-bast fibres) garments for cotton.[42] According to the ethnographer Yanagita Kunio, 'hemp garments began to fall rapidly out of use' during the Meiji era. One notable exception is cloth made from wisteria vines. Work clothes in the Shūchi area of Shizuoka prefecture were, until the late Meiji, referred to as *fujigimono* ('wisteria kimono'), woven from wild wisteria grown in the local mountains.[43]

In addition to cloth produced in and around the urban centres of Kyoto and Edo, locally produced rolls of cloth were recognized as speciality products associated with specific regions. In some cases, these regional productions served as exchange items in a barter-based economy. Certain types of bast fibres emerged and sustained their status as the cloth of the samurai class throughout the Edo period. A summer robe (*katabira*) from the first half of the eighteenth century attests to the value placed on garments made of high-quality bast fibres (illus. 49, 50). In this rare case, the dyer's marks inscribed on the inside front of the garment read 'number 766, very precious, high-quality summer garment' (*jōjō ontsuji*).

As early as the eighth century, another type of handcrafted, fine ramie cloth made of bast fibres, notably a type of fabric known as *Echigo chijimi* ('crepe ramie cloth of Echigo', present-day Niigata prefecture), was used to pay taxes. In later centuries, the military elite favoured Echigo cloth and requisitioned it for tribute and trade. As other fibres, particularly cotton, entered the common market in the mid-eighteenth century, diminished demand for Echigo cloth, coupled with increasingly mechanized production methods in the early nineteenth century and a move from home-based to factory-based production, led to the near demise of Echigo cloth production.[44] In the 1950s, Echigo cloth, like many other regionally produced textiles, was recognized by the Japanese government as a tradition worth preserving, and is today recognized as an Intangible Cultural Property.[45]

Wool has yet another history in Japan. By the late sixteenth century, Dutch, Portuguese and Spanish traders had introduced wool to Japan, but it was not readily available. Prior to Japan's expanded contact with the world outside its borders in the mid-1850s, wool was a relative novelty, confined to such uses as the fabric of military campaign coats (*jinbaori*), which celebrated their owner's ability to procure the rarest of materials (see illus. 26).[46] The military class promoted Western-style uniforms starting in the 1870s, yet Japanese wool consumption depended on imported fabrics from Germany and England through the late 1890s.[47] Japan was a valuable foreign market for England, though France's exports of worsted wool cloth to Japan eventually surpassed those of England.[48]

48 Girl's under-kimono with designs related to early Meiji period Yokohama, 1870s–80s, paste-resist dyeing on imported wool muslin.

It was not until the kimono-wearing consumer adopted woollens and worsted wool that one can speak of a wool industry in Japan. Increased demand for coats to be worn over the kimono – known *as tombi, nijūmawashi* and *azumakōto* – ignited the market, as many were made of woollen fabrics.[49] Lightweight muslin fabrics of wool (*mousseline de laine*) in hues of red or purple became the popular fashion choice for women's obi sashes and three-quarter-length *haori* jackets.[50] Women also favoured fine, lightweight wool for the warmth it offered when used for under-kimonos. A rare example of imported wool used for a young girl's undergarment is decorated with stencil-dyed paste resist motifs referencing historical events in Yokohama that occurred from the 1870s and 1880s, when the garment was likely produced (illus. 48).

As described later in this chapter, a Japanese artisan developed a technique of printing designs on the plain imported wool muslins that appealed to local tastes.[51]

These printed muslins – called Yūzen muslins – became extremely popular, and as a result, in 1896, muslins amounted to 40 percent of total imports of woolens and worsteds . . . When the technique of

49, 50 Woman's summer
robe (*katabira*) with design
of plovers above sandbars
and flowering plants, and
detail, 18th century, paste-
resist dyeing on ramie.

printing became mechanized in 1907 at the dyeworks of Inahata Katsutarō in Osaka, the use of these materials spread even further, and eventually led to the establishment of many large worsted mills – first weaving works and then also spinning establishments.[52]

Domestic production of wool muslins began in 1895, and other firms attracted by the potentially lucrative trade joined the field in the early 1900s.[53]

The import-substitute strategy of procuring fibres, yarns or cloth, followed by innovations in dyeing techniques that triggered increased demand and the subsequent mechanization of an industry, is a common pattern of transmission of foreign materials and technology to the Japanese market.[54] Wool mills represented the exception, in that the government-sponsored Senjū Woolen Mill established in 1878 under the direction of the government official Inoue Shōzo represented 'the only mill that introduced an entirely new branch of industry to Japan, and it was the only enterprise in the textile industry that retained its importance for many decades'.[55] But it was increased demand for lightweight wool muslins as a kimono fashion fabric that contributed to the successful integration of the wool industry into Japan's domestic economy.[56]

Adapting Foreign Materials and Technology

The Japanese government's participation in international expositions afforded an opportunity to promote their country's products and industry as well as to acquire new technology and materials from the West. The delegation sent to the Vienna International Exhibition in 1873 included artisans, merchants and experts in sericulture, who received government sponsorship to spend six months in Europe to visit factories and workshops.[57] They returned to Japan with samples of European fabrics, chemical dyes, the Jacquard loom, Kaye's flying shuttle and graph paper. Japan domesticated foreign technologies and materials, harnessing the power of the West to fuel its textile industry. Rather than adopting or copying Western tools and concepts wholesale, as is commonly assumed, Japanese weavers and dyers exercised an adaptive, innovative approach to modernizing the kimono industry.[58]

Japanese wares were exhibited in many international expositions including London (1862 and 1910), Paris (1867 and 1900), Vienna (1873), Philadelphia (1876), Chicago (1893) and St Louis (1904) (illus. 51).[59] Through encounters with the world beyond its borders, Japan became acutely aware of how presentation affected perception. The Japanese government strategically viewed expositions as a venue to display the nation's cultural capital and assess the

51 Kimono fabric exhibited at Paris International Exhibition of 1867 and purchased by the Victoria & Albert Museum (red bamboo and plum blossom design), *c.* 1860–67, stencilled paste-resist dyeing on silk crepe.

reception of its wares in a global context. The production of Japanese textiles in the last quarter of the nineteenth century and into the early twentieth century became a part of this cultural negotiation, reflecting Japan's attempt to absorb Western materials and technology while maintaining its own cultural integrity and identity.

The government, industry cartels and individuals often worked in tandem to continually improve the quality and output of Japanese textiles in an increasingly competitive world market. The dissemination of new materials, tools and technology continued processes begun in the eighteenth century, during the period often referred to as proto-industrialization. For example, the 'tall loom' (*takabata*) was a well-guarded secret of the Nishijin weavers in Kyoto. In the eighteenth century, select Kyoto weavers transferred their expertise to the nascent textile industry that was taking root in small towns, such as Kiryū, located in eastern Japan.[60] The 'tall loom' soon replaced the 'backstrap loom' (*izaribata*) in many of these regional areas. Regions with sustainable crops and by-employment attracted workers. Kiryū's population tripled between 1757 and 1855, and an 1835 document credits the growth to the weaving industry: 'Weavers who came to make a living hired women operatives to spin and weave, and people came crowding into the town from other provinces, renting houses there and even in surrounding hamlets.' In 1836, 'every peasant family was said . . . to practice sericulture, to weave silk cloth, or to work at paper making in the intervals of farming'. Neighbouring villages, such as Ashikaga, competed for skilled workers, luring them away with the promise of higher wages.[61]

Keen interregional competition and localized knowledge contributed to subsequent inventions. A Japanese wheelwright from Kiryū, Iwase Kichibei, is credited with the application of water power to large wheels used in the silk-throwing process.[62] The concentration of industrial effort in localized areas led to incremental innovations and improved products. A perceived need to ensure high-quality output led to the establishment in 1878 of the trade organization Kiryū Company (Kiryū Kaisha).[63] Thomas Smith convincingly argues that

> the modern textile industry grew mainly in districts of traditional manufacture; much of the growth occurred in villages and former 'country places'; entrepreneurs, plant managers, buyers, shippers, and labor contractors came from the same districts; and the labor came overwhelmingly from farm families.[64]

The infrastructure established in the Edo period provided fertile ground for the stimulus activated by foreign materials and technology.

Members of Japanese delegations sent to the United States and Europe conducted research abroad and returned with knowledge of new materials, tools and technologies. In 1872, the Kyoto city mayor Makimura Masanao dispatched the weavers Inoue Ihei (1821–1881) and Yoshida Chūshichi (?–1874), together with Sakura Tsuneshichi (1835–1899), to Lyon to study French weaving technology.[65] Sakura and Inoue returned with the Jacquard loom and a model of Kaye's flying shuttle that Japanese carpenters, most likely including Araki Kohei (1843–?), modified and replicated for use by the Nishijin weavers.[66] Yoshida died unexpectedly in 1874 when the boat that carried him, and many of the works returning to Japan from the 1873 Vienna Exhibition, sank off the coast of the Izu Peninsula.[67] When the weaver Date Yasuke IV (1813–1876) travelled to Vienna for the 1873 International Exposition, he took with him samples of woven silks in the hope of stimulating interest and garnering orders. Besides prizes awarded for his own work, he brought back at least two European sample books that included swatches of velvets, *chiné* and other woven silks, some of which incorporated Art Nouveau designs.[68] Date would later be named an 'Imperial Household Artisan' (*teishitsu gigeiin*).[69]

The Kyoto city government, home of the Nishijin weaving industry, recognized the need to compete with foreign merchants vying for the highest quality silk products. The Japanese government also hired foreign experts to teach in Japanese universities, research centres and factories. In 1876, Kyoto's mayor Makimura invited the British designer Christopher Dresser, then visiting Japan, to help promote Anglo-Japanese trade and advise on industrial developments.

The government – initially at the feudal domain level and later at the national level – also established spinning mills, utilizing a combination of foreign expertise and Japanese specialists who had trained abroad, coupled with imported machinery adapted to suit Japan's particular needs. In 1866, Satsuma domain officials contracted with the Platt Brothers of Oldham in England and a British engineer to set up a cotton mill in Kagoshima employing Western-style spinning mules.[70] When officials of the Maebashi domain made the decision to invest in the establishment of a silk-reeling mill based on Western models in 1870, they sought the advice of Hayami Kenzō (1839–1913), a man of samurai lineage who understood the Yokohama silk trade. Hayami brought in a Swiss technician named Casper Mueller to aid in the initial set-up of Italian equipment in the Maebashi domain.[71] The first private cotton spinning factory, the Osaka Spinning Mill, opened in 1883, made the decision to switch from the spinning mules commonly employed in British factories to the more recently developed ring-spinning technique and made adaptations to imported machines to suit Japanese conditions. Specifically, the government official Shibusawa Eiichi hired a Japanese engineer already in England, Yamabe Takeo, to gain first-hand experience of the spinning machines prior to importing them from Platt Brothers.[72] Private firms, such as the Osaka Spinning Mill, provided the initiative to adapt imported technology for domestic use.

One of the most famous model factories of the Meiji era was the Tomioka Silk Reeling Works, overseen by Itō Hirobumi and Shibusawa Eiichi in 1872. The Tomioka factory relied on French machinery and expertise. Ironically, although the government-established Tomioka mill hired the French expert

Paul Brunat to advise on the operations of the mill, the sponsors disregarded Brunat's recommendation to utilize locally produced machines made of domestic materials. Instead, they opted for a factory design that made use of the latest Western technology and techniques, however ineffectual, in order to showcase the government's efforts to modernize.[73] In 1890, the mill was privatized.

The first large-scale private silk factory, established in Tsukiji, Tokyo, in late 1871, was backed by the Ono family, one of the leading Kyoto-based merchant families (illus. 52).[74] Ono called upon the Swiss technician Mueller, who had been involved in setting up the silk-reeling factory in Maebashi, to create it. As Morris-Suzuki notes,

> although Tsukiji was foreign in inspiration, its technology was drastically modified to suit Japanese conditions. The machinery was wooden, built in Japan, and driven, not by steam or water power, but by the labour of human beings who spent their working days tied to the endlessly turning rows of drive-wheels.[75]

Eventually the equipment from the Tsukiji operation was transferred to other Ono-established silk filatures in Nagano prefecture, favoured for its proximity to local cocoon supplies. By 1920, Nagano prefecture had gained a reputation as a 'silk kingdom' and silk dominated the region's economy.[76] By the late twentieth century, only one silk spinning factory survived in Nagano, and only one household was still engaged in sericulture.[77]

52 Utagawa Yoshitora, imported silk spinning machine at Tsukiji in Tokyo, c. 1876, triptych of polychrome woodblock prints, ink and colour on paper.

Toyoda Looms is the classic example of Japanese ingenuity and adaptation. Its founder, Toyoda Sakichi (1867–1930), hailed from the cotton-weaving centre of Nagoya and was a carpenter by trade. Studiously observing different models of looms exhibited in government-sponsored industry exhibitions, Toyoda developed and patented an automated loom in 1916. He recognized that an enormous market existed for standardized, reliable quality products, and he tinkered with 30 prototypes tested over a period of several years in an effort to produce the loom. With the financial backing of the Mitsui conglomerate, Toyoda ultimately extended his cotton-spinning venture to China.[78]

By the 1920s, a large percentage of textiles was produced in privately owned factories, but factory-based textile production did not necessarily displace home- or regionally based productions. Home-based production continued to provide for a family's personal needs and also afforded supplementary income as by-employment for rural families that supplied silk or cotton products for local and distant markets. The increased demand for export silk in the early twentieth century may have prompted local communities to emphasize sericulture and silk reeling over less lucrative markets, such as lacquerware or ceramic production. Regional producers capitalized on labour-intensive, putting-out methods, and adapted their production to and were sustained by local and distant market demands. Some small-scale textile producers in rural areas thus managed to survive into the post-1945 era.

Patterns of Transmission

The macro-level changes of shifting values of fibres on the global market, the textile industry's integration of imported materials and technology, and a growing awareness of other modes of dress affected kimono production in numerous ways. Building on established domestic weaving and dyeing practices, kimono designers incorporated newly imported materials and technology into their repertoire. As will be discussed in more detail below, three innovative uses of a simple design tool – the stencil – coupled with the integration of newly imported chemical dyes into the kimono dyer's repertoire, exemplify the Japanese dyer's ability to modify imported materials and incorporate them with indigenous ingenuity to suit a variety of domestic markets.

First, the introduction of chemical dyes in the second half of the nineteenth century allowed kimono producers to create *yūzen*-dyed kimonos with stencils, today referred to as *kata-yūzen*. The Japanese delegation sent to the Vienna Expo in 1873 returned to Japan with chemical dyes.[79] In the 1870s,

the Japanese Chemistry Bureau was established in Kyoto. Chemists from
Germany and Holland supervised the initial establishment, and by 1875,
Nakamura Kiichirō (1850–1915), a member of the Vienna delegation, was
teaching Western dyeing techniques.[80] Stencil-dyed *yūzen* kimonos represent
a synthesis of modern chemical dyes with traditional designs produced by
artists who worked in the Japanese style of painting, known as Nihonga.
Rather than applying the paste-resist through the stencil, dyers could apply
actual dye colours through the stencil – an innovation that became possible
with the introduction of chemical dyes in the late nineteenth century. Within
the contours of their distinctive T-shaped outline, kimonos of the last quarter
of the nineteenth century reflect Japan's attempts to rapidly absorb Western
materials and technologies while maintaining its own cultural identity.

By 1879, the dyer Hirose Jisuke (1822–1890) had perfected a method
of mixing chemical dyes and rice paste to create a compound, or a dye-
imbued rice paste, that could be applied through stencils. The *kata-yūzen*
process revolutionized kimono design. Pictorial designs, made possible by the
eighteenth-century invention of *yūzen*, could now be produced in multiples
with the use of stencils and chemical dyes. To cut individual stencils for
each colour application was time-consuming and expensive. Some designs
required the application of more than 30 colours (illus. 53, 54). Yet the cost
was spread over the number of garments ordered, possibly as many as 20
or 30 if the design was popular. Gradations of colour and the chromatic
effects of painting could be simulated by this stencil-dyeing process.
Nishimura Sōzaemon XII (1855–1935), head of the Kyoto kimono company
Chisō, led the way by hiring leading Nihonga artists – those painters who
worked in the Japanese style – to produce designs for kimonos by utilizing
this process.[81]

As kimono producers entered into a technological and aesthetic dialogue
with the West in the latter half of the nineteenth century, the consumer base
shifted. The Meiji government formally abolished the four-tiered class system
of samurai, farmer, artisan and farmer. The establishment of a middle class
propelled changes in consumer behaviour. Whereas status trumped wealth in
early modern Japan, Meiji-era consumers gradually selected clothing based
on social and economic considerations, rather than sumptuary laws. Sartorial
choices were no longer dictated by birth but by the consumer's taste and
economic status. This newly unleashed consumer demand stimulated artisans
to create designs suitable to a diversified clientele.

As class-based aesthetic distinctions blurred, regional tastes became more
apparent. Preferences for certain colour schemes or compositions arose among
consumers in large urban areas, such as Kansai (Kyoto and Osaka) and Kantō
(Tokyo and its environs). Some of these regional distinctions emerged during

the previous Tokugawa era. Designs illustrated in the 'Pattern Book for Order Selections' (*Chūmon hinagata*, 1716, described in chapter One) presented styles appropriate for clientele in Edo, Kyoto and Osaka. Later, there emerged an emphasis on the 'Shimabara-style' or 'Miyako-style' of Kyoto in contrast to the 'Edo-zuma'-style of Edo. Within Tokyo, references to a *shitamachi* or 'low city' look, favoured by the merchants and artisans who lived in the physically lower region of the city along the Sumida River, were compared with the Yamanote (literally 'towards the mountain') style referring to the more affluent areas populated initially by the military class in service to the Tokugawa shogun. By the Taishō era (1912–26), when department stores set trends in *yūzen*-dyed kimonos, producers themselves exhibited designs emanating from a Kyoto-school or Tokyo-school style of painting. Masuyama Ryūhō's (dates unknown) kimono design of Ryōgoku Bridge, produced around 1919, is an exquisite example of a Tokyo-school-style kimono design (illus. 55). Masuyama's student Nakamura Katsuma (1894–1982)

53, 54 Design (*zuan*) for kimono with fans and poem cards, 1902, ink and colour on paper. The back (right) lists 34 different colours that were used in the production.

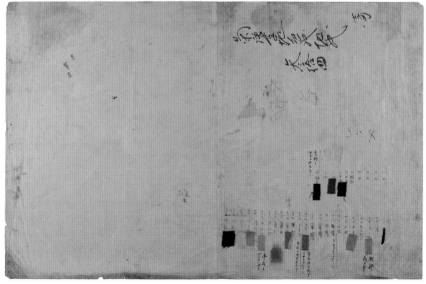

became a leader of the Tokyo-school style of *yūzen* designers, and in 1955 he was designated a Living National Treasure.[82]

A second innovative use of the stencil was the creation of intricately patterned designs known as *komon* ('small patterns'), once reserved for garments worn by members of the military and nouveau riche merchants, to form the background design for accents of hand-painted *yūzen*-dyed motifs favoured by women of all classes. Throughout the late nineteenth and early twentieth centuries, designers continued to perfect and expand the *yūzen* repertoire to include stencil dyeing, hand painting with dyes directly onto fabrics without outlines, as well as the conventional application of outlines within which dyes were applied by hand. In other cases, *yūzen*-dyed motifs were paired with other techniques to create new 'looks'. The combination of two techniques – a background of minutely patterned or *komon* designs, overlaid with hand-painted *yūzen*-dyed motifs – gained popularity from the late nineteenth century, particularly as decorative patterning for

55 Masuyama Ryūhō, woman's kimono with 'Evening by the Sumida River' design, *c.* 1919, stencilled paste-resist dyeing (*yūzen*) on silk.

women's kimonos. Minutely patterned *komon* stencil designs transgressed class and gender boundaries during the nineteenth century. Certain small-patterned motifs rendered in the *komon* technique, previously reserved for the decoration of male clothing of the military elite, were adapted into playful, witty motifs favoured by male actors and wealthy merchants, and eventually formulated the background patterning of a nineteenth-century woman's kimono. For example, a late nineteenth-century woman's kimono exhibits finely wrought paste-resist *yūzen*-dyed designs of bundles of brushwood, stylized snow roundels and weeping branches of cherry trees against a background of minute *komon* designs of pine needles and chrysanthemums (illus. 56, 57).

A third way in which stencils were employed in innovative ways to meet modern market demand was the production of a fabric marketed under the commercial name *meisen*. This fabric, initially produced in the regions north of Tokyo, was extremely popular in the first half of the twentieth century.[83] The production of some types of fabrics today referred to as *meisen* employed the stencil as a dyeing tool (but in a form distinct from the *kata-yūzen* developed by Hirose Jisuke) along with a combination of a *komon*-patterned background with applied motifs. With *kata-yūzen* and *komon*-patterned backgrounds, the dye or rice paste-resist is applied after the fabric is woven. If cloth is dyed after being woven, it is considered *atozome* ('after dyeing'). In *meisen* production, the yarns are dyed prior to weaving rather than dyeing the finished cloth. Yarn dyed prior to the weaving of the cloth falls into the category of *sakizome* ('before dyeing', or the equivalent of 'yarn-dyed'). In *meisen* production, the dye is applied through stencils onto the warp yarns, and as the process was refined, to both the warp and weft yarns, demarcating regional distinctions (illus. 58, 59). For one regional type, the pre-dyed warp yarns, stabilized by a loosely interwoven yarn in a zigzag pattern, are then secured to the loom, and the wefts are inserted in a plain-weave structure as the stabilizing yarn is removed. Traditional accounts identify *meisen*'s predecessor as the inexpensive silk fabric known as *futoori* ('thick weave') developed around 1835 by Katō Jizaemon of Isezaki (a small textile town north of Tokyo).[84] Other towns in the Kantō area, such as Chichibu, Ashikaga, Kiryū and Hachiōji, also excelled at *meisen* production.[85]

On a macro level, incremental improvements in the manufacture of silk and cotton bridged the divide between small-scale handcrafted production and factory-centred mechanical processes. On a micro level, changes in the use of a simple tool, like the stencil, or the burgeoning desire to produce recognizable regional styles such as Iyo *kasuri* and Oshima *kasuri,* stimulated weavers and dyers to create novel patterning for the kimono.

Modern Kimono Modes

Macro-level changes in the textile industry reverberated through the kimono industry. The narrow loom width required for kimono fabric of approximately 35 cm provided a built-in trade barrier that protected and insulated the weaving industries of Japan.[86] Imported cloth rarely met domestic demand for the specific widths and lengths required by the kimono industry.[87] The kimono industry adopted and adapted imported materials and technology for the various stages of kimono manufacture, but it was a selective process driven by domestic desires rather than external pressures.

At the beginning of the nineteenth century, reeled silk continued to command the highest market prices, followed by spun silk and ramie cloth. Consumption of silk and fine-quality ramie was restricted to samurai and wealthy merchants, perhaps 20 per cent of the total population at that time. Striped and patterned cotton were valued above plain white cotton cloth, and garments made from cotton cloth were worn by approximately 80 per

Overleaf
56, 57 Woman's kimono with design of weeping cherry trees, bundles of brushwood, and stylized snow roundels, and detail, late 19th century, minute stencil-dyed patterns of pine needles and chrysanthemums in white with fine paste-resist dyed and embroidered designs against a black, plain-weave silk ground.

Pages 86–7
58, 59 Woman's kimono with design of castles and maple leaves, and detail, 1930s, stencilled paste-resist dyeing on raw silk.

cent of the population.[88] The output of patterned and striped cotton kimono fabric grew until the end of the nineteenth century when other fabrics developed within the kimono industry, such as *meisen*, printed cotton flannel, printed wool muslin and other inexpensive fabrics vied for the kimono wearer's attention and purse.[89] While the implementation of imported materials and technology in the textile industry may have contributed to reducing processing costs, it also stimulated creative impulses and generated new products.

As noted, the importation of chemical dyes in the second half of the nineteenth century led to new applications of traditional techniques, as well as new product lines. Around the same time that Hirose Jisuke invented stencilled paste-resist dyeing, a textile artisan from Osaka, Horikawa Shinzaburō (1851–1914), developed a similar method of printing on woollen fabrics.[90] The newly developed product was named *mosurin yūzen* ('muslin *yūzen*').

60 Woman's under-kimono (*juban*) with design of modern paintings, late 1920s–early 1930s, stencilled paste-resist dyeing on wool muslin.

Wool muslin fabric was first imported to Japan in the 1860s as undyed cloth, and later in dyed colours. From the 1880s, Japanese dyers patterned this fabric with chemical dyes using coloured paste applied through stencils in the direct-print dyeing method (*iro nori nassen zome*), and sold their products in the domestic market.[91] Roller printing technology also developed at a rapid pace during this time and was applied to various types of fabrics.[92] The desire for muslin *yūzen* for kimonos, kimono linings and under-kimonos from the mid-nineteenth to the early twentieth centuries ensured a steady demand for domestic production (illus. 60).

Another type of cotton cloth favoured for kimonos and under-kimonos appeared in the late 1880s.[93] The cloth was dubbed *neru*, derived from the final syllable of the English word 'flannel'. First woven in the early 1870s in Kishu, where a similar fabric, *monpa-ori*, was already in production, cotton flannel production spread to Kyoto, Osaka, Sakai and Wakayama from 1879 to 1900.[94] Whether the virtually simultaneous development of stencil and chemical dye printing on silk and wool challis was coincidental or collaborative, or whether the development of under-kimonos of striped and printed cotton flannel was a logical market response to the popularity of wool printed under-kimonos has yet to be documented. Certainly the web of brokers involved in the production process, the networks of distribution, the mobility of a skilled workforce that transported technical knowledge across regional borders and the widespread dissemination of new trends through the media (including woodblock prints, illustrated books and later photographs) contributed to an expanded network and increased efforts to gain a competitive advantage in the new large-scale market economy.

Trends in overall design compositions and the layering of kimonos changed in tandem with dyeing processes. In the third quarter of the nineteenth century, the lower sleeve, lower half and front overlaps of the kimono monopolized designers' attention. Silk kimonos for young women were decorated on the lower sleeves and around the skirt area; for married women, designs pooled around the hem; and for mature women, patterns were confined primarily to the front overlaps. The overall height of the patterned area, measured from the hem up, also shifted with prevailing fashions. In the 1870s, designs were generally concentrated on one front overlap, rising to a level approximately 20 cm from the hem. When both front overlaps were patterned, the design reached a height of approximately 30 cm. From the 1910s, the design element stretched from the front overlaps across the entire back of the garment (illus. 61, 62). Demand for silk kimonos with *komon* resist-dyed backgrounds, enhanced with diminutive applied designs scattered around the hem and front overlaps of the kimono, were commonly worn as formal wear throughout the Meiji period by wealthier members of society.[95] Regional differences emerged as well, with women from the Kansai area favouring designs that swept across the back of the garment's hem, while those in the Kantō area continued to favour the Edo-zuma style in which the front hem areas were the focus of attention.

In addition to novel design compositions catering to regional tastes, the appeal of fresh products permeated the textile industry. Clever manufacturers recognized that each innovation warranted its own unique name. *Meisen* is but one of many examples in which a new type of fabric was christened with a new name or brand. While the pronunciation of the word *meisen* was constant, in written works the two Japanese characters used to denote the term were modified to capture the spirit of the times. The term was in flux throughout the first decade of the twentieth century, as documented in the 1908 Mitsukoshi magazine 'Trends of the Times' (*Jikō*) in which the term *meisen* is written with different characters on facing pages. But nomenclature, particularly in the service of marketers, is an inexact science. Japanese textile terminology is especially intractable, as the meaning of the Japanese terms shifts over time and with use. Once the vaguely defined Japanese term is translated into a suitable English equivalent, the term's original meaning is often lost in translation.

Overleaf
61, 62 Woman's long-sleeved kimono (*furisode*) with design of phoenixes amid paulownia and roses, and detail, first quarter of 20th century, paste-resist dyeing on silk crepe ground.

For example, *chirimen* refers to cloth woven of silk in a plain-weave structure with highly twisted wefts that imbue the finished cloth with a crepe texture. Modifications to this simple crepe weave led to a plethora of new types of cloth. Although traditionally woven in a plain-weave structure with highly twisted wefts that alternated every two shots, a bewildering array of textures blossomed throughout the late nineteenth and early twentieth centuries. *Kabe chirimen*, woven with untwisted warps and highly twisted thick and thin yarns plied into a single weft yarn, resulting in a fabric that is less supple than *chirimen*, came into fashion from the late 1870s. The term *uzura chirimen*, literally 'quail crepe', alluded to the mottled texture of a quail's feather patterning, created by alternating highly twisted wefts every four to six shots. Other crepe-type fabrics included *hitokoshi chirimen* (untwisted warps with highly twisted wefts alternating every single shot), *mon-chirimen* (silk crepe with woven designs) and *nuitori chirimen* (silk crepe woven with discontinuous supplementary wefts). Certain crepe textures were considered suitable for particular dyeing processes (illus. 63).

Omeshi, another slippery textile term, refers to a stiff, thick silk crepe produced with yarns that are dyed prior to weaving. Iwase Kichibei, who hailed from the textile-producing region of Kiryū, developed a water-powered spinning machine that produced highly twisted yarns, enabling weavers to harness this newly developed material to the imported Jacquard loom in order to produce a distinctive type of cloth which they named *omeshi*.[96] According to the textile scholars Yamanobe and Fujii, *omeshi* was 'most in demand by all the classes from the Meiji . . . to the Taishō period'.[97] From about 1884, a double-weave, silk crepe cloth known as *fūtsū-omeshi* gained popularity. A single roll of kimono *fūtsū-omeshi*, composed of 340 examples, enabled kimono retailers to compactly transport multiple samples for their customers' perusal. *Fūtsū-omeshi* demand peaked in 1895 to 1896, to be replaced by a variation, a supplementary weft-patterned woven silk (*nuitori-omeshi*), and was only revived in 1927.[98]

63 Length of fabric with design of trains and bridges, c. 1918, stencilled paste-resist dyeing on silk crepe.

Other silk-producing areas developed regionally specific products to sell on a national scale. *Akashi-chijimi*, a thin plain-weave silk crepe woven in Akashi, was sought after for summer kimonos due to its airy, lightweight quality. The vertical-stripe patterning resulted from the reflective quality of the material and the method with which the silk was processed – reeled, raw silk for the warp and glossed, twisted wefts. As the fabric gained national recognition, weavers in Nishijin, Kyoto and other areas, such as Tokamachi (Niigata prefecture), capitalized on the increased demand for this product.[99] Tokamachi weavers, already familiar with the production of another type of fine silk, known as *sukiya*, adapted their skills to produce *Akashi chijimi*. *Sukiya*, originally woven with a silk warp and ramie weft, itself evolved into a cloth woven of reeled, unglossed silk for both warp and weft.[100] Not surprisingly, it was produced in Echigo (Niigata prefecture), also renowned for its *Echigo chijimi*, the lustrous crepe made from ramie once favoured by the military elite.

Whereas urban centres of fashion in the past coexisted with regional styles of dress, the impetus to gain competitive advantage by producing recognizable regional specialties and increase sales resulted in a plethora of new kimono designs in all types of materials. Books filled with swatches of cotton dyed in myriad patterns, as well as the establishment of cartels or trade groups associated with specific regions, indicate the growing commercial market for kimono fabrics. The weaving of cloth, once produced primarily for personal consumption, became a lucrative business as seasonal side employment for farmers.

The role of trade associations or cartels, modelled after the Edo-period guild system, allowed regional groups to engage in discussions aimed at improving cultivation and production processes, promoting local products and maintaining quality standards. For example, an 1886 gathering of the Iyo Woven Textiles Improvement Association (Iyo Orimono Kairyō Kumiai) comprising local merchants, weavers and dyers, allowed members to exchange information and coordinate efforts to acquire improved technologies.[101] Traditional accounts credit Kagiya Kana (1782–1864) of Shikoku with introducing *kasuri* weaving – a technique believed to have been transmitted to Japan from Southeast Asia via the Ryūkyū Islands (modern-day Okinawa) – to the Iyo region (present-day Ehime prefecture) where it developed a distinctive patterning, appreciated today for its pictorial designs.[102] *Kasuri* is one of the *sakizome* (yarn-dyed) processes. To create patterns, warps and wefts are tied off with an impermeable material to prevent the dye from penetrating in discretely bound areas. The yarns are repeatedly dipped in an indigo dye-bath, the number of dips determined by the desired intensity of the colour. The loom is warped, and as the weaver inserts the pre-dyed wefts, the pre-determined patterns emerge. Other regions produced cotton *kasuri*-patterned

64 Length of fabric with design of steam train, *c.* 1870s, thread-resist dyeing (*Kurume gasuri*) on cotton ground.

cloths that bear their geographic labels, such as *Kurume gasuri* and *Bingo kasuri* (illus. 64).

Regional specialities with converging historical developments are *Miyako jōfu, Oshima tsumugi* and *kasuri*, and *Isezaki meisen*. The cloth today known as *Miyako jōfu*, a fine ramie cloth appreciated as a high-grade summer kimono fabric in the Meiji period, was originally known as *Satsuma jōfu* in the Edo period. Primarily patterned with warp stripes, from the early twentieth century *Miyako jōfu* weavers and dyers learned the practical application of the *kasuri*-patterning technique from artisans on the neighbouring island of Amami-Oshima.[103]

From about 1877, weavers in Oshima produced *Oshima tsumugi* as a commercial product. *Oshima tsumugi* weavers in turn had looked to the *kasuri*-weaving traditions and expertise of nearby Kurume, recognized for its cotton *kasuri* products known as *Kurume gasuri*, and transferred those dyeing techniques to the silk of *Oshima tsumugi*. Initially woven on the backstrap loom of hand-spun silk threads, innovations led to *Oshima kasuri* manufactured of high-quality reeled silk being woven on the counter-balanced, treadle *takabata* loom.[104] The importation of the Jacquard loom and a simple design tool – the graph paper used by weavers in Lyon, France to produce *chiné* – enhanced *Oshima kasuri* weavers' ability to produce increasingly intricate designs at a lower cost.[105] *Oshima kasuri* followed the established fashion preference for small patterns on stylish kimono or *osharegi* – a new category of kimono that bridged the realm between formal and casual wear. On a practical level, the use of graph paper for designing *Oshima kasuri,* which flourished from 1927 to 1941, had the added advantage of recording a weaver's designs in a form more tangible than individual memory. Knowledge of graph paper use that began in Nishijin was transmitted to the weaving district of Isezaki in 1914, and from there to Amami Oshima in 1919. Coincidentally, Isezaki is also one of the production centres for another type of textile that prized designs with blurred outlines – *meisen*.[106] The aspiration to transfer technical information on graph paper may be correlated with the transmission of other weaving and dyeing techniques from region to region.

This overview of the diversity of kimono fabrics available in the modern era serves as the historical background for the production of kimonos in our own time. The disruptions caused by the war years to kimono production, the lives of its makers and the attendant values of the kimono will be taken up in chapter Five. It is worth noting, however, that the materials, processes and transfer of technology in the modern era generate issues that resonate in our own time. In the era of mass mechanization, Japan's relatively segmented production system and division of labour – production of fibres, spinning, weaving, dyeing – allowed for changes to be made in one step of the process without requiring that the entire system be shut down. The weakening of certain segments of a horizontally integrated system may eventually have led to the demise of the kimono industry in the post-Second World War era. Ironically, the 'specialization of tasks' jeopardized the production of speciality fabrics in the post-war period, as older craftspeople died without apprentices to carry on their work. The newer system of vertical integration allowed for a single entity to control all aspects of production and thereby enhance the producer's longevity through continuous training and replacement of aged or retired workers. With the conventional and historically based proclivity towards horizontal manufacturing processes, in contrast, the loss of a single link or artisans' skills in the production chain eventually led to the decline or disappearance of certain textile craft traditions; the livelihood of stencil-cutters in the Ise Shiroko region who produced the renowned Ise *katagami* stencils is but one example.

Post-Second World War government-supported initiatives to preserve the production of specifically named fabrics or kimonos made by Living National Treasures parallel Empress Shōken's support for Japanese cloth and clothing producers in a world when fashion trends were moving towards Western styles. Today's government-sponsored programmes help sustain an industry whose initial demand as kimono-to-wear is waning. The continued production of kimonos and traditional Japanese fabrics, whether as clothing to wear on special occasions, as examples of 'traditional Japanese craftsmanship' or as works of art, raise further questions about the rationale for preserving 'traditions'. When, for example, does assimilation of the novel cross over into the realm of 'tradition', regardless of whether the original source of inspiration was domestic or international? Imported materials and technology, incorporated in incremental innovations into the large-scale Japanese textile industry, stimulated urban and regional kimono designers to develop new products for the burgeoning national market. Competition among neighbouring villages, which both shared and stole knowledge of industrial improvements through trade associations and cartels, resulted in the production of regionally specific speciality fabrics, sometimes today referred to as 'named things' (*meibutsu*). In the post-Second World War era, many of the *meibutsu* considered the cultural heritage of a particular prefecture or region are craft traditions practised by cooperative associations, and have been designated as Intangible Cultural Properties by the Japanese government in order to sustain their production. Individual artisans perceived to have preserved distinctive weaving or dyeing techniques have been recognized by the government as Living National Treasures.

The effects of Empress Shōken's call for her subjects to don Western-style apparel of Japanese material and manufacture are debatable, given the small percentage of the population that could then afford the costly fabrics and tailoring of Western dress. There is no doubt, however, that imported Western materials, technologies and styles of dress massively influenced the Japanese textile industry as a whole, reverberating throughout urban and regional kimono production centres.

In the next chapter, we turn our attention to major changes in the promotion and marketing of kimonos, and shifting consumer demands, coinciding with Japan's exposure to the West and integration into the global market.

THREE

Shopping for Kimonos,
Shaping Identities

We may mention, in passing, that this idiosyncrasy of [Japanese who adopted European] dress was actuated by a love of symbolism. It was the expression of a desire on the part of the progressionist to cast off the shackles of the decadent East and identify himself with the advance of Western civilization. Our kimono meant leisure while the European dress meant activity and became the uniform of the army of progress, like the *chapeau rouge* in revolutionary France. Nowadays, a reaction has set in, and native costume is more generally worn by the progressives. Few of our ladies affect European costume except at court.

Okakura Kakuzō[1]

O kakura Kakuzō (also known as Tenshin, 1862–1913) was an influential teacher and cultural critic who assumed the mantle of translator of Japanese art and aesthetics to the English-speaking world. In 1904, he observed that a reactionary sentiment towards 'things Western' had taken over Japan. This growing sense of national pride is not surprising, given that Japan had nine years earlier defeated its largest Asian neighbour in the Sino–Japanese War of 1894–5 and was embroiled in the Russo–Japanese war of 1904–5. During this tumultuous time Okakura published his now classic *The Ideals of the East: With Special Reference to the Art of Japan*, which began with the profound assertion that 'Asia is one'.[2] In 1904, he completed another influential volume, *The Awakening of Japan,* which nods towards his pan-Asian perspective. A year later, Japan would emerge victorious over Russia and embark on the colonization of its Asian neighbours.

Japan's struggle for an identity distinct from other Asian nations and for recognition among the then-dominant Western countries often revealed itself in the clothing of its citizens. Nativist attitudes were visually manifest by clothing one's body in Japanese dress – an expression of pride in Japanese culture. Donning Western-style garments symbolized Japan's aspirations to be recognized as an equal.

Yet decoding the symbolic meanings of Japanese wearing kimonos, or suits and bowler hats, was far more complex than meets the eye. When travelling abroad, Okakura often deliberately and defiantly chose to wear kimonos, even if it subjected him to criticism from his own countrymen, including the influential Japanese ambassador to the United States, Kuki Ryūichi. As the scholar Christine Guth notes: 'By donning such attire, Okakura sought to assert some measure of symbolic resistance to the West's cultural colonization of Japan.'[3] Okakura's exceptional command of the English language and knowledge of Western cultural norms allowed him

> to dictate the terms of his interactions with the West. As [Okakura] explained to his son, 'From my first trip to Europe, I wore kimono most of the time. I suggest you travel abroad in kimono if you think that your English is good enough. But never wear Japanese costume if you talk in broken English.'[4]

Okakura engaged in a form of self-orientalizing; he fully recognized the impact his wearing of Japanese-style garments would have in a Western setting. A journalist for the American magazine *The Critic* commented that Okakura was 'one of the most interesting foreigners now visiting this country', adding, 'Mr. Okakura continues to wear his native costume, his sense of the artist being too great to allow him to don the clothes of European civilization.'[5] In contrast, in the 1930s, the acclaimed theoretician Kuki Shūzō – son of the statesman Kuki Ryūichi, who had earlier criticized Okakura for wearing Japanese-style dress – would wear dapper Western-style garments as he strolled the campus of Kyoto Imperial University, distinguishing himself from colleagues who continued to wear kimonos.[6] Distinct differences in sartorial approach were apparent in this period.

A woodblock print of 1874 by Utagawa Hiroshige III (1843–1894) is telling in its detailed depictions of men and women strolling along the Ginza (illus. 65). Some are dressed in Japanese-style garments – kimonos and *hakama* (split trouser-like skirts). Others appear in Western modes – dresses, trousers and uniforms. Most interesting are the ensembles pairing Japanese-style garments with boots or bowler hats. While the mixing and matching of boots and *hakama* may appear strange to twenty-first-century eyes, the fusion of fashions from around the world during this era became a familiar sight in daily life, in the same way that one might sit in a Western-style chair at the office and then recline on a *tatami*-mat floor in the comfort of one's private space.

Newly established emporiums of the early twentieth century assisted consumers in navigating the tides between domestic and foreign merchandise. Department stores used marketing strategies to launch themselves as the new arbiters of taste in modern Japan.[7] In contrast to conventional kimono shops

65 Utagawa Hiroshige III, scenic view of Tokyo enlightenment, the Ginza from Kyōbashi, December 1874, triptych of polychrome woodblock prints, ink and colour on paper.

of the previous Edo era, in which shop boys retrieved rolls of silk for examination by individual customers, department stores of the early twentieth century were palaces of display in which merchandise was exhibited in glass cases and shop windows. Customers could browse freely without feeling the pressure to purchase, and newly imported goods were domesticated by sales staff trained in making the foreign familiar. In a series of woodblock prints, considered by many to be a precursor to modern advertising, the kimono purveyor Echigoya was featured in the series 'Contemporary Beauties in Summer Garments' by Kitagawa Utamaro (1753–1806), discussed in chapter One (illus. 66).

In the early twentieth century, Echigoya, still recognizable by its emblematic logo but renamed 'Mitsukoshi', continued to lead the way in stimulating demand with novel advertising strategies.[8] Mitsukoshi sponsored poster design competitions that featured the season's upcoming fashions. In one updated version of promotional material, Mitsukoshi's in-house magazine featured a woman dressed in a kimono seated in a chair surrounded by Art Nouveau-inspired interior designs and furnishings, perusing a woodblock-printed book with images of Edo-period figures (illus. 67). The poster, designed by Hashiguchi Goyō (1880–1921), won the poster competition in 1911. The cartouche on the right reads 'Mitsukoshi *gofukuten*' (kimono shop) with the store's logo prominently displayed above. Goyō's prized poster is an amalgam of juxtaposed symbols – traditional and modern – that visually fused native and exotic for the Japanese consumer.

Western or Japanese, conventional or contemporary, or an amalgam of some sort, these stylistic choices were not simply a question of garment choice, but of decorative motifs. In 1905, the design theme for kimonos promoted by the Mitsukoshi department store harkened back to the Genroku era (1688–1704), a time romanticized by the Japanese for its flourishing culture propelled largely by the nouveau riche merchant class.[9] Mitsukoshi's campaign of 1905 was so influential and effective that the cultural critic Hayashida Shunchō felt compelled to comment on the political implications of the Genroku-design revival in the arts and literary magazine 'Venus' (*Myōjō*), which served as an early forum for discourse on Western and Japanese cultural tastes.[10] Indeed, art, politics and fashion converged on the bodies of the Japanese people and in the newly established emporiums.

Emerging artist-designers, notably Sugiura Hisui (1876–1965), himself a collaborator in the promotion of a fusion of Japanese and Western aesthetics in the pages of 'Venus', left their mark on the graphic arts and forged new directions in consumer trends. Hisui, who rose to become chief designer of Mitsukoshi from 1910 to 1934, and Takahashi Yoshio (1861–1937), director

66 Kitagawa Utamaro, 'Suited to Crepes Stocked by Echigoya', from the series 'Contemporary Beauties in Summer Garments' (*Natsu ishō tōsei bijin*), *c.* 1804–06, polychrome woodblock print, ink and colour on paper.

67 Hashiguchi Goyō, Mitsukoshi department store poster, 1911, colour lithograph.

68 Sugiura Hisui, Mitsukoshi department store poster, 1914, colour lithograph.

of Mitsukoshi, are credited with the 1905 Mitsukoshi marketing campaign to revive the Genroku style.[11] The dissemination of information on fashion trends, aided by the publication of pattern books, store advertisements and women's magazines, the promotions and exhibitions sponsored by department stores, as well as improved transportation between the major cities, created ideal conditions for the textile industry to cater to its expanding consumer base.

Hisui masterminded the 'face of Mitsukoshi'.[12] Hisui's designs reflect formal training in Nihonga ('Japanese-style') painting, but also reveal knowledge of Western artistic movements, likely resulting from his encounter with the *yōga* ('Western-style') painter Kuroda Seiki (1866–1924). Hisui's poster of 1914, submitted for the 'Meeting to Display New Designs' (*Shingara chinretsukai*), like Goyō's poster of 1911, depicts a seated woman wearing a kimono (illus. 68). The up-to-date woman in Hisui's poster, however, has a copy of Mitsukoshi's magazine resting in her lap. She leans towards a vase filled with tulips, an increasingly popular motif in Japan at the time due to their recent cultivation there. Tulips became very popular in the kimono design repertoire of the mid- to late 1920s. The room's interior decor has noticeably mutated from Goyō's Art Nouveau style to the Secessionist style, reflecting the shift in taste.

Department stores collaborated with textile manufacturers to commission artists to design advertising, a triangular relationship seemingly originating in Utamaro's time. Posters prominently displayed the store's name above a chic woman dressed in a fashionable kimono made from a specific type of textile. For example, the Ashikaga Meisen Association commissioned well-known painters and print designers, many of whom specialized in *bijinga* ('pictures of beauties'), such as Yamakawa Shūhō (1898–1944), to design posters of women wearing kimonos made of *meisen* fabric.[13] Renowned artist-designers were also employed to design covers for women's magazines and participated in kimono design research groups.[14] As discussed in detail in chapter Five, artists trained primarily as painters were also commissioned to design patterns for kimonos.

望展の裳衣美和調

着物……金糸入東雲縮緬社交服
　漆茶裏地に花の丸、觀世水の調和よく、單に效果を呈す

帯……錦織名古屋帯
　生地能衣裳調の最も分たく、巧彩と品味を加ふ

着物……西　陣　お　召
　納戸地に濃淡の縞、疊付きて見ゆ、精黄の變た浮き出づ
　また明春のさわやか

帯……眞　砂　錦　織
　白地に濃き伊豆貴人形の福々丹青の妙味た見立
　の美し

着物……美裳縮緬社交服
　納戸雲取絞り藍の表現やさしく、花
　見快き花たの世ご香る魅示

帯……こうけつ織名古屋帯
　生地に制代模様青海波のつの絞り風の表現に上品さ

着物……西　陣　お　召
　爲色青地の縮緬の色につけ大籟に銀色の白縞一段
　見明快な樽

帯……錦織名古屋帯
　眞地に制風の華紋とほかして武士の番左服ぶ天、牡丹の
　榮とし見事取り

着物……鳥帽子縮緬社交服
　栗種色地の濃淡に白く秋の花た用ひ、色調の巧
　みにほほ

帯……錦織名古屋帯
　ピンク地に結ばれし蝶五彩の巧みは、皆春の美しさ
　なあらば

着物……美裳縮緬小紋着尺

着物……綸子縮緬社交服
　泉地に黒が白ぬける子弟な横に、絞の自調快さ意敷の閒
　見す

帯……金茶地錦織名古屋帯
　金銀原子重丹莊風粕分横誕した方促美作

着物……美裳縮緬社交服
　淺黄裏地に納戸濃淡の竹絡風に見開一木藤ぐく物の情真美し

帯……錦　地　壽　織
　臨層地善文様に光花の詰凝化ゆ妙調和よ

着物……綸子縮緬絞り訪問服
　錦納戸地に縮緬ぼかし、絞り花の丸の續模様に技巧の冴え見す

帯……金茶地錦織名古屋帯

帯……眞砂錦織名古屋帯
　白地に盛蓮色調のなか

着物……西　陣　お　召

着物……綸子縮緬社交服
　黒地に黒かが白ぬけて、朱色の牡丹た便化
　た張る刺る表現

帯……錦織名古屋帯
　うすピンク地に赤、黄の唐獅子の出威な浴と
　て銀糸の有職刺映ゆる

69 Pamphlet for Matsuzakaya
department store, March 1937.

Department store posters prominently displayed fashions current during a particular year or season, visually promoting a new 'look' intended to stir consumer desire and increase sales.[15] Department stores and textile manufacturers also promoted their products through seasonal trade shows that for the first time featured ready-to-wear kimonos displayed on mannequins (illus. 69).[16] In some cases, each was labelled as an ideal type of woman.[17] The marketing tactic of promoting a specific look enfranchised the customer by cultivating and appealing to her imagined or idealized taste.

Department stores and their wholesalers featured popular actresses and singers, such as Tanaka Kinuyō and Mizutani Yaeko, modelling the latest kimono fashions (illus. 70). As early as 1896, Mitsukoshi had established a precedent for employing Japanese 'celebrities' to market kimono designs when it introduced its 'dandy-pattern' (*date moyō*) and distributed kimonos decorated with this new motif to the geisha of Shinbashi, who wore them when performing.[18] A geisha wears a Genroku-revival-style kimono in a 1907 poster, itself a promotion devised by Mitsukoshi's marketing team (illus. 71). Mitsukoshi also featured photographs of well-known customers on the covers of its in-house magazine 'Trends of the Times' (*Jikō*).

Beyond the kimono patterns featured in the popular images of geishas and celebrities, modern kimono designs reflect the multi-faceted role of women during the late nineteenth and early twentieth centuries. In this transitional era, working women typically were employed as waitresses in the city's cafes, shop girls, factory hands in the textile mills, clerical workers, telephone operators, teachers or nurses.[19] As a sign of this labour trend, Mitsukoshi hired its first female clerk in 1901.[20] Urban middle-class wives constituted another consumer category. The model 'good wife, wise mother' (*ryōsai kenbo*) often wore a kimono.[21] The 'ordinary woman' (*tada no onna*) wore kimono patterns that were traditional and familiar so as not to draw attention to herself. Her more liberated and modern sister, the emerging 'modern girl' (*modan gaaru*), might on occasion choose to wear a trendy kimono with her hair modishly permed in a Western-style bob.

70 Poster for Ashikaga Honmeisen with actress Tanaka Kinuyō as model, 1932, colour lithograph.

71 Mitsukoshi department store poster with Shinbashi geisha dressed in the 'Genroku style', 1907, ink and colour on paper.

Tucked into the pages of the 1910 issue of the in-house advertising magazine for the Mitsukoshi department store was a 'New Game of Fashion for the Family' (*Shin-an katei ishō awase*) (illus. 72).[22] Profiles of family members aligned horizontally across the top of the page, read from right to left, depicted a husband, wife, grandfather, grandmother, young girl, young boy, baby and maid. Below each figure were five frames enclosing articles of clothing or accessories appropriate for each person. The insert, created by Mitsukoshi's chief designer, Hisui, graphically categorized items suitable by gender and age for members of an urban, elite family. In the first decade of the twentieth century, clothing for various family members incorporated an amalgam of Japanese- and Western-style items. Notably, however, Japanese-style garments dominate selections for mother, grandmother, young girl and maid, intermingled with a few Western-style accessories such as parasols and shawls. For the men, clothing items and accessories, such as hats, gloves, pocket watches, shoes and overcoats show a favouring of Western-style dress.

Age, generation and gender often determined who wore kimonos and who didn't. In a 1925 poster by Hisui, designed to advertise the unveiling of Mitsukoshi's Shinjuku store, a woman with bobbed hair carries two trendy imports: a parasol in her right hand and a handbag in her left (illus. 73). She is simultaneously conventional in her kimono and up-to-date in her selection of Western-style accessories. Although she is wearing a kimono, her slender, willowy figure, cinched at the waist by her obi, and her gently fluttering garment are reminiscent of the flapper-style silhouette popular in Western fashion at this time. The little girl standing beside the woman, in contrast, is outfitted from head to toe in Western-style clothing. While the two appear to be mother and daughter on a shopping outing, they are gazing off in different directions, possibly foreshadowing the divergent paths their future clothing purchases might follow, though at this time both styles coexisted harmoniously in the Japanese mindset.

73 Sugiura Hisui, poster for the Shinjuku branch of the Mitsukoshi department store, 1925, colour lithograph.

72 Sugiura Hisui, 'New Game of Fashion for the Family' (*Shin-an katei ishō awase*), supplement to *Mitsukoshi Times* magazine, VIII/1 (January 1910).

Takabatake Kashō's (1888–1966) illustration for the magazine 'Ladies' World' (*Fujin Sekai*) reveals the eclecticism prevailing in this moment in history. Two women seated in chairs and playing cards are depicted in his illustration. Both women sport Western-style bobs, but whereas one figure is wearing an orange dress, red scarf and shoes, the other is wearing a kimono, her feet demurely hidden beneath the folds of cloth. Notably, the kimono's design has been updated with the imported tulip motif rising from the lower edge of the kimono's sleeve, offering a taste of the exotic. A woman might wear Western-style dress from head to toe, while her companion might choose to wear a kimono decorated with newly imported Western motifs. Despite their different clothing choices, both could be viewed as modern Japanese women. Some observers were sceptical of the significance of these developments, regardless of whether then-emerging modern Japanese fashions were categorized as Japanese-style, Western-style, or a hybrid. The feminist writer Yamakawa Kikue commented in a magazine article, 'exchanging the Japanese clothing the commodified woman is wearing for Western clothing . . . is only modernization on the surface'.[23]

Although Takabatake's image depicts women at leisure, throughout the first half of the twentieth century, more and more women found gainful employment in the growing economy, particularly in the textile industry. As the economic historian Janet Hunter observes, 'both before 1914 and afterwards, textile work was consistently seen by most participants in the labour market as a phase in a woman's life cycle'.[24] From 1894 to 1912, female labour accounted for an average of 60 per cent of Japan's industrial labour force.[25] In 1900, women comprised 77 per cent of the labour force in the cotton industry.[26] In 1909, 52 per cent of factory labourers were female textile workers.[27] By 1911, more than 190,000 women found employment toiling at the silk-reeling machines in major production centres.[28] Powered by women, the textile industry provided much-needed capital to fund the government's efforts to industrialize and modernize.

No longer constrained by government-imposed sumptuary laws or the dictates of her class, the modern Japanese woman was relatively free to style herself as befitted her personal taste. The upsurge in women's participation in the textile manufacturing industry, as well as the increasing prominence of women in the literary world, is encapsulated in the selected motifs that decorate a single kimono – open books to signify women's access to higher education and spools of thread to signify their status as makers of textiles and clothing (illus. 74). In addition to working as migrant labourers in one of the many textile mills, women were often responsible for making clothing for themselves and the members of their households. As recounted in the personal diary of one Kyoto merchant's wife, whether the kimono fabric was purchased from travelling salesmen, at kimono shops or received as gifts, the sewing of the roll of cloth into kimonos was still part of a woman's household duties.[29]

The launching of women's magazines in the 1910s and their proliferation in the 1920s catered to women with improved literacy rates and increased discretionary income from their participation in the work force. These attributes made them perfect targets for publications such as 'The Housewife's Companion' (*Shufu no tomo*), 'Ladies' Club' (*Fujin kurabu*), and 'Ladies' Pictorial' (*Fujin gahō*).[30] While print runs for individual publications ranged in the tens of thousands when first launched, the women's magazine industry grew to an estimated 1.2 million issues in 1925.[31] The focus, content and layout of each magazine reflected its attempt to garner a particular niche of the women's magazine market. Publishers meticulously classified constituencies based on region, class, marital status and age. Certain publishers targeted married women and focused on the attendant issues, such as being a good wife and running a household, while others targeted single, working women. Some focused on the urbane and the elite; others directed their attention to women in rural areas, and even to Japanese emigrants living in other countries.[32] What all these magazines had in common was their aim to encourage women to consider their role in Japanese society and the world at large. Many of these magazines incorporated images of women at work and at play, and featured articles on how to behave and dress. Both explicitly and subversively, these publications cultivated the readers' perception of the ideal woman at a time when the role of women in Japan, like the nation itself, was undergoing sweeping transformations.

Strolling Around the Ginza

The Rokumeikan era (1884–9) signalled the embrace and subsequent dismissal by many women of Western fashions. Between this era and 1923, when the

74 Woman's kimono with design of open books and spools of thread, first half of the 20th century, stencilled paste-resist dyeing and silver threads on silk.

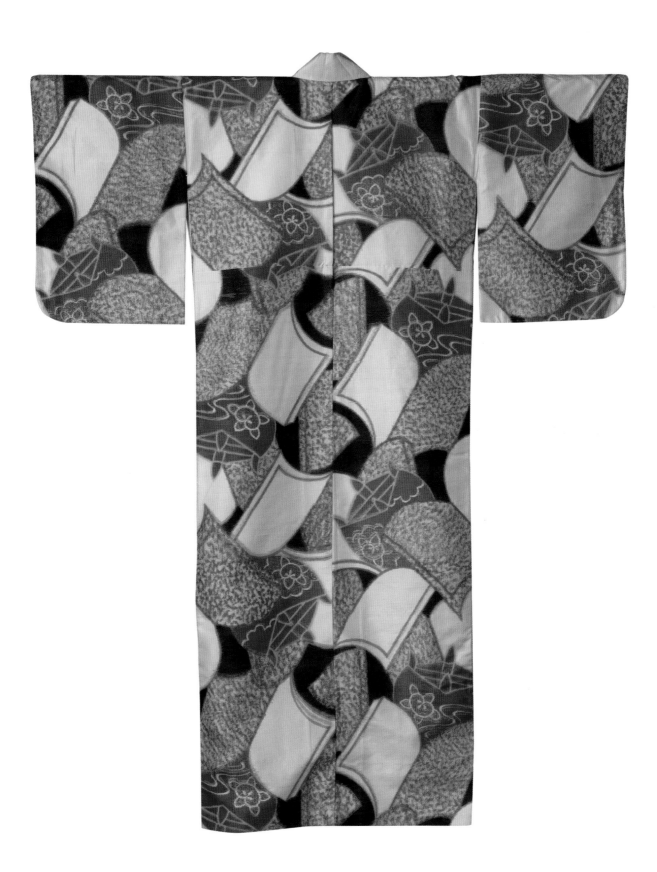

Great Kantō Earthquake levelled most of the city of Tokyo and its environs, the denizens of Tokyo existed in a rapidly changing urban society. Reverence and nostalgia for tradition, exemplified by continued wearing of the kimono, was tempered by a fascination with the new, as embodied by Western-style architecture and dress. The tension generated by these two forces characterized the transitional years of the beginning of the twentieth century.

Two years after the devastating Kantō Earthquake and subsequent fires that turned much of Tokyo to ash, the city had begun to recover as people rebuilt and resumed their daily activities. In 1925, the ethnographers Kon Wajirō and Yoshida Kenkichi, together with their assistants, surveyed individual articles of clothing worn by men and women strolling through the Ginza, an upscale shopping area of Tokyo. Of the 1,180 people observed cruising the Ginza, 'sixty-seven percent of the men wore Western clothing, while all but one percent of the women were in Japanese dress' (illus. 75).[33] Kon's objective was to observe 'the everyday practice of the cultured people of the present'.[34] Similar to his larger project known through his neologism 'modernology'

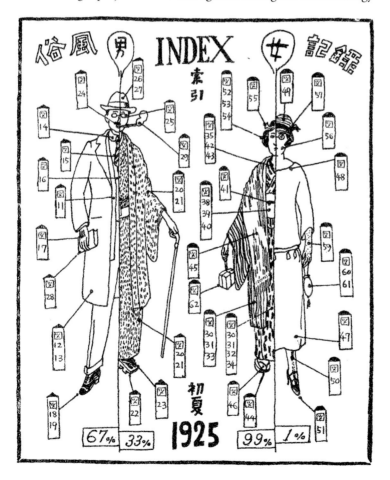

75 Kon Wajirō, 'Index' of Japanese- and Western-style fashion, *1925 Survey of Customs in Tokyo Ginza in Early Summer*, 1925, published in *Fujin Kōron* magazine.

(*kōgengaku*), Kon engaged in a quasi-scientific study and observation of the present – life as it was played out in the realm of clothing choices.

As Miriam Silverberg notes in her study of Kon and fellow ethnographer Gonda Yasunosuke, both active in the 1920s and '30s,

> The writing, drawings, and photographs of the Japanese ethnographers open up to us a new vision of how Japanese women and men of different classes integrated the relationship between East and West in different ways, not through borrowing or a double life enabling them to switch back and forth from white-collar suit to kimono, but via the construction of a complex identity informed by a type of cultural code-switching whereby elements of Western material and mass culture were integrated into everyday practice.[35]

Distinctions between Western and Japanese modes of dress, housing and food choices were less acute than when Western options were first introduced in the preceding decades. Rather, a form of daily living that not only subsumed Western things into a Japanese context, but also subjugated the concept of Asian (*toyō*) things, reflected a new mindset for the Japanese people. Department stores not only introduced these Western goods to Japanese consumers, they were also crucial translators who educated Japanese consumers in how to use and assimilate into their daily lives objects previously viewed as 'exotic'.[36]

As an ethnographer, Kon was interested not only in what people wore, but also in what they bought and how they used these objects in their homes. Whether or not Kon was aware of Thorsten Veblen's *Theory of the Leisure Class* (1899) and his theory of conspicuous consumption, Kon's innate curiosity as to how status anxiety relates to consumption patterns led him similarly to study consumers' behaviour in department stores.

What did the newly established emporiums offer and how was the merchandise displayed in order to optimize sales? According to Kon's study of department stores of 1928 that was published in the women's magazine 'Ladies' Companion', Mitsukoshi provided a climate designed to entice shoppers and those out for a leisurely stroll by offering warmth on colder days and a cooling respite from the heat of summer.[37] As one entered from the street level, the shopper or casual stroller might encounter items suitable as gifts or souvenirs (*miyagemono*), foodstuffs, cosmetics and personal accessories. Escalators, first installed in 1914, glided customers up to the various floors with slow-moving ease at the same time they invited shoppers to survey the floor they were leaving. Shoppers could peruse the second and third floors, stocked with an array of kimono fabrics: cotton and muslins (*merinsu*) on the second floor and the better quality silks, such as *omeshi* and *meisen*, as well as obi on the third floor. Western-style clothing and hair accessories could be found on the fourth floor, and home furnishings and appliances on the fifth.

In Kon's study, he divided his consumer subjects into three groups: those passing through or just looking around; those admiring merchandise; and those seriously engaging with or actively selecting merchandise. On one particular day, Kon and his survey team, positioning themselves near the famous lions that guard the entrance to Mitsukoshi Department Store in the Ginza, counted 1,077 men, 1,065 women and 92 children entering and leaving the store within a 30-minute time span. Of the women, 84 per cent wore kimonos, whereas only 39 per cent of the men were garbed in Japanese-style dress.[38] Women clearly continued to favour kimonos, even after the devastating earthquake of 1923 destroyed many of the personal belongings of Tokyo's inhabitants. Women, at least, seemed to have opted to replace their ruined kimonos not with Western-style garments, but with new kimonos. According to Kon's study, 51 per cent of the women strolling the Ginza wore *meisen* kimonos.

Stylish women wearing kimonos that incorporated Western accessories continued to be featured in posters, woodblock prints and magazines. In Watanabe Ikuharu's (1895–1975) series 'Comparison of Shōwa Beauties' (*Shōwa bijo sugata kurabe*, circa 1930s), the woman featured in his print for the twelfth month wears a bold purple- and brown-striped kimono patterned with bright red bamboo (illus. 76). She sports two flowers at the nape of her neck that accentuate her permed, bobbed hair. Her Western-inspired shawl, red clutch and grey gloves mark her as a fashionable, modern woman.[39]

76 Watanabe Ikuharu, 'Comparison of Shōwa Beauties: December, Snow, Sky' (*Shōwa bijo sugata kurabe-harumachizuki, yukizora*), *c.* 1920s–30s, polychrome woodblock print, ink and colour on paper.

Department Stores and Their Precursors

Many kimono purveyors converted their shops into modern-day department stores in the early twentieth century to more widely serve this evolving modern feminine ideal. A well-documented example is the transformation of the Edo store of Echigoya, established in 1673 by the Mitsui family, and subsequently renamed Mitsukoshi (illus. 77). Daimaru, established by the Shimomura family in 1717, converted in 1908, and Matsuzakaya, founded in 1611 by the Itō family, converted in 1910.[40] Takashimaya, established in Kyoto in 1831 as a shop that specialized in selling used kimonos, began selling new merchandise in 1855, and by 1907, converted its shops into department stores.[41] In most of these cases, not only the physical establishment, but also the merchandise was updated and modernized. Shirokiya, one of the established kimono shops featured in Utamaro's 'Contemporary Beauties' series, led the way when it became the first to sell Western-style clothing in 1886.[42]

The representational politics of display emerged during the 1860s as international expositions allowed Japanese manufacturers to promote their nation's wares. Indeed, as Japan jockeyed for position among national powers, a nation's goods served as markers of nation building in the competition for

77 Utagawa Hiroshige, 'View of Suruga-chō' (showing the Echigoya fabric and kimono shop), from 'Series of Famous Places in the Eastern Capital', *c.* 1844, polychrome woodblock print, ink and colour on paper.

international prominence. The commercial aspects of this relationship are highlighted in Peter Kornicki's study of public display, where he notes:

> 'nations' exhibited themselves at the exhibitions, packaged and prepared for an 'international' audience. But the components of the national exhibits were there principally as commodities, that is, either manufactured articles in search of export markets, exhibited to compete with each other for prizes valued for their advertising potential, or objects and people transformed into commodities by being displayed commercially. The latter were not for sale, but the opportunity to view them was for sale. Commodities were an inescapable facet of participation in the Great Exhibitions.[43]

Advertising a nation's wares served to demonstrate its industrial prowess.

As early as 1862, a member of a Japanese delegation to a London exposition recognized that 'the objective is to make known one's country's products to the peoples of each country.'[44] The Iwakura Mission report of 1871–2 echoed the value of displaying a nation's goods, in this case within a museum setting rather than at an international exposition. Based on eighteen months observing life in the United States and Europe, Ōkubo Toshimichi, a member of the delegation, noted that

> When one goes through a museum, the order of a country's enlightenment reveals itself spontaneously to the eye and heart. If one studies the basic reason when a country flourishes, one learns it is not a sudden thing. There is always an order. Those who open their eyes first awaken those who wake later . . . There is nothing better than museums to show that order.[45]

Thus, international expositions provided a model for the development of Japanese department stores and later, for another venerable cultural institution – the museum.

In addition to their relationship to expositions, the birth of the department store is also viewed as an outgrowth of another Meiji period phenomenon: the *kankōba*.[46] As Edward Seidensticker points out, the neologism *kankōba* referred to a

> place for the encouragement of industry [where] numbers of small shops would gather under a roof or an arcade . . . The first bazaar was publicly owned. It opened in 1878 selling products left over from the First Industrial Exposition, held at Ueno the preceding year.[47]

Products exhibited at *kankōba* served to stimulate desire by exhibiting wares previously unfamiliar to the Japanese people alongside recognizable but improved domestic products.

The Japanese government proceeded to foster the promotion of industry through an array of public exhibitions. In 1871, the Kyoto city mayor Makimura Masanao wrote in the preface of a catalogue that exhibitions were for 'contributing to the spread of knowledge rather than showing off one's possessions'.[48] In their solicitation of items for exhibit, the organizers circulated a leaflet explaining that

> in the countries of the West there is an excellent custom of holding what are called *hakurankai*. Newly developed machinery, antiques, and various other things are put on display to all and sundry, thus spreading knowledge and encouraging people to innovate and to profit from their inventions. Wishing to follow this good example, we sought the prefectural governor's permission to hold something similar, and now plan to exhibit to the public a collection of old and unusual things from Japan and China.[49]

Interestingly in this case, the emphasis is on old and unusual things, and while acknowledging their indebtedness to Western practices of display, the organizers solicited objects of Japanese and Chinese manufacture, not necessarily Western imports. In any case, the experiences gleaned by kimono purveyors, who were increasingly aware of new display modes and product promotion methods, hastened the transformation of kimono shops into department stores.[50]

During his two-decade-long relationship with Mitsukoshi, Hibi Ōsuke (1860–1931) would transform Mitsukoshi into a cultural citadel as well as a shopper's paradise.[51] Like his predecessor Takahashi (who studied at the respected Keiō University in the shadow of the writer Fukuzawa Yūkichi), Hibi journeyed abroad to study department stores. Unlike Takahashi, whose model was the Philadelphia-based store Wanamaker's, Hibi went to London, and was impressed by what he observed at the long-established Harrods. Takahashi was mainly concerned with identifying and later generating trends that would enable his store to sell more products. While Hibi expected Mitsukoshi to prosper as a profit-making venture, his motives were also altruistic; he believed that Mitsukoshi should contribute to the betterment of society and the country. To this end, he arranged for Mitsukoshi to host visits from foreign dignitaries and established research groups of well-known intellectuals.[52]

Through the ongoing efforts of Takahashi and Hibi, Mitsukoshi began to fashion its store identity through in-house publications: 'Floral Robes' (*Hanagoromo*) issued in 1898 included information on Mitsukoshi's business practices, as well as articles on woven and dyed goods and the differences between purveyors of Japanese and Western-style clothing. The success of 'Floral Robes' prompted the issuance of 'Summer Robes' (*Natsugoromo*) that same year, followed by 'Spring Patterns' (*Haru moyō*) and 'Summer Patterns' (*Natsu moyō*), all under the editorship of Hibi.[53] In 1903, Mitsukoshi began publishing 'Trends of the Times' (*Jikō*), which included articles about popular fashions, new products and store events, and essays written by noteworthy writers.[54] Mitsukoshi sponsored writing contests and awarded cash prizes for the best essays: even Mori Ōgai's satirical essay entitled 'Trends' (*Ryūkō*, 1911), about a man controlled by the latest fashions, brought attention to Mitsukoshi.[55] Recognizing the invaluable branding opportunities these publications afforded, the eponymous *Mitsukoshi* magazine made its debut in 1911 and, with the exception of an interruption caused by the 1923 earthquake, was issued monthly until 1933.[56]

Other department stores followed Mitsukoshi's lead. Shirokiya launched 'Household Guidance' (*Katei no shirube*), 'Trends' (*Ryūkō*) and 'Shirokiya Times' (*Shirokiya taimusu*); Takashimaya issued 'New Apparel' (*Shin ishō*); and Daimaru circulated 'Apparel' (*Ishō*) and 'Ladies' Club' (*Fujin kurabu*).[57] Filled with information on the latest trends, products, events and literary articles, these publications crafted and disseminated information on standards of taste. In a world where newly imported appliances were lined up alongside the latest modes of dress, these publications informed consumers about what new products were available and simultaneously stimulated the readers' desire to elevate their lifestyles through mechanization and modernization.

Modernization and mechanization proved to be a fatal blow to one former kimono purveyor – Daimaru. Established in the Nihonbashi area in the mid-eighteenth century, at one time Daimaru rivalled even the Mitsui-backed Mitsukoshi. In 1935, the playwright and critic Hasegawa Shigure reminisced that 'the Daimaru . . . was the center of Nihonbashi culture and prosperity, as the Mitsukoshi is today.' As the historian Edward Seidensticker pointed out, however,

> the Daimaru did not lie, as its rivals did, on a main north–south trolley line. By the end of the Meiji it had closed its Tokyo business and withdrawn to the Kansai, whence only in recent years it has returned to Tokyo, this time not letting the transportation system pass it by. It commands an entrance to Tokyo Central Station.[58]

In 1929, the Hankyū Railway Company founded the world's first railway store when it opened a department store in a bustling Umeda station in Osaka.[59] Then as now, location was a critical component of a business's

financial success, and the newly established 'railway stores' rivalled the established department stores. In order to differentiate themselves, the larger
department stores continued to cater to an elite clientele, while the railway
stores concentrated on the mass market of commuters flowing through their
terminals.[60]

Mitsukoshi blazed many trails in order to establish itself as an arbiter of
taste. In 1895, Takahashi wrote an essay criticizing kimono designs as stagnant
and tied to conventional Edo-period designs. In an effort to invigorate kimono
production, Takahashi set up an in-house design department (*ishōbu*), inviting
Nihonga artists to create fresh kimono designs. Visual materials such as painted
handscrolls and screens produced by renowned pre-modern painters from the
Tosa school, Sumiyoshi school, Rinpa tradition and the *ukiyo-e* tradition were
used as models for this endeavour. In 1901, Mitsukoshi sponsored a display
of new patterns and awarded monetary prizes for fresh designs, kindling
excitement throughout weaving and dyeing communities in Japan.[61]

From 1905 to 1924, Mitsukoshi sponsored meetings among a group
of select intellectuals, writers and 'people of culture' (*bunkajin*). Known as
the Ryūkōkai ('Trend Gatherings'), the group initially focused its efforts on
administering annual design contests held in the spring and fall and conduct-
ing research on merchandise. Following the lead of Takahashi, who promoted
the Genroku style in the boom after Japan's victory in the Russo–Japanese
War, the Ryūkōkai sponsored discussions centring on contests for a revival of
the Edo-period artist Kōrin's designs in 1909, and a Taishō-style motif contest
in 1915.[62] The group also conducted surveys of clothing trends, documenting
the number of men and women wearing Japanese or Western-style clothing.
Although their unscientific methods drew criticism from some quarters, their
survey revealed that in Tokyo in 1910, a majority of males surveyed wore
Western-style clothing, whereas a majority of the women wore Japanese-style
clothing, or a combination of Japanese-style clothing with Western elements.[63]
The Ryūkōkai held intellectual discussions on the meaning of the term *ryūkō*
(trend, fashion or mode) itself and attempted to understand prevailing trends in
order to predict and shape new ones.[64] The group also brainstormed exhibition
plans that would allow the general public to visually assess new trends, with
exhibited objects later becoming featured products.[65] In 1916, in honour of
the 200th anniversary of the death of the celebrated designer Ogata Kōrin
(1658–1716), Mitsukoshi promoted an exhibition of objects related to him,
and sponsored a design contest with 'Kōrin-style' motifs as its theme.[66]

In contrast to the longevity of the Kōrin-style campaign and despite
the blessing of the Ryūkōkai and the backing of Mitsukoshi advertising, other
initiatives, such as a promotion of the Gothic style, fizzled within a year. The
logic for promoting the 'Gothic style' came in partial response to an interest in

Overleaf
78 Kitano Tsunetomi,
poster for Ashikaga
Honmeisen, 1927, colour
lithograph.

79 Okada Saburōsuke,
Chiyoko, the wife of
Mitsukoshi's director, in a
poster for the Mitsukoshi
department store, 1909,
ink and colour on paper.

neo-Gothic architecture abroad. Certain members of the Ryūkōkai claimed that the Gothic style harkened back to Japan's own medieval period, the Warring States period (*sengoku jidai*, 1467–1568), and captured the warrior's spirit.[67] Whether its campaigns succeeded or failed to stir consumer interest, Mitsukoshi used its prominent position to influence kimono design trends.

At the executive level, department store managers also adapted newly imported technology in their efforts to promote their products and company's name. Advances in printing technology and the recognition of posters as an effective form of advertising created new avenues for store promotions. Replacing woodblock-printed handbills and single-sheet prints, such as Utamaro's 'Contemporary Beauties' series, were large-scale posters, often designed by established artists, and featuring celebrities or famed beauties. In addition to Nihonga painters such as Kitano Tsunetomi (1880–1947), who designed posters for the Ashikaga Meisen group (illus. 78), other collaborative examples of known painters designing posters for department stores include Ishikawa Toraji's 1914 design for Shirokiya; Ikeda Shōen's 1915 poster design for Daimaru; and Kaburagi Kiyokata's 1916 design for Matsuzakaya.[68] An extant 1916 photograph of Matsuzakaya's window display prominently featured Kiyokata's poster, with rolls of kimono fabric draped in the foreground.[69]

Posters designed by well-known painters often featured female celebrities. A 1909 poster advertising the Mitsukoshi department store was designed by the Western-style painter Okada Saburōsuke (1869–1939) and depicted Chiyoko, the wife of Mitsukoshi's director Takahashi Yoshio. She is wearing a kimono in the Genroku style, which was the focus of a Mitsukoshi retail campaign (illus. 79).[70] A postcard of 1931 for Chichibu Meisen Cooperative pictured the stage actress Mizutani Yaeko wearing a bold, colourful *meisen* kimono (illus. 80). The film actress Tanaka Kinuyō, later to become the first Japanese female film director, was selected as the model for the True Meisen of Ashikaga

80 Actress Mizutani Yaeko modelling a Chichibu Meisen kimono, 1930s, postcard.

(*Ashikaga Honmeisen*) poster of 1932.[71] It has been claimed that the popularity of *meisen* kimonos stemmed from their relatively low cost during an economic downturn.[72] But the high production quality and cost of the posters advertising *meisen* suggest that demand may have been cultivated by a sophisticated marketing campaign. With the imprimatur of a store or textile conglomerate's sponsorship, a known painter's design and a celebrity's endorsement, these posters provided a visual link across people, products and places.

From Named Things to Branded Goods

The association between place and product is well established in Japanese culture. From the mid-sixteenth century, primers for elite children included lists of places and their best-known products, resulting in such items acquiring 'name and fame because of an excellence of expressive local genius'.[73] Primers not only taught school-aged children the writing system, but also shaped their minds to recognize their country's best manufactures and the locales that produced them. In the early seventeenth century, a traveller's diary lists 'famous products' (*meibutsu*), such as dyed cloth from Narumi (*Narumi shibori*), available as souvenirs (illus. 81).[74] The practice of linking product to place led to the development of a

> mini-genre of guides to named goods – with titles like the *Shokoku meibutsu kanoko* (Dappled Fabric of Famous Things) – [that] took off in the eighteenth century . . . While geographical textbooks had long included basic lists of products, primers such as *Banmin chōhō meibutsu ōrai* (Everybody's Treasures of Famous Things) focused sole attention on the country's resources, arts, and crafts. They taught popular piety toward the land, even as they introduced children to economic values, and perhaps, the lure of consumption.[75]

By the mid-nineteenth century, regional products with 'brand' identities were so well established that they bypassed the central market in Osaka and were shipped directly to loyal consumers nationwide.[76]

Commercial directories of the major cities appeared in the form of self-guided shopping tours (*hitori annai*) as early as the 1670s, listing a shop's address and crest, and the types of goods sold. These publications continued to be viable sources of information into the nineteenth century.[77] Many of the textile products listed in primers and commercial directories, such as crepe fabric from Akashi (*Akashi chijimi*) or brocades from Kyoto (*Kyoto nishiki*), survive not only in local guidebooks but in the modern lexicon. Visitors to the city could immerse themselves in the guide-books, indulge in fantasies of owning objects they previously hadn't known existed and educate themselves on the requisite material trappings in their efforts to adapt from rural to city life, or from one socio-economic level to another.

Travellers from rural regions to big cities crossed paths with city dwellers seeking new experiences in the countryside. Improved transportation systems not only allowed for increased domestic travel, but also made previously remote areas accessible to a greater number of people of all classes. The well-trodden routes between Tokyo and Kyoto, such as the famous Tokaidō route, as well as more obscure pilgrimage routes, were lined with shops catering to tourists' need to return home with souvenirs of their adventures (*omiyage*).[78] The rise of the new middle class with a penchant for leisure travel fuelled a burgeoning market for these named *meibutsu* or regional products.

Awareness of the variety of domestic products available to the modern Japanese consumer was embedded in a general recogni-tion of an expanding global marketplace. Coupled with a concomitant sense that traditional Japanese culture was increasingly threatened by foreign forces, a renewed appreciation of Japanese arts and crafts grew among intellectuals and elites.[79] By the 1920s and into the '30s, intellectuals such as Yanagi Sōetsu (also known as Muneyoshi, 1889–1961) followed the lead of Okakura Kakuzō by collecting Korean pots and clothes. Yanagi took his endeavour one step further by incorporating – colonizing – these Korean objects into the newly forming 'people's crafts' (*mingei*) movement. Indeed, the rising awareness of the value of regionally produced crafts existed both within Japan's borders and beyond, reaching Japanese-occupied territories: the northern areas now known as Hokkaido in 1869; Okinawa (formerly the Ryūkyūan Kingdom), annexed in 1879; Formosa (now Taiwan), annexed in 1895; Korea, as a protectorate in 1905 and annexed in 1910; and southern Manchuria, established as a Japanese puppet state after the Manchurian Incident of 1931.[80] As Kim Brandt notes,

81 Utagawa Hiroshige, 'Narumi: Shop with Famous Arimatsu Tie-dyed Cloth' (*Narumi meisan Arimatsu shibori mise*), from the series 'Famous Sights of the Fifty-three Stations' (*Gojūsan tsugi meisho zue*), 1855, polychrome woodblock print, ink and colour on paper.

in the 1930s, with the sharpening of Japan's appetite for imperial expansion on the Asian continent and the outbreak of war with China . . . it became clear that an effective Japanese challenge to the West required a return to a Japan positioned within an Orient from which it remained sharply distinct. This is not to say that most Japanese had not long assumed a distinction between Japan and the rest of Asia, nor that Yanagi did not remain highly conscious of the West as a location of alterity. Rather, people took positions along a range that attempted to identify Japan and Japaneseness in relation to various and shifting 'others'.[81]

The construction of the *mingei* movement emanated from a nationalist sentiment to define Japan and its craft products within a larger cultural sphere.

Within Japan, proponents of *mingei* partnered with department stores and capitalized on their marketing expertise to showcase regional products within urban centres. As Brian Moeran points out, 'stores were clearly designed to be tourist, as well as shopping attractions; and thus to be palaces of culture as well as consumption.'[82] From the mid-teens of the twentieth century, Mitsukoshi sponsored exhibitions of arts and crafts on their premises. In their efforts to promote regionally produced goods, as Kim Brandt notes, 'it might well be argued that the *mingei* reformers actually managed to encourage the development of a relatively homogenous aesthetic at the expense of genuine local diversity.'[83] In a backlash against this perceived homogenization, rural producers were urged in the early 1930s to

> replace the consumption of imported fibers such as wool and cotton with locally produced hemp and (waste) silk . . . [while publications such as] *Ie no hikari* (The Light of the Family) emphasized the idea of a special rural aesthetic associated with clothing manufactured at home of hand-woven and hand-dyed textiles.[84]

In other words, regional specificity was tied to a rural identity that should not be relinquished in a quest to mimic urban lifestyles and goods. Japan's internal struggles to preserve regional identity within the larger national enterprise echoed Japan's efforts to resist the Western ways that were seeping into Japanese modes and customs. Tellingly, the readership of 'The Light of the Family' was not limited by regional or national borders, but extended to Japanese emigrants to Brazil and other nations.[85]

In this increasingly nativist climate, Itō Shinsui's (1898–1972) woodblock-printed image of a woman dreamily gazing into the distance belies the complex conception of the contemporary ideal female beauty (illus. 82). The woman from the series entitled 'Twelve Figures of Modern Beauties: Woman

82 Itō Shinsui, from the series 'Twelve Figures of Modern Beauties: Woman from Oshima Island' (*Shin bijin jūni sugata: shima no onna*), 1922, polychrome woodblock print, ink and colour on paper.

from Oshima Island' (*Shin bijin jūni sugata: shima no onna*) wears a garment of indistinct cut, decorated with a pattern of white crosses. Her dark-coloured fingerless gloves appear to match her garment and what, at first glance, appears to be a French-inspired beret. A bucket of water in the lower right corner of the print slightly obscures her right elbow. Upon closer inspection, however, we discover that rather than a chic, modern woman, she is likely a woman from rural Ōshima Island, known as an *anko*.[86] The apparent beret is actually an indigo-dyed cloth that *anko* wrapped around their heads when transporting buckets of water. Her 'fingerless gloves' are actually arm protectors similar to those worn by Ōharame women of the Ōhara region who transported firewood and other necessities from the countryside into urban areas. The obi sash worn by these working women is typically tied in front, as it is in Itō's print. As the print suggests, female beauty in the early 1920s was not limited to the sophisticated city woman dressed in a silk kimono. A woman wearing a simple, indigo-dyed cotton kimono and engaged in labour could appear traditional yet up-to-date, pastoral yet urbane. In contrast to

83 'Custom of Oshima Peoples' [*sic*], 1930s, postcard.

Itō's print, contemporaneous postcards targeting an English-speaking audience show women transporting buckets of water on their heads in the countryside. The women are not positioned as pastoral yet urbane; rather, they and their form of dress unambiguously evoke the traditional and the rural (illus. 83).

Depending on the context in which it was worn, the kimono evolved to become a distinct symbol of national ideals, and at the same time a 'named' product linked to a specific place – Japan. With the wave of Western-style clothing entering Japan in the mid- to late nineteenth century, new conceptual categories were constructed: *wafuku* for Japanese-style clothing and *yōfuku* for Western-style clothing.[87] By assimilating the novel concept of a Japanese-style robe into the broader conceptual category of clothing available in the global marketplace, the kimono was gradually redefined as a uniquely Japanese garment. As previously noted, within the Japanese context, different types of similarly shaped and constructed garments each had specific names or labels attached to them. The kimono ideal, partly shaped in Japan but more dominantly in the West, subsumed the more specific types of garments. The word *kimono* became a recognizable catch-all term for the multiplicity of robe-like garments worn primarily by the Japanese. The complex signals sent and received by those donning kimonos – Japanese as well as Westerners, within Japan's borders or in an international setting – will be further discussed in chapter Four.

Aesthetics of Taste in the Marketplace

As suggested by the quotation from Okakura Kakuzō at the beginning of this chapter, the strategic selection of garments in order to define national identity was practised by key figures in early twentieth-century Japan. For Japanese nationals living in European or American cities, the issue of what to wear was emblematic of an increasingly global consciousness. Kuki Shūzō, the progeny of Hatsu (wife of the Japanese ambassador to the United States, Kuki Ryūichi), serves as a case in point. Before marrying into Kuki Ryūichi's provincial samurai family, Hatsu was 'rumored to have a past in the Kyoto geisha district of Gion'.[88] Kuki Shūzō's biography, therefore, included an official paternal lineage to a samurai family, a maternal lineage to the pleasure quarters of Kyoto and a more tenuous link to his 'uncle' and 'spiritual father' (reputed to be his biological father), Okakura Kakuzō, who fervently promoted his ideas regarding the position of Japanese art and culture within a global context.

Kuki Shūzō left Japan in 1921 to see the world. It was during his European sojourn that he read Okakura's *Ideals of the East* and subsequently penned in Paris what was to become Kuki's most well-recognized manuscript 'The Structure of *Iki*' (*Iki no kōzō*, 1930). *Iki* is a slippery Japanese term that describes an aesthetic taste, attitude or sensibility that meant different things at various moments in history. In general, *iki* suggests the ability to convey an attitude of playful delight in an understated, subtle manner. As defined by Kuki Shūzō in 1930, *iki* of the late nineteenth century signified a kind of urbane chic that drew simultaneously on both flirtatious behaviour (*bitai*) and daring bravado (*ikiji*) but dissolved into resignation or acquiescence (*akirame*).[89] It was an attitude or ideology that he claimed was manifest in visual gestures, such as the type of clothing one wore or the manner in which it was worn. For example, to display the nape of a woman's neck in a certain way was considered an expression of *iki*, as was lifting one's kimono slightly to expose a leg or the

84 Design no. 21 with plovers over waves, page from pattern book *Shin hinagata chitose sode* (1800), woodblock-printed book, ink on paper.

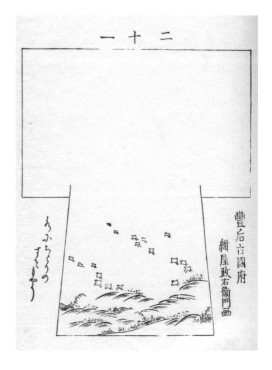

red lining hidden beneath the kimono. *Iki* is a specific affect or sensibility. While it is primarily a nineteenth-century concept, Kuki's revival of the *iki* aesthetic represents his attempt to define a distinctively Japanese sensibility that glorified the tastemakers of the Edo period. Not coincidentally, this yearning for a 'return to Japan' after a period of intense cultural borrowing and assimilation of Western ideals was coupled with an increasingly nationalistic agenda.

Conventional motifs enjoy longevity in the Japanese design repertoire. Reiteration of those specific motifs, within both literary and visual traditions, links pre-modern and modern design. By observing particular motifs – such as plovers hovering above waves – over time and across various media, we can learn much about shifts in Japanese design and aesthetic sensibilities. We can also observe how strategies to market kimonos adapted to these changes.

In kimono pattern books of the mid-eighteenth century, designs of plovers and stylized waves cover the entire garment, rising from the hem and curving upward across both shoulders (see illus. 27). But by the early nineteenth century, the design space had been compressed to the lower half of the garment, with designs concentrated mainly around the hem and on the front overlap of the kimono, as is apparent from a pattern book design dating from the 1800s (illus. 84). Infused with an *iki* sensibility, a kimono of the late nineteenth to early twentieth centuries (illus. 85, 86), when seen from a distance, barely allows the viewer to appreciate the beige mist against the misty blue background. Upon closer inspection, however, the fabric is revealed as a very

85, 86 Kimono with design of plovers over waves, late 19th–early 20th century.

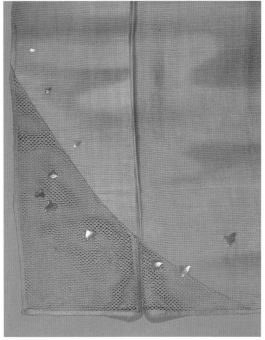

87, 88, 89 Woman's three-piece kimono ensemble with design of plovers over waves, and details, early 20th century, woven with supplementary gold metallic threads, hand painted with dyes, inks and pigment, brushed shaded dyeing, silk embroidery with seed pearls and coral beads on silk crepe.

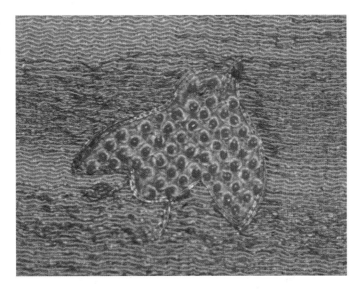

open, gauze-like weave similar to European lace drawn work, resembling a net. Tiny plovers composed of mother-of-pearl fly above the water. This attention to detail and the masking of time-consuming, labour-intensive effort and expensive materials epitomize the *iki* aesthetic preference for understated elegance.

As suggested by this example, challenging the viewer's ability to recognize the value of a garment's concealed worth was an important dimension of the *iki* aesthetic. Changes in aesthetic taste are evident in kimono ensembles comprising two or more layers of silk. A late nineteenth-century kimono ensemble decorated with designs of plovers and waves beckons the viewer to examine its finely wrought details (illus. 87, 88, 89). Plovers rendered in seed pearls and coral beads fly against a background of fine *yūzen*-dyed wave patterns. The layered format and the execution of details in fine materials and exquisitely rendered techniques mask the expense of the ensemble. The application of jewel-like accents on kimonos may evoke images of the robe purportedly designed by Ogata Kōrin with *nanten* berries of rare coral beads, as discussed in chapter One. Produced in layers consisting of an inner, middle and outer kimono, silk kimono ensembles with designs compressed in the kimono's lower half emerged as a fashion statement during the late nineteenth and early twentieth centuries.[90] By the 1920s, embroidered plovers hover over vertically oriented waves that radiate outward from the centre front of the kimono (illus. 91, 92).

Much of the shift in kimono design composition reflected changes, not only in the kimono's relation to the obi, but also to the environment in which the kimono was worn. By the early twentieth century, when women wearing kimonos to formal functions found themselves seated on chairs rather than on *tatami*-mat floors, the upper portion of the kimono received more attention as it became the most visible design space. Design elements decorated the shoulder areas of the front left and back of the kimono, with complementary motifs circling the kimono's hem. Unlike the 'shoulder and hem' (*katasuso*) compositions of the Momoyama era (1573–1600), in which the middle section was deliberately left undecorated and considered to be outside the design space, the modern compositions engaged the entire kimono as a canvas but devoted particular attention to the adornment of the shoulder and hem areas.

Certain kimono motifs gained popularity when kimono designers, employed by kimono manufacturers or department stores, promoted them and became the arbiters of taste. Department stores such as Mitsukoshi attempted to cultivate a particular taste among its customers by 'wed[ding] the image of the department store to the concept of *ryūkō* or "fashion"'.[91] Information and inspiration garnered from the world at large set new design fashions in Japan. Western flora appeared as motifs on kimonos, for example,

90 'The fragrance of Waseda' (*Waseda no kaori*), design with orchids, postcard advertisement for the Mitsukoshi store, inscribed 1909, colour lithograph.

after designers returned from the 1904 exposition in St Louis. In 1906, Mitsukoshi commissioned the designer Hirata Shūho (dates unknown) to sketch orchids growing in the garden of Ōkuma Shigenobu, the founder of Waseda University. The kimono manufacturer Chisō labelled these designs the 'fragrance of Waseda' (*Waseda no kaori*), and they appeared on postcards distributed by Mitsukoshi (illus. 90). Begonia flowers sketched in Baron Iwasaki's garden and other flora previously unfamiliar to Japanese dyers, such as lily-of-the-valley, tulips and clover, made their debut in paste-resist dyed kimono designs around this time. In 1907, the well-known author Natsume Sōseki wrote 'Field Poppies' (*Gubijinsō*), a story serialized in the *Asahi Shinbun* newspaper from 1907. Interest in Sōseki's story inspired a kimono design of field poppies by the Daihiko Dye Shop of Tokyo and Mitsukoshi's promotion of their summer kimono (*yukata*) with a similar design.[92] Other kimono designs were promoted in similar ways. In 1929, for example, the Nishihonganji temple in Kyoto sold poetry cards decorated with motifs associated with the famous selection of poets known as the Thirty-six Immortal Poets. One of the immortalized poets, Fujiwara Michinaga, who flourished in the Heian era (794–1185) and who is said to have epitomized courtly elegance, was repackaged into elegant designs that decorate a kimono of the late 1920s, purportedly worn by the painter Uemura Shōen (1875–1949).[93]

What began in department stores – especially Mitsukoshi – as trend-spotting or a search for what was in vogue (*ryūkō*), evolved into a more focused surveillance of and interest in consumer taste. The Japanese term that best reflects the English word 'taste' is *shumi*. Like other terms for aesthetic

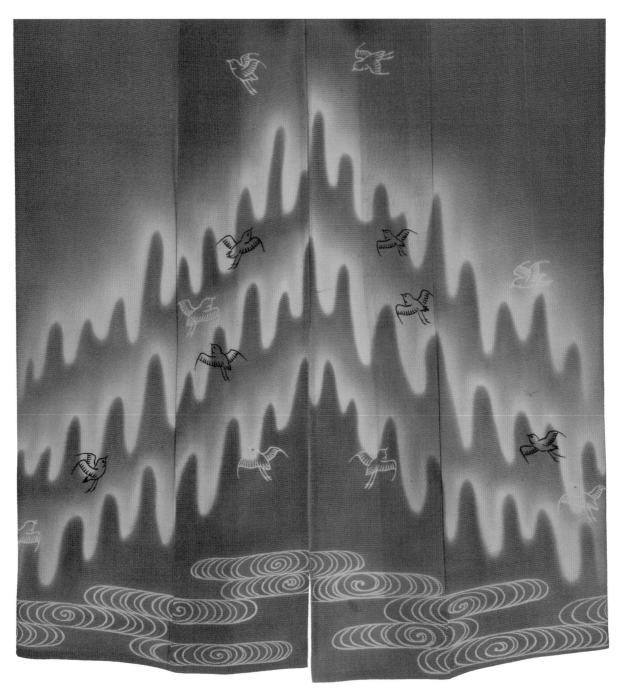

91, 92 Woman's summer
kimono (*hitoe*) with design of
plovers in flight over stylized
waves, and detail, 1900–1925,
silk embroidery and metallic
thread on silk ground.

preferences, such as *iki* ('urbane chic'), discussed above, *shumi* possesses its own historical context of usage. The term came into common parlance in the first decade of the twentieth century, around the same time that department stores proliferated in the urban landscape. As Jinno Yuki argues, it was during this period that the aesthetic concept of taste infiltrated the upper- and middle-class Japanese lexicon.[94]

Shumi would also take on the more informal connotation of 'hobby' or 'pleasurable pastime', a meaning it continues to have today. Collecting textile objects fell under the rubric of *shumi*. (Although as seen from the above discussion, motivation for collecting objects can range from 'pleasurable pastime' to the more serious, such as to garner national prestige by exhibiting objects in an international exhibition, to exemplify the 'order of a country's enlightenment' in a museum display or to preserve the traditions of one's own or other cultures, as the *mingei* founders attempted.)

From the late nineteenth century, as trade in Japanese goods expanded, collecting and selling antique Japanese textiles burgeoned and developed as a separate market from the buying and selling of newly produced kimonos. In the pre-Second World War era, there were at least two groups that engaged in the organized bartering and trading of antique textiles: the Suehiro-kai and the Chingire-kai. Suehiro-kai meetings took place on the second floor of antique dealer and collector Nomura Shōjirō's (1879–1943) shop in Shinmonzen, the antique district in Kyoto (illus. 93).[95] Wearing formal black silk kimonos, an exclusive group of twelve to twenty dealers and collectors gathered to present their individually treasured textiles for inspection. In front of each participant were placed an ink brush, ink pot and small lacquer bowl turned upside down. After close inspection of an object up for auction, each member would write his bid inside the bowl and slide it to the appointed auctioneer. The object would then be sold to the highest bidder. Over time, the monetary value attached to textile objects was established through these auctions. The auctions may also have served to enhance the prestige of individual participants, who were able to demonstrate that they possessed valuable objects and the skills of a connoisseur.

Collectors' motivations determined the way objects were categorized, catalogued, organized and displayed. These motivations continue to shape cultural memories and inform notions of 'taste'. Japanese artists formed one professional group actively engaged in the study, collection and display of Japanese textiles and costume in the modern period. In order to produce historically accurate representations of their subjects, painters relied on scholars and collectors to provide them with information and models of textiles to use in their paintings. The dealer and collector Nomura Shōjirō collaborated with other scholars and organized exhibitions, published books and held sketch classes for artists using the objects in his collection. With the publisher Unsōdō in Kyoto, Nomura reproduced his kimono collection in seven volumes of colour plates between 1927 and 1939. The painters Itō Shōha, Uemura Shōen and Nakamura Daizaburō reportedly sketched objects from Nomura's collection.[96] The Western-style painter Okada Saburōsuke (1869–1939) studied, collected, painted and wrote about Japanese textiles. In fact, although Okada painted with oils on canvas, his models were often Japanese women dressed in kimonos.[97] The kimono designer Tabata Kihachi (1877–1956), who studied Japanese-style painting under Konō Bairei and later Takeuchi Seihō, amassed a textile collection that was admired by many artists and continues to be revered today. The mounter of Seihō's paintings had a vast collection of antique textiles that other painters, including Uemura Shōen, used as resource material in their work.

Japanese antiquarians, artists, antique dealers and painting mounters, who evidently shared their knowledge and collections of Japanese textiles, increasingly recognized the historical and economic value of new and old Japanese garments and fragments. As they studied and collected ancient and antique garments and fragments, they developed systems of classification, ranking and grading individual pieces for the market, modulated by their specialized knowledge of the rarity of the object, its relative quality and the current demand for the object based on contemporary taste. In doing so, they created categories for the things that pleased their own tastes. This circumstance is not unique to textiles; examples of blurred categories in Japanese art have existed in many realms. Categorizing terms such as *yamato-e* in painting,

93 Postcard of Shōjirō Nomura, manufacturer of silk embroideries, no. 25 Shinmonzen, Kyoto, late 19th to early 20th century, collotype.

Oribe in ceramics or *iki* in aesthetics has consistently proved to be elusive and problematic.[98] In textiles, a prime example is *tsujigahana,* the label given to a category of rare and exquisite sixteenth-century textiles, discussed more fully in chapter Five. From the 1930s to the '50s, a group of predominantly male textile connoisseurs collected, named and preserved these textiles, constructing the cultural memory of *tsujigahana.* This process affected the perceived historical, aesthetic and economic value of the objects so classified. At the beginning of the twenty-first century, fragments labelled as *tsujigahana* sold at auction for over U.S.$70,000.

The current market for antique kimonos fluctuates considerably, but prices are generally rising as supplies diminish. The dearth of information on modern kimonos, a subject only recently garnering attention from collectors, dealers, connoisseurs, curators and academics, is a result of hierarchical attitudes towards objects. Modern kimonos are still available in flea markets within Japan and beyond, relegating them to the category of 'collectibles' rather than 'art'. National museums in Japan do not actively acquire modern kimonos because they are not yet old enough, rare enough or 'valuable' enough to justify their collection. While the economic value of modern kimonos, particularly those dating from the 1850s, may still be open to question, their historical value is clear. They reflect the aesthetic choices of the Japanese during a critical moment in Japanese history; their preservation reflects the collecting tastes of our own time.

When Japan encountered the West in the mid-1850s, the two cultures collided with a velocity and intensity that created, for a time, a hybrid culture incorporating elements of both. Eventually, as knowledge of Western customs and costumes in Japan deepened, a more refined and sophisticated response to the new fashion emerged. At the turn of the twentieth century, and well into its first few decades, the simple act of donning a kimono could signal a reaction to a perceived threat in Japan's external environment, a display of national pride or a return to traditional values. Opting for Western-style dress, on the other hand, signalled a desired alignment and equality with Western powers, or a rejection of antiquated Japanese ideals. For the elite and well-educated members of Japanese society, wearing kimonos was no longer a necessity, but a conscious choice. The symbolic separation of 'us' and 'them' through personal choice of attire expressed distinctions of taste.

The French sociologist Pierre Bourdieu has noted that 'tastes (i.e. manifested preferences) are the practical affirmation of an inevitable difference':

> Like every sort of taste, [the aesthetic sense] unites and separates. Being the product of the conditionings associated with a particular class of conditions of existence, it unites all those who are the product of similar conditions while distinguishing them from all others. And it distinguishes in an essential way, since taste is the basis of all that one has – people and things – and all that one is for others, whereby one classifies oneself and is classified by others.[99]

Building on Bourdieu's thesis, sociologist Yuniya Kawamura explains,

> in any differentiated society, individuals, groups and social classes cannot escape this logic, and it brings them together while separating them from one another. The boundaries that we create are symbolic. Cultural consumption plays a central role in this process. Therefore, analyzing the different relations that people have with cultural objects helps us understand domination and subordination. Fashion can be used as a conceptual tool to understand the nature of symbolic activity.[100]

Leslie Pincus, a historian of modern Japan, has analysed Kuki's deployment of taste through Bourdieu's lens. She concludes that 'Bourdieu's insights into the social uses of taste suggest that the distinction drawn by *Iki no kōzō* between Japan and the West might well conceal other distinctions within the boundaries of Kuki's imagined community.'[101] To Pincus, 'though Kuki presented his argument as a polemic against the leveling of differences between national cultures – that is, against the assimilation of Western cultural forms – the implicit object of his criticism was the leveling of social difference within Japan.'[102]

Japanese dress, and the kimono in particular, exemplifies this argument. The kimono physically enveloped the body and signalled not only the 'differences between national cultures' but also the 'leveling of social differences within Japan'. Over time, the kimono – whether as clothing or collectible object – has revealed and concealed the ambiguities and anxieties in Japan's quest to formulate a national identity during a tempestuous period.

MODERN STYLE OBI ADDS GAY NOTE AND PERFECT HARMONY TO
SIMPLE, FASHIONABLE COLOUR SCHEME OF SPRING COSTUME

KIMONO

BY
KENICHI KAWAKATSU

TOKYO
MARUZEN COMPANY LTD
1936

FOUR

THE KIMONO IDEAL
MIGRATES WEST

I do not know whether it was an Oriental vision depicted by the kimono itself
or a lovely mirage engendered by the model wrapped in the kimono, or a reflection
of the yearning for Japan burning in my heart. But through the graceful lines
of the kimono, I had discovered a new life, a bewitching mystery, in the body.

Monsieur B as described by Kawakatsu Ken'ichi[1]

While the fictional Monsieur B expressed a romantic notion of the kimono (illus. 94), Commodore Matthew Perry's assessment of Japanese female attire nearly 100 years earlier was less flattering (illus. 95). Perry described the women serving him in the household of the mayor of Yokohama as 'barefooted and barelegged, dressed very much alike in a sort of dark nightgown secured by a broad band passing round the waist'.[2] Perry's journal further notes that 'the costumes of the various classes are as unchangeable in fashion, cut, and color as are unchangeable their laws and customs, and the rank and condition of the wearer are known by their dress'.[3] Perry's comments suggest that he viewed the kimono as unbecoming, and that he believed the garment itself was frozen in time.

Two centuries prior to Perry's arrival, the Portuguese Jesuit João Rodrigues had a similar impression of the kimono. While Perry recognized distinctions of rank, based on dress, Rodrigues observed:

The principal robe invariably worn by the nobility and ordinary folk, both men and women, in the whole of this realm is called *kimono* or *kirumono*. It is a long garment after the fashion of a night-gown, and it used to reach down to the middle of the leg or shin, but nowadays it is considered more elegant and formal to wear it reaching down to the ankles.[4]

94 Frontispiece to Ken'ichi Kawakatsu, *Kimono: Japanese Dress* (1936), published by the Board of Tourist Industry, Japanese Government Railways.

Perhaps Western sensibilities that associate the kimono with 'nightgowns' and Japan with the 'unchangeable' were initiated by the Portuguese Jesuit and perpetuated by later observers, such as Perry. Indeed, the streamlined, narrow-cut kimono as a formal garment must have appeared to Western eyes as more akin

95 Woman's over-robe (*uchikake*) with design of pine, plum and bamboo (purportedly given to a member of Commodore Perry's crew on the second expedition to Japan, *c.* 1854), *c.* 1825–50, gold-wrapped threads couched on silk satin.

to a nightgown than to the full-skirted and highly tailored style of formal dress to which they were accustomed.

Visual sources from the mid-nineteenth century onwards reinforced the Western perception of the kimono as a dressing gown or bathrobe. In 1864, James Tissot completed the painting entitled *La Japonaise au bain* (illus. 96). In the painting, a Caucasian woman emerges from the bath, seductively draped in a very realistic rendition of a kimono. A garment of similar design to the one depicted in Tissot's painting is referred to in Japan as an *uchikake* (outer garment). However, this type of garment would never have been worn as a bath or lounging robe. Rather, this type of robe, decorated with a specific array of motifs embroidered in silk and gold-wrapped threads, was a formal garment worn by wealthy women of the military class. This apparently mattered little to Tissot; it was the exotic nature of the design, silhouette and materials that stirred his interest, not the original function of the garment.

But what happens when one culture appropriates an object from another? In its new context, divorced from its social, economic and political meaning, the object takes on a new life. In Tissot's rendering, for example, the prized robe of a wealthy Japanese woman of the elite military class has traversed the globe from Japan to Europe. In its new context, the kimono has been transformed into a novelty. In a European painter's imagination, the kimono is used to embody an exotic Japan.[5]

Nineteenth-century paintings by European and American painters differ in their portrayals of the kimono as a symbol of an exotic Japan. In Tissot's painting, the combined effect of the kimono serving as a bathrobe, the woman being partially unclothed and the interior setting including Japanese sliding paper doors, cherry blossoms and an open window in the background clearly position the kimono in a fantasized exotic–erotic setting. In 1882, several years after Tissot completed *Japonaise au bain*, Auguste Renoir painted a portrait of Madame Hériot wearing a kimono over a high-necked, concealing red blouse (illus. 97). The kimono is belted at the waist with a gold buckle. Madame Hériot is seated on a Western-style chair. The interior setting suggests she is a wealthy, upper-class woman. In Renoir's portrayal, the kimono appears to represent an accoutrement of a well-travelled, affluent woman who may have purchased the kimono as a souvenir or received it as a gift. The kimono in the portrait by Renoir signals the exotic, but not the erotic. In both paintings, the original Japanese meaning of the kimono as a marker of a woman of military status is lost.

One of the most salient images of the kimono in the Western imagination links the garment with alluring women. The well-known story of Madame Butterfly, resplendent in her kimono, is but one example. The autobiographical novel of Pierre Loti (a pseudonym for Julien Marie Viaud), which recounts the

97 Pierre-Auguste Renoir,
Madame Hériot, 1882,
oil on canvas.

love affair between a naval officer and a geisha in Nagasaki, was published in
1887 as *Madame Chrysanthemum* and was performed as an opera five years later.
Soon after, the story became the basis for Puccini's famous opera, which prem-
iered in 1905. *Madame Butterfly* continues to be produced today, perpetuating a
stereotype rooted in a French naval officer's romantic experience in the 1880s.

Beauties of the Edo-period pleasure quarters, depicted in the large
numbers of *ukiyo-e* paintings and prints that found their way into the hands of
Western collectors in the late nineteenth century, were naturally garbed in
kimonos. The subtle distinctions in the patterning and styling of the kimonos
in these meticulously rendered images distinguished courtesan from geisha,
teahouse maiden from merchant's wife. Yet these nuances were impenetrable
to the average Western viewer.

96 James Tissot,
La Japonaise au bain,
1864, oil on canvas.

143

Fervent and frequently misguided associations between the kimono, the geisha and the courtesan were formulated during this period and persist today. Common misperceptions of the geisha (literally 'person of the arts') and her association with kimono culture have distorted Western perceptions of both the wearer and the garment. The socio-cultural practices behind both object and figure have been misunderstood. Conversely, the Japanese have themselves engaged in a form of auto-exoticizing in relation to the kimono, manipulating Western perceptions of the garment to their own advantage.[6]

Demystifying the Kimono

In 1879, a frontispiece designed for a set of booklets commemorated the visit of General Ulysses Grant and his wife Julia (Dent Boggs) Grant to Japan (illus. 98). The image depicted Kabuki dancers wrapped in kimonos decorated with the stars and stripes.[7] Donning the American flag was intended as a welcoming gesture by the Japanese, but using a representation of the national banner as clothing likely bemused or upset American viewers. Moreover, Julia Grant is depicted with the American flag, displayed in reverse, while General Grant is shown with the Japanese flag. Given the socio-historical tendency of Western audiences to position Japan as feminine and 'quaint', juxtaposing the American flag with a feminine personality and the Japanese flag with a male American military figure may have been jarring to American viewers.

The representation of Japan through the medium of woodblock prints was generally controlled by the Japanese themselves; but with the introduction of photography in the 1850s, Westerners gained the ability to manipulate images of Japan. For example, the Austrian-born photographer Raimund von Stillfried opened a studio in Yokohama initially known as Stillfried & Co. (later renamed Stillfried & Andersen when he partnered with Hermann Andersen in 1876). Under the auspices of Stillfried & Co., von Stillfried compiled a book of photographs entitled *Views and Costumes of Japan*.[8] According to the art historian Allen Hockley,

> Stillfried purposefully indulged Westerners' general fascination with Japanese women by producing erotically charged portraits . . . Stillfried's role in promoting the sexuality of geisha, although perhaps indirect, cannot be understated.[9]

Many of Stillfried's subjects were photographed wearing kimonos, often with bared breasts.

98 Utagawa Kunisada III, fold-out frontispiece from 'Japanese Biography of Mr Grant' (*Gurandoshi den Yamato bunsho*) – visit of General Ulysses Grant and his wife to Japan in 1879 (July 1879), polychrome woodblock-printed book, ink and colour on paper.

To gain a historical understanding of how the exotic–erotic associations between geishas and kimonos developed, it is imperative to distinguish the geisha from the courtesan. In his efforts to dispel the mistaken Western notion that geishas sold sexual favours, the British theatre historian and critic Osman Edwards wrote in 1901,

> Convention having banished the actress from the Japanese stage, the geisha takes her place as the natural recipient of masculine homage. She is much courted, and sometimes makes a brilliant match. There are a large number who make the profession an excuse for attracting rich admirers, just as the name of 'actress' in more Puritan climes will cover a multitude of sins. But a professional courtesan she is not: her favors are not always for sale to the highest bidder.[10]

A geisha was first and foremost an entertainer, trained in music, dance and the art of conversation. As Edwards points out, she 'sometimes makes a brilliant match', often by cultivating a relationship with a patron (*danna*), but the primary role of a geisha was and is to entertain through her artistic refinement.

As arbiters of taste in their own right, geishas were often at the forefront of fashion, setting trends. When Western clothing became available to the Japanese populace in the 1860s, 'a geisha from the Maruyama district of Nagasaki created a sensation by being photographed in a flouncy Western frock and crinoline'.[11] By the first decades of the twentieth century, the tides had turned. Imitating Western ways was considered disloyal and insulting to the Japanese way of life:

> By the 1930s [geishas had] stopped trying to be mainstream fashion innovators, reverted to wearing the kimono, and settled into their new role as curators of tradition by working to preserve the classic arts and dress.[12]

The cultural critic and theoretician Kuki Shūzō – mentioned in the previous chapter, whose biological mother was purportedly a geisha from the renowned Gion district of Kyoto – 'argued for a return to cultural authenticity in the name of the Edo geisha'.[13] The rise of the cafe girl, with her modishly Western dress and deportment, may also have prompted the geisha's retreat to more traditional ways. From this time, the tandem promotion of the alluring female figure – often in the guise of the misunderstood geisha – and the kimono secured their conflated image in the West as symbols of Japanese tradition.

This association is not surprising, given that a number of Japanese states-men who were highly visible personalities in Europe and America had married geishas, or had geishas as mistresses.[14] Alice Mabel Bacon commented on the trend of women whom she considered to be of low social status circulating with the political elite. In her *Japanese Girls and Women*, penned in 1891, Bacon writes:

> Yet so fascinating, bright and lively are these geisha, that many of them have been taken as wives by men of good position, and are now the heads of some of the most influential households. Such marriages were especially frequent in the wild period at the beginning of Meiji when all social restraints broke down temporarily.[15]

Itō Hirobumi (1841–1909), who rose from the title of count, to prince, and later to prime minister, was married to a former geisha named Umeko (dates unknown), ostensibly raising her status from geisha to 'first lady of the realm'.[16] Itō Umeko's geisha training served her well in her new role as the wife of a government official. Umeko instructed women of the Rokumeikan era (1884–9) in the arts of ladies' etiquette, guiding wives of officials through the unfamiliar territory of social interaction between men and women in public.[17]

Like Itō Umeko, the geisha formerly known as Yakko – who became the internationally celebrated stage actress Sada Yacco (1871–1946, alternatively

known as Sadayakko, a combination of her samurai family birth name of Sada and her geisha name Yakko) – also had ties to a prominent family.[18] After Sadayakko's husband and her theatre troupe's director Kawakami Otojirō died in 1911, Sadayakko became the mistress of her first true love, Iwasaki (Fukuzawa) Momosuke. Iwasaki was the adopted son of the influential writer Fukuzawa Yūkichi, having once been married to Fukuzawa's daughter, Fusa.[19] In the rapidly changing world of the twentieth century, while some geishas retreated into the role of cultural preservationists, symbols of Japan's traditional arts, others like Sadayakko transformed themselves into modern-day actresses. She went on to perform with her troupe in San Francisco, Seattle, New York, London, Brussels, Vienna, Paris and other overseas venues. All the while, Sadayakko wore kimonos on stage, and often when she appeared about town (illus. 99).

The Japanese government commissioned Sadayakko's husband to orchestrate the troupe's performance at the 1900 Paris Exhibition:

> [Sadayakko's] performances, extensively reviewed in the popular press, captivated widespread public interest including that of several artists, notably Pablo Picasso, who made sketches of her, and William Nicholson, who featured her in his woodblock prints.[20]

Another geisha-cum-actress, Ōta Hisa (1868–1945, also known as Hanako), was spotted by the sculptor Auguste Rodin in Marseilles in 1906. Rodin persuaded her to pose for a series of sketches and figure studies.[21] Featured in posters, on stage and in works produced by well-known European artists, images of geishas wearing kimonos were disseminated widely and further solidified the fusion of the ideals of the kimono and the alluring Japanese female body.

Capitalizing on Sadayakko's fame in Paris, a Parisian shop by the name of Au Mikado purchased the rights to use her name to market perfume, skin cream and a kimono named the Kimono Sada Yacco. In contrast to the more expensive kimonos available on the market, the

Kimono Sada Yacco sold for one-tenth the price, about twelve to eighteen francs, and was also made available to consumers outside of Paris via mail order. An extant Kimono Sada Yacco in the Kyoto Costume Institute suggests that the format (long-draping sleeves and crossover collar) and the designs of phoenixes may derive from a Japanese model, but a few oddities in construction indicate that the Kimono Sada Yacco was clearly tailored by seamstresses to suit Western taste.[22] Like the hybrid dramas Sadayakko and her husband created by adapting several different Kabuki plays into a single, shorter version designed to entertain Westerners who could not understand the original script, the Kimono Sada Yacco was altered to play to stereotyped Western perceptions of the kimono.

After Sadayakko retired from her life as a stage actress, she and Iwasaki (Fukuzawa) Momosuke built a house in Nagoya, where neighbours included the Toyoda family that was engaged in the loom-making business.[23] During her years in Nagoya, Sadayakko established her own textile business, the Kawakami Silk Company, and produced silks under the brand names Yakko Meisen and Yakko Silk until declining sales in the aftermath of the earthquake of 1923 drove her out of business.[24] Sadayakko's long career as a geisha, stage actress and silk producer not only reveals the highs and lows experienced by Japanese women during this tumultuous era, but also attests to the innovative ways in which women extended the life of the kimono.

With the advent of radio, film and television, the talents of former geishas began to attract scouting agents. The Victor Recording Company discovered the former Tokyo geisha Ichimaru (1906–1997) and signed her to an exclusive contract in 1931. Ichimaru's success as a recording artist induced her to relinquish her geisha status, though the effects of the war caused her to stop recording in 1944. When the war ended, Ichimaru earned the honour of being the first Japanese singer to be invited to perform in Hawaii, and later became a national television celebrity in Japan in the late 1950s.[25] In a testament to Ichimaru's cultural impact on the arts, her kimono and other possessions migrated west in 2001 when they were given to the Art Gallery of Greater Victoria and later exhibited there in 2006.

Japanese Textiles in the West

Orientalist portrayals of kimono-clad women in paintings by James Tissot, Claude Monet and James Abbott McNeill Whistler provide evidence of historical circumstances related to the kimono. For example, the conspicuousness of kimonos in these paintings points to the accessibility of Japanese textiles on the international market in the mid-nineteenth century. In a letter to his mother

from Paris dated 12 November 1864, the English painter Dante Gabriel
Rossetti recounts his visit to a Parisian shop selling Japanese goods:

> I have bought very little – only four Japanese books . . . but found all
> the costumes were being snapped up by a French artist, Tissot, who it
> seems is doing three Japanese pictures which the mistress of the shop
> described to me as the three wonders of the world, evidently in her
> opinion quite throwing Whistler into the shade.[26]

The competition for these objects among artists must have been keen.
Artists in Europe were clearly enamoured with kimonos, often incorporating
them into their works with little regard for the garment's original social functions.
Painters working in Paris frequented La Jonque Chinoise, a curio-shop on the
Rue de Rivoli, as well as La Porte Chinoise, an antique shop on Rue Vivienne.[27]
As is obvious from the names of the shops and the variety of objects they sold,
distinctions between Japanese and Chinese objects were not clear: Japanese
kimonos were sold at La Jonque Chinoise. Even today, the reverse circumstance
of Chinese-style garments mistakenly referred to as kimonos persists. The Japanese
encouraged and even capitalized on the Westerners' inability to distinguish
differences between Chinese and Japanese goods. Aligning their merchandise
alongside those catering to the Chinoiserie and Oriental craze, Japanese merchants
enhanced the cachet of their country's wares.

Many Americans' first encounter with Japanese art occurred at the
Philadelphia Centennial Exposition in 1876. The industrialist Henry O.
Havemeyer (1847–1907) was one such American. The textiles purchased by
Havemeyer and his wife Louisine (1855–1929) in 1876 were used over a
decade later to decorate the ceiling of their library, the walls of their music
room and their reception room.[28] In her book *Sixteen to Sixty: Memoirs of a
Collector*, Louisine Havemeyer described the circumstances surrounding the
purchase and design of the library ceiling:

> In 1876, Mr Samuel Colman with Mr Havemeyer visited the Centennial
> Exhibition in Philadelphia. They became interested in the exhibits of
> China, and especially of those of Japan, with the result that my husband
> bought many beautiful objects of art and a collection of Japanese textiles,
> a wonderful lot of brocades of lustrous gold and silver, and rich blues,
> reds and greens . . . 'Some day I will make you a ceiling out of these
> beautiful silks,' said Mr Colman to my husband, and true to his words,
> in 1889, thirteen years later, Mr Colman had all these remarkable
> stuffs sent to his home in Newport, where in his studio, with the
> help of many nimble fingers, he had them made into the design he

wanted for the various panels of our library ceiling.[29]

Over 2,000 fragments of Japanese textiles of the eighteenth and nineteenth centuries were ultimately given to the Metropolitan Museum of Art by the Havemeyers.[30]

    In addition to the Japanese products featured at international expositions, the increased exposure to Japanese works in the international art market, some of which were of very high quality, was stimulated by the domestic policies of the Japanese government in the early Meiji period, roughly the 1870s. When Meiji government policy began to promote Shintō as the state ideology, Buddhism suffered. A proclamation required Buddhist influences to be removed from Shintō shrines. Temples associated with Buddhist traditions lost much of their previous stature and financial support. While many Buddhist statues, implements and other ritual objects were destroyed as a result, others, including textiles, found their way into the burgeoning art markets. A Buddhist priest's vestment, or *kesa*, now in the Metropolitan Museum of Art, documents the physical transmission and transformation of a Japanese textile. In this case, fabric originally designed for a woman's robe was remade into a *kesa* and later migrated from its sacred sanctuary in Japan to a museum in New York (illus. 100).[31]

    In 1871 the Meiji government abolished feudal domains and established a prefectural system. As a result, many land-owning military families were divested of their holdings. Some of these families were generously pensioned, but others began to sell off their family possessions. Thus, objects previously preserved in the storehouses of wealthy families suddenly appeared on the market. In her book *Japanese Girls and Women*, Alice Mabel Bacon recounts her quest for 'procuring the old-fashioned embroidered kimonos, which are now entirely out of style in Japan and which can only be obtained at second-hand clothing stores, or at private sale'. She acquired a 'curious garment' that 'rightfully belonged in the wardrobe of any lady-in-waiting in a daimio's [*sic*]

100 Buddhist vestment (*kesa*) with design of maple leaves and fans, 1750–1850, paste-resist dyeing, silk and metallic thread embroidery and shaped-resist dyeing on crepe silk.

house'.[32] Antique textiles were one of the many categories of objects that now found a niche in the market among collectors in Japan and internationally.

Japanese textiles became more accessible to Western audiences through the businesses of men such as Yamanaka Sadajirō (1866–1936) and Nomura Shōjirō (1879–1943). In 1895, Yamanaka opened his first shop in Manhattan, and went on to establish branch offices in a number of major cities including

Boston, Chicago, London and Beijing, through which he offered an array of Asian art and antiques.[33] He garnered the support of three men, William Sturgis Bigelow (1850–1926), Edward Sylvester Morse (1838–1925) and Ernest Francisco Fenollosa (1853–1908).[34] Today referred to as the triumvirate of Bostonians, they, as well as collectors such as Henry Havermeyer, helped to establish the appreciation of Japanese art among the East Coast social elite.

Yamanaka and Nomura, among others, recognized that kimonos, produced from sumptuous silks lavishly embellished with labour-intensive dyeing and decorative techniques, had long been treasured for their material value. Extant garments from the late sixteenth and early seventeenth centuries, many previously owned by elite families of the military class, owe their survival to the tradition of preserving clothing as family heirlooms. Indeed, Nomura's world-renowned collection resulted from his penchant for acquiring altar cloths from Buddhist temples and reconfiguring them into their original kimono format. Similarly the vast Tabata textile collection, discussed in more detail in chapter Five, grew out of a family kimono-making business: impoverished military families of the late nineteenth century relinquished their valuable robes in exchange for newly created designs from the Tabata kimono house. Today, collectors of Japanese textiles active both within and outside Japan contribute to a heightened appreciation of these garments – as evidence of Japan's social history, as examples of the virtuosity of Japanese weavers and dyers, and as prized objects of art.

Nomura Shōjirō remains one of the most renowned collectors and dealers of Japanese textiles, both in the United States and Japan. Descending from a family of cloth merchants, Nomura acquired his first robe at age thirteen, on a trip to visit an aunt in Nagoya.[35] As he passed a vendor's stall on the way to Nagoya Castle, he noticed an early Edo-period robe and turned over all of his travel money in order to acquire it. His mother had no choice but to send him additional funds for his return trip to Kyoto. In 1908, Nomura's mother helped him establish a shop in Kyoto, and from there Nomura began selling antiques to foreigners. Soon, he became an internationally recognized dealer serving clients in China, India, Australia and the United States. In fact, Nomura advised many public and private American collectors of Japanese textiles. Many objects that passed through his hands found their way into the collections of Lucy Truman Aldrich (1869–1955), whose collection was donated to the Rhode Island School of Design, and Bella Mabury (1871–1964), whose collection is now held by the Los Angeles County Museum of Art. The Metropolitan Museum of Art and the Museum of Fine Arts, Boston, also house Japanese textiles previously owned by Nomura, including many *kesa* which were featured in Nomura's catalogue of 1914 for an exhibition at

Previous pages
101 Buddhist vestment (*kesa*) with design of autumn grasses and butterflies (made from a Noh costume), 1750–1850, silk and metallic threads in supplementary weft-patterned twill-weave silk.

the Copley Society of Boston. An exquisite example purchased by the Metropolitan Museum of Art was constructed of fabric usually reserved for Noh theatre costumes (illus. 101).

Kesa were originally made to be worn by Buddhist clerics and nuns who wrapped them around their bodies. In a Western context, they were often transformed into textiles to decorate the interior spaces of wealthy patrons. Abby Aldrich Rockefeller (1874–1948), sister of Lucy Truman Aldrich, displayed Japanese textiles in her Maine home, known as The Eyrie. An inventory of 1936 notes that 'there were three "priest robes" in the library, four in the Buddha room, and two in the living room.'[36] The Buddha Room was outfitted with 'Buddhist sculptures and paintings, and East Asian furniture, rugs and textiles'.[37] In a photograph of the room, the *kesa* are hung vertically, side by side on the back wall, rather than in their more proper horizontal orientation (illus. 102).

102 Interior of the Buddha Room, The Eyrie, Seal Harbor, Maine (the Rockefeller summer home on Mount Desert Island), 1960, colour photograph.

Japanese textiles migrated into Western hands, not only in the form
of finished garments and *kesa*, but also as bolts of fabric purchased in Japan.
Ernest F. Fenollosa, one of the three Bostonians celebrated for their impact
on the appreciation of Japanese art in the West noted previously, travelled to
Japan in 1878 where he taught at the prestigious Tokyo Imperial University.
He later became the first curator of Japanese art at the Museum of Fine Arts,
Boston, and lectured widely on the arts of Japan and China.[38] A diary entry
dated Thursday 8 October 1896 records that Fenollosa and his wife, Mary
McNeil Fenollosa, visited the Takashimaya department store in Japan where
they bought both Japanese and Western-style clothing. According to the diary
entry, they viewed 'an assortment of rich and superb textiles [that] France
cannot begin to equal'.[39] A dress once owned by Mary Fenollosa and now in
the Philadelphia Museum of Art collection appears to have been crafted with
Japanese materials to suit Western taste. The dress is said to have been worn
by Mary Fenollosa for presentation at the Japanese Imperial Court. The dress,
which bears no label, was acquired by the museum at the same time as one
designed by Charles Frederick Worth that bears his label (circa 1886–7).
The dress worn by Mary Fenollosa is of the same cut as the Worth dress.[40] The
fabric, a chrysanthemum-patterned silk, may have been purchased in Japan and
later made by another dressmaker, perhaps based on a copy of the Worth dress.

Takashimaya also recognized a potential market for kimonos as souvenirs.
An early example of a Takashimaya kimono designed for export, purchased
by the Victoria & Albert Museum in London, is made of crepe silk (*chirimen*)
fabric, similar in texture and design to a roll of crepe silk *chirimen* fabric
displayed at the Paris Exposition in 1867 (see illus. 51).[41] Unlike kimonos
for Japanese consumers, this kimono has additional panels inset into the side
seams that effectively widen the skirt area and a loop inside the collar for ease
of hanging on a hook. It bears a label which reads, 'S. Iida Takashimaya, Kyoto,

103, 104 Takashimaya
department store, woman's
kimono gown for the
Western market with design
of clouds silhouetted with
cherry blossoms, and detail
of label, late 19th century,
paste-resist stencil-dyeing
on silk crepe.

105 Exterior view of the
Takashimaya store in Kyoto,
1893, photograph.

Tokyo & Yokohama' (illus. 103, 104). Other styles of kimono made for export,
in addition to inserts at the side seams, also left the sleeve edges unstitched and
a braided cord was inserted around the entire sleeve edge. In lieu of the ornately
tied obi sashes worn with kimonos in Japan, the export kimonos were sold
with a matching sash with fringed edges. The S. Iida Takashimaya Silks and
Embroideries store displayed Western-style dresses next to kimonos made for
the export market (illus. 105). The same style is one of six different formats
that appear in a book of hand-drawn designs in the Takashimaya Shiryōkan
Collection titled 'Kimono Designs for Foreigners' (illus. 106).[42] Favoured
motifs illustrated in this design book include what came to be considered
quintessentially Japanese motifs thought to be especially desirable to foreigners:
wisteria, butterflies, cherry trees, birds and maple leaves. Similar in construction
and design to one of the designs in the 'Kimono Designs for Foreigners' book,
an extant silk kimono gown decorated with maple leaves has been personalized
with the embroidered name 'Emmie' (illus. 107).

The kimono, whether as a souvenir or collectible object, was a referent to
Japan as imagined by its owner, not as lived within a Japanese context. As these
examples discussed above demonstrate, Japanese textiles migrated to the West
in the form of dealers' merchandise, as products for international exhibitions,
as bolts of silk that were later fashioned into Western-style clothing and as
travellers' souvenirs and collectible artefacts. The notion of possessing or
experiencing Japan in some way is captured by Susan Stewart's reflections
on the meaning of a souvenir. For Stewart,

106 Kimono designs for foreigners (*Gaijin muke kimono zuan*), 1909–16, underdrawing, ink and colour on paper.

> The souvenir speaks to a context of origin through a language of longing for it is not an object arising out of need or use value; it is an object arising out of the necessarily insatiable demands of nostalgia. The souvenir generates a narrative which reaches only 'behind,' spiraling in a continually inward movement rather than outward toward the future.[43]

The kimono's owner could project onto this garment his or her longing for a Japan that was 'traditional', exotic, unchanging or whatever image suited his or her fancy, regardless of the kimono's function and symbolism within Japan. This type of longing or nostalgia was later adapted by the Japanese in their quest for a national costume to suit their preferred identity in an international context.

Designers Inspired by the Kimono

In 1889, in an oft-repeated quote, Oscar Wilde declared, 'In fact, the whole of Japan is a pure invention. There is no such country, there are no such people. The Japanese people are simply a mode of style, an exquisite fancy of art.'[44]

To be sure, Japan as envisioned in the West differed markedly from reality. Yet the tangible objects created by Japanese weavers and dyers sparked the imagination of designers in Europe and America. Notable examples of how Japanese aesthetics, and in particular Japanese textiles, have influenced Western taste in subtle ways can be demonstrated by a review of major designers who adopted and adapted Japanese textiles and designs for the Western market.

The self-identified 'decorative artist' Christopher Dresser (1834–1904) travelled to Japan in 1876–7, less than a decade after the fall of the Tokugawa shogunate and the establishment of the Meiji government. In 1882, Dresser published his findings from the trip in the volume *Japan: Its Architecture, Art and Art Manufactures*.[45] Dresser's opinions on Japanese design, however, pre-date his sojourn to Japan. He is known to have purchased a kimono at the 1873 Vienna International Exhibition, and later used it as an example of good design, praising it as 'the finest dress that I have ever seen'.[46] Dresser was particularly enamoured with the Japanese craftsperson's ability to bring nature to life through design. In two different publications, he describes the design of a kimono, remarking:

> No one can look upon this beautiful dress without feeling the influence of the sunny ground, of the profusion of richly coloured bloom, of the gay and glorious insects which appear to hover over the flowers, and the influences make us feel that it is summer while we gaze.[47]

Reflecting a romantic view of Japan in Victorian England, Dresser heralded the Japanese affinity for nature displayed in the vitality of their designs. Dresser praised the kimono, and lamented the adoption of European dress by the Japanese, fearing that the incorporation of Western elements into Japanese aesthetic principles would corrupt the purity of the design he so appreciated. In her essay on Dresser, Elizabeth Kramer – herself reflecting on Eric Hobsbawm's notion of the 'invention of tradition' – notes that the 'kimono served as a potent visual sign of Japanese identity and tradition, and, as tradition relates to a set of interacting practices, to disrupt one, disrupts all'.[48] The Japanese, too, were grappling with the issue of balancing domestic productions to suit Japanese taste against the incorporation of design ideals they believed would appeal to the burgeoning and lucrative markets abroad.

107 Woman's kimono
gown and sash for the
Western market with
design of maple leaves,
early 20th century, silk
embroidery and knotted
silk fringe on plain
weave silk.

Dresser's activities in Japan and his opinions about Japan's domestic products proved to be a double-edged sword: on the one hand, he encouraged the Japanese to protect their native craftsmanship, and on the other, his mere presence and expressed preferences served as barometers for the Japanese of the differences between their own tastes and those of the West. In writing about Japanese textile designs (see illus. 108), he commented:

> by flatness of treatment and evenness of distribution they achieve the production of effects having all necessary qualities of repose, although, at the same time they bid defiance to all the canon of European art.
>
> What would an English artist think were he asked to produce a pattern from telegraph posts and wires, or to arrange a design in outline and flat colours which should consist wholly of little boys at play? Yet with such materials the Japanese figure fabrics! Japanese art seems to laugh at the canons by which the European designer is bound, and to hold our method in derision. Clearly without law and without order, patterns can be constructed which are quite as acceptable as those which other nations with fixed rules have produced.[49]

After praising the efforts of Japanese weavers and dyers, Dresser admonishes British designers for not taking advantage of combining various techniques, such as printing and weaving, or printing and embroidery, for more interesting effects:

> Nothing can be more stupid than our pig-headed persistence in old methods. Progress is no longer possible if we do only what our forefathers did; and the gulf which separates one manufacture from another must be crossed if we are to advance as we should. We have yet to learn the need of so using all processes and all materials as to achieve the best possible results. In so doing we may meet with trade opposition and the difficulties which spring from prejudice and ignorance, but these must be encountered and overcome or our manufacture will ultimately be to a great extent replaced by those of Japan.[50]

108 Kobayashi Gyokunen, 'Pattern Sketches' (*Moyō-e*), 1901, polychrome wood-block-printed book, ink and colour on paper.

Dresser encouraged his compatriots to breach the walls of a guild mentality that dissuaded weavers from collaborating with dyers, or embroiderers with printers, in order to achieve the kinds of decorative effects visible in Japanese textile products. His comments also reveal anxieties about the potential strength of Japanese industries and their competitiveness in global markets.

In 1880, Thomas W. Cutler (1841/2–1909) also looked to Japanese objects as a source of inspiration when he published the popular book

A *Grammar of Japanese Ornament and Design*.[51] Cutler's stated aim was to present

> a carefully selected series of characteristic examples of the natural and conventional ornament of the Japanese which shall furnish a general and comprehensive view of the leading features of their Decorative work.[52]

Cutler's drawings were 'all faithfully copied from the originals, and produced by the process most calculated to retain their spirit, all reductions having been made by photography'.[53] His parade of insects, copied from a hanging scroll (illus. 109), depicts

> a procession of grasshoppers, wasps, and other insects; in the cage is borne a beetle, and various grasses and flowers are carried as insignia; the mantis beetle is ridden as a horse. The whole is a caricature of a *Daimio's* [sic] procession.[54]

109 Illustration (plate 20) from Thomas W. Cutler, *A Grammar of Japanese Ornament and Design* (1880), published by W. Batsford, London.

This parody of the pomp and circumstance of a *daimyō*'s procession could only have been executed once the feudal lord had fallen from power. A kimono from the second half of the nineteenth century bearing the same processional motif demonstrates how designs migrate: this motif appears on a Japanese hanging scroll, in a British book on ornament, and on a kimono (illus. 110, 111).[55] Cutler's assessment of Japanese textiles was laudatory:

> Textile fabrics constitute a class of art productions for which the Japanese are well known . . . In the colours of their grounds, and in the contrasts and harmonies of their designs, the taste of the Japanese is absolutely perfect, combining the most delicate gradations of tints, with equally delicate harmonies or richest contrast.[56]

Candace Wheeler (1827–1923), often hailed as one of the first women in the United States to run a successful design firm, appreciated the Japanese penchant for naturalistic designs. An essay she wrote in 1893 entitled 'Decorative and Applied Art' for the magazine *Household Art* explains her attraction:

> This is where Japanese design has obtained, and well deserves to obtain, world-wide popularity. Every flower or leaf or plant which appears in Japanese design is absolutely an individual specimen, true to its individualism as well as its species and while there is little composition in the sense of large and regularly recurring groups or masses in Japanese design, the absolute truth and grace of drawing, and the unerring taste in placing ornament, has given Japanese art a foremost place in influence and favor in the world.[57]

Prior to establishing her own company, Wheeler, together with Louis Comfort Tiffany, Samuel Colman (who designed the Havemeyers' library) and Lockwood de Forest collaborated under the firm name Associated Artists (*fl.* 1879–83).[58] One of the earliest textile designs produced under the aegis of Associated Artists, which depicts carp frolicking amid swirls of water, appears to have been inspired by Japanese stencils of a similar design.[59] Other designs also exemplified the Associated Artists' reliance on Japanese textile products, or Japanese design reference books, such as Cutler's *A Grammar of Japanese Ornament and Design*.[60]

Edward C. Moore (1827–1891), chief designer for Tiffany & Co., is credited with encouraging Tiffany's initial interest in interior decoration.[61] Moore collected Asian and Islamic objects, many of which served as inspiration for his own designs and some of which may have been actually purchased by Christopher Dresser during his trip to Japan.[62] Japanese textiles were among

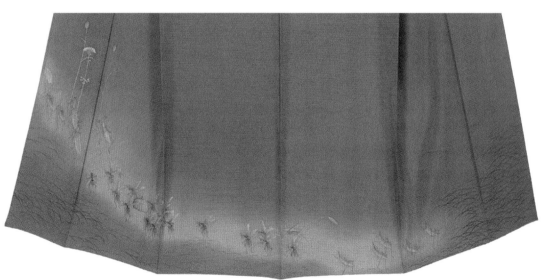

110, 111 Woman's summer garment (*hitoe*) with design of insect procession, and detail, 1850–1900, paste-resist dyeing and embroidery on silk.

the many objects Moore bequeathed to the Metropolitan Museum of Art in 1891. While one-to-one correspondence between Japanese objects in Moore's collection and his designs can only be conjectured, clearly his visual repertoire included Japanese works. A water jar by the potter Makuzu Kōzan (1842–1916), previously owned by Moore and bequeathed to the Metropolitan Museum of Art in 1891, depicts a procession of grasshoppers that parodies *daimyō* processions similar to those illustrated in Cutler's book.[63]

Designers transformed Japanese motifs, techniques and formats to suit their needs, or the needs of their clients. Arthur Lasenby Liberty, a British merchant who founded Liberty & Co. in 1875, visited Japan in 1888–9. In his 1898 Yuletide Gift Christmas catalogue he advertised 'Japanese dressing gowns'. The gowns illustrated – quilted floor-length gowns with leg-of-mutton-style sleeves and front button closures – do not resemble Japanese garments in format, sleeve style or material. In small print, the advertisement's description for the gowns reads: 'The shapes are reproductions of models sent out to Japan by Messrs. Liberty & Co. for the guidance of the native manufacturers. The Shapes, Styles, and Fittings are adapted for Western use.'[64]

Liberty's use of the word 'Japanese' in this instance appears to refer simply to the country of manufacture rather than the style of dress. Liberty also sold kimonos similar in fabric and construction to those sold within Japan. In 1891, the Victoria & Albert Museum purchased a kimono from Liberty with stylized designs of swirling water patterns and bamboo against a figured silk ground (illus. 112). The swirling water pattern was reinterpreted within the Art Nouveau design repertoire and then re-appropriated by Japanese kimono designers, as shown on the woman's summer kimono (illus. 25) in chapter One.

Stores in the United States that specialized in 'Oriental goods', such as A. A. Vantine & Co., often relied on Japanese companies to provide custom-ordered merchandise to which the Vantine logo was applied.[65] Based on modifications to the T-shaped kimono silhouette, embroidered silk gowns elaborately embellished with roses and cherry blossoms, butterflies and wisteria, or peacocks were produced to suit the taste of female consumers outside of Japan. As with the kimono made for export by Takashimaya, these kimono gowns for the export market differed from kimonos for the domestic market not only in their decorative motifs and techniques, but also in construction. Labels placed inside the collar, such as 'S & Gump' of San Francisco or 'Sing Fat & Co.' of Los Angeles, referred to the company responsible for marketing, but not necessarily manufacturing, the kimono gown. Japanese-owned companies, such as S. Nishimura and Takashimaya, produced kimono gowns under their own labels for export. A number of Yokohama-based companies also competed in what many perceived to be a lucrative market.

Not all customers, however, were enamoured with the kimono silhouette. A client's rejection of a black wool cloak 'cut along straight lines like the kimono' prompted the French couturier Paul Poiret (1879–1944) to establish his own house in 1903. At the time of the client's rejection of the order, Poiret was employed by the House of Worth, founded by Charles Frederick Worth. Poiret's emphasis on draping rather than tailoring, according to costume historians Harold Koda and Andrew Bolton, followed the cutting and construction principles of the 'Greek chiton, the Japanese kimono, and the North African and Middle Eastern caftan'.[66] Similar to Japanese kimono construction, which exploits the integrity of the two-dimensional cloth through draping and minimizes waste with straight-line cutting, Poiret's designs harnessed planar modules and unleashed them to dramatic effect through strategic draping around the body.[67] Hailed as the designer who liberated women from the constrictions of the petticoat and corset, Poiret appears to have been inspired by the kimono.

The designer Madeleine Vionnet (1876–1975) is known for her garments that fold, wrap or drape around the body. Many see her trademark bias-cut dress, launched in 1919, as being inspired by the principle of minimizing fabric waste, as with the kimono.[68] Vionnet's bias-cut dresses valued the materiality and form of the two-dimensional fabric. One scholar has speculated that Vionnet 'must have discovered the kimono materials as well as crepe de Chine (silk crepe) and mousseline de soie (muslin) that she loved to use in her later designs' while 'searching through the mountain of cloth kept at the Callot Soeurs fashion house'.[69] Vionnet was also in Paris during the 1900 Paris Exposition, when Sadayakko's performance in a flowing kimono caused a great stir. While a direct correlation between Vionnet's bias-cut dress and the kimono design principles is difficult to document, the similarities are too great to ignore.

Women in kimonos made lasting impressions on performance artists as well. The American pioneer of modern dance Ruth St Denis (1879–1968), enthralled by a performance by Sadayakko, remarked that it 'haunted me for years and filled my soul with such longing for the subtle and elusive in art that it became my chief ambition as an artist. From her I first learned the difference between the words astonishing and evoking.'[70] St Denis often wore kimonos – authentic or copies modelled on originals – for her performances and was often seen wearing kimonos off stage as well (illus. 113).[71]

The world-renowned American architect Frank Lloyd Wright had a well-publicized passion for Japanese art and amassed an impressive collection of woodblock prints. Less well known is his respectable collection of Japanese textiles and stencils. An extant child's kimono, now in the John C. Weber collection, was a gift from Wright to his son, Llewellyn, after his 1905 trip to

112 Woman's kimono with design of swirling water, bamboo and birds, 1850–1900, paste-resist dyeing and embroidery in silk and metallic thread on silk, purchased by the Victoria & Albert Museum at Liberty's of London in 1891.

Japan (illus. 114). Wright used Japanese textiles, from futon covers to Buddhist vestments, as accents to highlight the interiors of his architectural spaces. A photograph of the living room of Taliesin II (*c.* 1916–24), shows a Japanese textile featuring the phoenix and paulownia in its design, probably originally a futon cover, draped over furniture. Wright is only one example of a long line of innovative industrial designers, clothing designers, dancers and architects across Europe, Britain and the United States who have been drawn to Japanese textiles and the underlying technical and aesthetic principles of their production.

114 Child's kimono with design of wisteria and lattices, early 20th century (before 1905), stencilled paste-resist dyeing on silk crepe.

Capitalizing on the Ideal

Responding to the mid-nineteenth century craze for 'things Japanese', one Japanese advocated 'that the new Western interest in Japonesque commodities made it imperative that Japanese production for export cease to imitate Western goods and return to [our] true, characteristic spirit and unique technology'.[72] This comment was made by Kunii Kitarō, director of the Ministry of Commerce and Industry's Industrial Arts Research Institute. Kunii was responding to the German architect Bruno Taut's assessment of objects on view at the Mitsukoshi department store, which Taut described as including 'some things of good quality – but very few, about two or three. The rest was sloppy and makeshift. From first to last, these were sketchy imitations of European and American [objects] for "export taste".'[73]

Alice Mabel Bacon had a different perspective, having lived in Japan for some years. She commented that

> much surprise is evinced by foreigners visiting Japan at the lack of taste shown by the Japanese in the imitation of foreign styles. And yet, for these same foreigners, who condemn so patronizingly the Japanese lack of taste in foreign things, the Japanese manufacture pottery, fans, scrolls, screens, etc., that are most excruciating in their sense of beauty, and export them to markets in which they find a ready sale, their manufacturers wondering, the while, why foreigners want such ugly things. The fact is that neither civilization has as yet come into any understanding of the other's aesthetic side, and the sense of beauty of the one is a sealed book to the other. The Japanese nation, in its efforts to adopt foreign ways, has been, up to the present time [the 1890s] blindly imitating, with little or no comprehension of underlying principles. As a result, there is an absolute crudeness in foreign things as attempted in Japan that grates on the nerves of travelers fresh from the best to be found in Europe and America.[74]

Having criticized the Japanese on one hand, and 'foreigners' (in this case Europeans and Americans) on the other, Bacon generates a more positive outlook: 'There are signs, however, that the stage of imitation is past and that adaptation has begun.'[75] After describing Japan's initial clumsy attempts to adopt Western dress and its increasing refinement and cultivation of sartorial styles, Bacon declares that the 'genius of the [Japanese] race will triumph over the difficulties that it is now encountering'.[76] Reflecting on Japan's absorption of other cultural traditions, Bacon pronounced:

> As no single element of the Chinese civilization secured a permanent footing in Japan except such as could be adapted, not only to the national life, but to the national taste as well, so it will be with European things. All things that are adopted will be adapted, and whatever is adapted is likely in time to be improved and made more beautiful by the national instinct for beauty.[77]

But Bacon could not help but judge Japan and the nation's aesthetic sensibilities through the lens of 'European standards'.

In his book *The Awakening of Japan*, Okakura Kakuzō captured Japan's unique position vis-à-vis the 'West' and within 'Asia'. Written while Japan was at war with Russia, a 'Western' adversary, and only a decade after Japan triumphed against its largest Asian neighbour in the Sino–Japanese War,

Okakura attempts to chart a course for Japanese art that is neither Asian nor Western, traditional nor modern, inferior nor superior, but distinctively, and uniquely, Japanese. Okakura states:

> The possibility that Japanese art may become a thing of the past is a matter of sympathetic concern to the esthetic community of the West. It should be known that our art is suffering not merely from the purely utilitarian trend of modern life, but also an inroad of Western ideas. The demand of the Western market for dubious art goods, together with the constant criticism of our standard of taste, has told upon our individuality. Our difficulty lies in the fact that Japanese art stands alone in the world, without immediate possibility of any accession or reinforcement from kindred ideals or techniques. We no longer have the benefit of a living art in China to excite our rivalry and urge us on to fresh endeavors. On the other hand, the unfortunately contemptuous attitude which the average Westerner assumes toward everything connected with Oriental civilization tends to destroy our self-confidence in regard to our canons of art. Those European and American connoisseurs who appreciate our efforts may not realize that the West, as a whole, is constantly preaching the superiority of its own culture and art to those of the East. Japan stands alone against the world.[78]

The Japanese designer Kamisaka Sekka (1866–1942) specifically advocated for a return to indigenous motifs. He travelled to Europe and recognized the interest there in Japanese art, particularly the painting style known as Rinpa. Upon his return to Japan, he engaged in the design and promotion of kimonos. In 1913, he served as a judge for the Hyakusenkai (Association of the Selected One Hundred) competition sponsored by Takashimaya department store (illus. 115). Sekka's role was to provide a liaison between the producers and the consumers. 'The Hyakusenkai centered on high quality kimono and traditional clothing articles and was established for the purpose of encouraging new styles and trends in fashion.'[79]

Sekka also designed pattern books and series of prints, most notably the 'Faces of the Old Capital' (*Miyako no Omokage*, 1890), which depicted new textile designs, and 'Change of Clothes' (*Koromogae*, 1901).[80] Sekka drew inspiration from both the Shijō and Rinpa-styles of painting, following perhaps in the traditions of Matsumura Goshun and Ogata Kōrin.[81] Like his contemporaries who hailed from the world of painting, he supplied designs for the commercial enterprises of Takashimaya, Kawashima and Chisō.[82] Sekka's refreshing flair for design invigorated his work with a vitality representative of a modern Japan steeped in its own traditions (illus. 116, 117, 118).

115 Hyakusenkai (Association of the Selected One Hundred): kimono design competition sponsored by the Takashimaya department store, 1916.

As with Sekka's eye on indigenous aesthetic appeal, other Japanese began to manipulate Westerners' appreciation of the kimono to suit their own interests. A photograph of a woman admiring her stylishly bobbed hair and fashionable kimono reflected in a full-length mirror serves as the opening of a book published in 1936 and entitled simply *Kimono: Japanese Dress* (illus. 119). Published by the Board of Tourist Industry and Japanese Government Railways, the book targeted 'the foreigner interested in Japan' and aimed to provide 'a basic knowledge of various phases of Japanese culture'.[83] The book's first chapter opens with the author describing to the Parisian painter Monsieur B the history and beauty of the kimono. By the end of the book, the cultivated Monsieur B exclaims, 'Japanese kimonos are really moving paintings. In the name of all the women of the world, I would therefore sing, "All honor to the Japanese kimono!"'[84]

The book is a distinct reflection of its time. The book was written by Kawakatsu Ken'ichi, then managing director of the Takashimaya department store. The commercial benefits Kawakatsu would derive from his promotion of the kimono in this publication were not considered suspect. More likely, these were the unstated and presumed goals of the project. His Occidentalist portrayal of a fictional Parisian painter, named Monsieur B in the characteristic style of early twentieth-century Japanese literature, was likely modelled on contemporary European painters who incorporated women dressed in kimonos into their work – a trend that, as described earlier, was very popular at the beginning of the twentieth century. Upon encountering a painter's model draped in a kimono, Monsieur B makes the declaration quoted at the

116 Kamisaka Sekka, design of the Thirty-six Immortal Poets, illustrated in 'A Thousand Grasses' (*Chigusa*, 1899/1900), polychrome woodblock-printed book, ink and colour on paper.

117 Length of fabric with design of Japanese dolls after a design by Kamisaka Sekka (1866–1942), early 20th century, stencilled paste-resist dyeing on silk crepe.

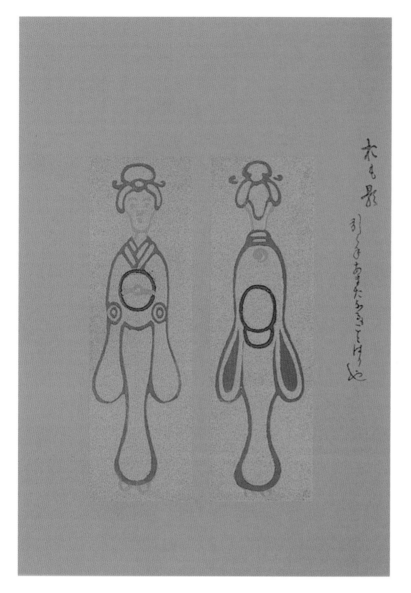

118 Kamisaka Sekka, design of Japanese dolls from 'A Collection of Humorous Designs' (*Kokkei zuan*, 1903), published by Yamada Unsodo (Kyoto), polychrome woodblock-printed book, ink and colour on paper.

outset of this chapter. Monsieur B questions whether the 'graceful lines of the kimono' evoke an 'Oriental vision depicted by the kimono itself', or 'a lovely mirage engendered by the model wrapped in the kimono', or 'a reflection of the yearning for Japan burning in [his own] heart'.[85]

 Aimed at the Western tourist venturing to Japan, *Kimono: Japanese Dress* crystallizes the collaboration between the government and marketers in the dissemination of the kimono ideal to the West. Written by a Japanese business-man and romanticized through the eyes of a foreigner interested in Japanese culture, *Kimono: Japanese Dress* perpetuated the idealized kimono as the embodiment of a 'traditional' Japan.

119 Ken'ichi Kawakatsu, illustration from the book *Kimono*: *Japanese Dress* (1936), published by the Board of Tourist Industry, Japanese Government Railways.

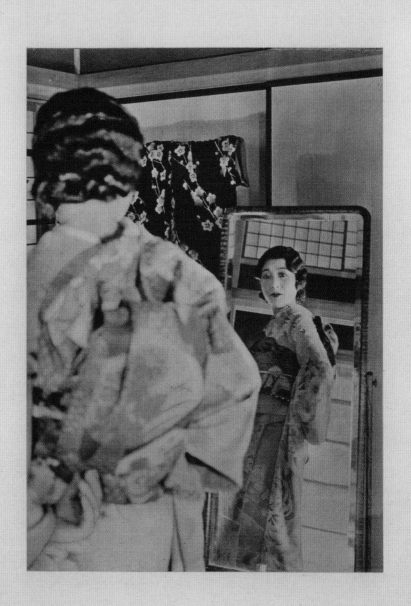

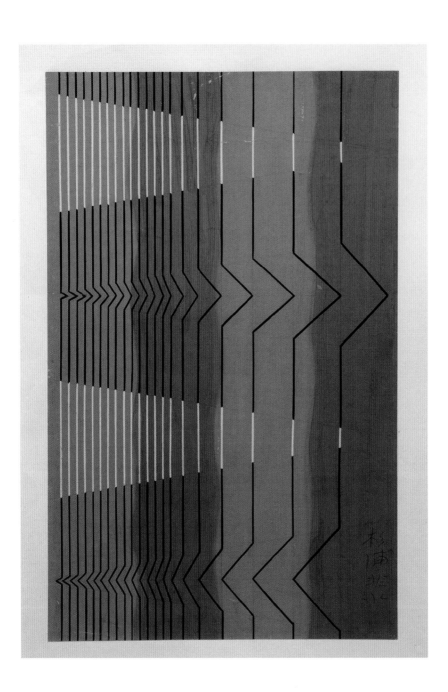

FIVE

KIMONO DESIGNERS

We have to answer the challenge of modernity:
what is a kimono, or what will it become, if it ceases to be a thing worn?

Moriguchi Kunihiko

By the first decade of the twentieth century, kimono shops had diversified their array of merchandise, and thus began to resemble modern department stores. Although customers could still request kimonos made to their specifications, they increasingly followed trends that were either forecast or dictated by designers employed by kimono makers and in-house design sections of department stores. One such in-house design from Matsuzakaya is shown overleaf (illus. 121, 122). Initially, department stores such as Takashimaya, Mitsukoshi and Matsuzakaya purchased designs produced by kimono manufacturers and wholesalers, such as Chisō and Marubeni. In turn, Chisō and Marubeni commissioned painters to draft kimono designs.[1] Eventually, Chisō proceeded to hire graduates from recently established design departments of prestigious art academies to create the most up-to-date fashions.[2] Unlike their predecessors who studied in art departments and tended to rely on conventional subjects, the graduates of recently established design departments infused kimono design with a refreshing repertoire of motifs.

During the first quarter of the twentieth century, in-house design sections established in department stores became so specialized that as early as 1909 Mitsukoshi separated its applied design unit (*ishōbu*) from its graphic design (*zuanbu*) department.[3] Although both *ishō* and *zuan* are translated variously as 'design' or 'pattern', they have slightly different connotations that have evolved over the years. The word *zuan*, coined in 1874 by the pottery painter Nōtomi Kaijirō who attended the Vienna Exhibition, initially referred to sketches or preliminary drafts of designs, and *ishō* to the design applied to the finished product.[4] By the first decade of the twentieth century, however, the word *zuan* encompassed more than just design sketches.

Mitsukoshi was again at the cutting edge, having established their *zuanbu* in 1909 under the guidance of Sugiura Hisui (1876–1965), who would go on to

120 Sugiura Hisui, design (*zuan*) of 'Lines', 1930, underdrawing, ink and colour on paper.

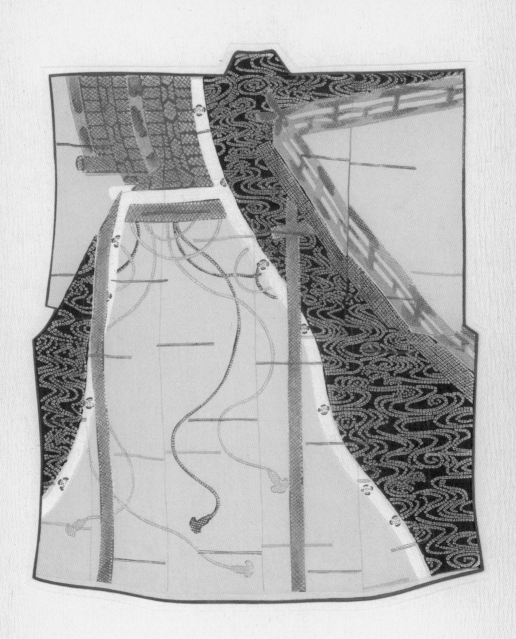

create a whole new field in commercial design (illus. 120). The *zuanbu* at Mitsukoshi produced trademarks, advertisements, inserts, covers for all public relations materials and even the menu for the in-house restaurant. Members involved in this division of the design department formulated and promoted the Mitsukoshi 'look'. Where previously the primary responsibility of a designer emphasized the production of patterns or models for objects, Hisui carved out a name for designers by promoting distinctive creations imbued with an individual designer's style.[5]

This emphasis on an individual designer's achievements rather than group productions, and its concomitant emphasis on originality, echoes the Western Romantic notion of the Artist with a capital 'A'. The revolution in woodblock-print designing that occurred from the early twentieth century parallels this emphasis on individuality and originality. During the Edo period, the designer of the print was beholden to the publisher, who coordinated the efforts of the designer, block carver and printer in order to produce a single-sheet print or series of prints. In the early twentieth century, woodblock-print artists continued to draw their prints, but also began to carve the block themselves, and then print their own designs, effectively taking on every portion of the multi-step process in a new movement called *sōsaku hanga*. Some print designers still relied on publishers for distribution, but the *sōsaku hanga* ('creative print') makers sold limited editions of individual prints. In general, the creative print movement promoted recognition of an individual designer's talents as an artisan as well as an artist, distinguished for his or her original, artistic achievements.

Similar trends materialized within the kimono design world as individual designers began to emerge from design departments and as established kimono houses promoted their family's designs. Some kimono designers – previously working as anonymous craftsmen, many labouring within workshops or under the direction of a producer (*shikkaiya*) responsible for coordinating the various stages of a kimono's production or the wholesaler (*ton'ya*) – became recognizable as individual designers in their own right. Some even established followings among a select clientele. For example, a kimono with a design of Mount Fuji rising above two pine trees bears the seal and signature 'Totsugen' (illus. 123). Tanaka Totsugen (1767–1823) was an artist active during the late Edo period. Whether the kimono was actually painted by Totsugen or was produced in the style of Totsugen has yet to be determined. In either case, the importance of branding the work with Totsugen's seal suggests an emerging interest in identifying individual designers who worked in the kimono format.

A handful of pre-modern and exceptional precedents to the anonymous craftsman tradition exist. Ogata Kōrin is the most notable.[6] An extant kimono with ink-painted designs of autumn grasses is attributed to this well-known

123 Tanaka Totsugen,
woman's over-robe
(*uchikake*) with design of
pines at Miho, 1850–1900,
paste-resist dyeing and
painting in ink and pigments
on silk.

painter and designer. As previously mentioned, Kōrin-style motifs abound in posthumously published pattern books of the eighteenth century. A few other exceptional examples of painters designing kimonos have been recorded, but generally speaking, pre-modern kimonos were produced by anonymous crafts-people who specialized in particular phases of a kimono's production or in a certain type of dyeing or weaving. Well-established divisions of labour made it unlikely that one person could create the entire kimono from start to finish.

The emergence of the individual designer in the modern era can be linked to department store and government-sponsored contests, and to incentive awards and honours presented to individuals rather than groups. In 1911, Mitsukoshi sponsored a poster contest and offered a cash prize of the unprecedented sum of 1,000 yen for the winning entry.[7] Trading companies also sponsored competitions in order to gain a foothold in new markets. The

Marubeni Company of Kyoto, for example, began their Exhibition of Weaving and Dyeing Arts (known as 'Biten', an abbreviation of *Senshoku Bijutsu Tenrankai*) competition in 1927.[8] Many of the submissions for the Biten competitions are preserved in the Marubeni Collection. A kimono of 1935 executed in a new *yūzen* technique developed by Kimura Uzan (1891–1977) is one of many examples (illus. 124).[9] Marubeni also sponsored a textile exhibition in Tokyo and invited painters and designers to submit their drafts for display. The Nihonga painter Kaburagi Kiyokata often submitted his designs for such exhibitions.[10] Kaburagi was also a member of a group that created woodblock prints of modern Japanese beauties for the publisher Watanabe Shōzaburō, whose business was targeted to appeal to the burgeoning export market.

International art movements, historical revivalism and the quest for modernity enlivened, enriched and complicated the world of design, propagating neologisms for newly emerging artistic movements. Hamada Masuji

124 Kimura Uzan, woman's long-sleeved kimono (*furisode*) with design of roses and fans, 1935, paste-resist dyeing and embroidery on silk.

represented the voice of 'commercial art' (*shōgyō bijutsu*), a word coined around 1926 and defined as a 'design theory [that] combined modernist fine-art aesthetics with the "progressive" values of industrialism'.[11] In contrast, the ethnologist and folklorist Yanagita Kunio addressed rapid social change by establishing his folklore studies (*minzokugaku*) that 'advanced a "new nativism" that aimed at restoring archaic religious beliefs to the centre of national life [which], he believed, would solve the problem of unevenness between city and countryside that resulted from modernization.'[12] In the face of increasingly mechanized and urbanized surroundings, Yanagita and some of his contemporaries stressed a nostalgia for the 'traditional' and 'rural' by constructing an unchanging and imaginary Japanese country 'folk'. Around the same time, the *mingei* movement drew attention to 'crafts' in an unprecedented fashion. Yanagi Sōetsu (also known as Muneyoshi, 1889–1961), one of the prominent founders of this craft movement, invented the word in 1925.[13] Inspired by the Arts and Crafts Movement in England, and in reaction to Japan's own industrial revolution occurring around him, Yanagi revered utilitarian, hand-made objects produced by anonymous artisans. He prized the work of the 'unknown craftsman'. By contrast, Hamada cultivated the status of the 'artist-designer' engaged in commercial design. As Gennifer Weisenfeld discusses, in the late 1920s commercial design

> was a more inclusive term, comprising three-dimensional forms such as show windows, and architectural structures used for advertising, such as kiosks and storefronts. It also overlapped with elements of industrial design, known as '*sangyō bijutsu*' or '*sangyō kōgei*,' which included product design. Japanese design historians identified a gradual conceptual shift around the turn of the century from the long-standing artisanal notion of design (*ishō*) to one which implied more personal intentionality and professional standing on the part of the designers, expressed in the increasingly common terms *zuan* (design), *dezain* (design) and *shōgyō bijutsu* [commercial art].[14]

Further complicating the charged relationship between 'art' and 'craft' was the term '*kōgei bijutsu*', or 'craft art', which was also coined in the 1920s.[15] Coexisting in a modern, industrial world, the people who produced and promoted 'craft', 'art' or 'commercial goods' in the first half of the twentieth century continuously redefined the boundaries among these newly constructed categories. Kimonos, notably, were represented in all three categories.

Yanagi Sōetsu later banded together with two potters, Hamada Shōji and Kawai Kanjirō and in 1926 founded the Japan Folk Art Association. Yanagi met the English potter Bernard Leach, who visited Japan in 1907; as the standard-bearer for Japanese ceramics, Leach promoted Yanagi's *mingei* ideals on an international scale. More significantly, Leach promoted his own work, and dubbed himself a descendant of the potter Ogata Kenzan, Ogata Kōrin's younger brother. Leach's desire to be seen as a disciple of Kenzan in order to claim legitimacy for his own work is a modern example of how name recognition, sponsorship and lineage shape views of Japanese arts and design. Leach wrote in one diary entry from 1953:

> I spent this day at the Kenzan-Kōrin exhibition at the Mitsukoshi [Tokyo Department Store] Gallery talking to visitors and members of the Kenzan Society. The opening of the exhibition had been set so that I, as one of the two living representatives of the school, the other being Tomimoto Kenkichi (1886–1963), could take part in it.[16]

To be sure, many potters like Leach, and subsequently weavers, dyers and other craftspeople, rose to prominence through the display and promotion of their work at department store exhibitions.[17] It was considered a passport towards greater recognition.

In Japan, displaying art and crafts in department stores enjoys a long history, so the idea of retail stores promoting art, as well as artists promoting retail products, is quite normal. It was only in the 1870s that the terms *bijutsu* (the equivalent of 'fine art') and *kōgei* (the equivalent of 'decorative arts', 'industrial arts' or 'applied arts') were coined. If one considers the Edo-period artist Ogata Kōrin painting a kimono for his client or the woodblock-print artist Hashiguchi Goyō creating advertising posters for the Mitsukoshi department store, it is apparent that distinctions between high and low art or hierarchies ranking fine arts (typically painting and sculpture) above the decorative arts or crafts were relatively foreign to the Japanese until such Western Beaux Arts ideals were imported in the 1870s.

Appreciation of the kimono as a commercial product to be worn, as a craft object prized for its technical mastery and as an art object coveted by both private and institutional collectors, is entangled with this moment in history when definitions and categories for objects – industrial art, *mingei*, craft and art – were being constructed. As noted previously, department stores not only sold kimonos but also sponsored kimono design competitions and exhibitions, thereby blurring distinctions among these categories. In the 1920s and '30s, the proliferation of magazines, newspapers and other forms of printed information contributed to the media marketing of kimonos. The stars and trendsetters in this new form of advertising were often actresses, some of whom were formerly geishas, and in one notable case, a female writer. The cult of the celebrity provided these women a stage from which to define and parade their personal styles. Uno Chiyo (1897–1996) distinguished herself as a writer before entering the world of kimono design. While not as well known in the kimono design world, she was influential in the fashion world through the publication of her magazine, 'Style' (*Sutairu*), and her later publication entitled 'Kimono Primer' (*Kimono dokuhon*). Uno, the quintessential 'nail that stood out' in the relatively male-dominated worlds of both literature and kimono production, capitalized on her celebrity status through cross-over marketing of her magazine, books and kimono designs.

In addition to department store promotions and other types of media marketing, another venue for exhibiting one's designs that affected kimono designers and the network of craftspeople supporting them arose in the form of government-sponsored programmes. In 1955, the Japanese government instituted a system whereby individual artisans could be designated as 'holders of intangible cultural properties'. Today, recipients of this honour are more popularly referred to as Living National Treasures (*ningen kokuhō*), the government's highest honour for artistic achievement. Tabata Kihachi III, Serizawa Keisuke, Inagaki Toshijiro, Moriguchi Kakō and his son Moriguchi Kunihiko, all profiled below, represent only a few of the many textile artisans who have enjoyed this status.

Other kimono designers claimed to have revived waning or extinct textile traditions, yet have not been recognized with the honour of Living National Treasure. Some, however, distinguished themselves among kimono designers by seeking a cosmopolitan audience for their works. As discussed below, within some circles in Japan, an aura of controversy surrounds Itchiku Kubota, his kimono designs and the decision to label his designs 'Itchiku Tsujigahana'. Yet Itchiku's works have been promoted in exhibitions both within Japan and internationally, and a museum bearing his name with a view of Mount Fuji enshrines his creations.

From the 1930s and through the '40s, Japan was engaged in what is commonly referred to as the Fifteen Year War (1931–45), but the country was actually involved in three major conflicts: the Manchurian Incident in 1931–2 that resulted in the occupation of Manchuria and the establishment of the puppet regime known as Manchukuo; the China War (known elsewhere as the Sino–Japanese War, 1937–45); and the Pacific War (1941–5) between Japan and the Anglo-American powers. A kimono design with military imagery from this period is shown overleaf (illus. 125). The 1920s and '30s were a time of great ferment in kimono production, as Western influences mingled with traditional Japanese designs (illus. 126). Yet by the early 1940s, the kimono had come to symbolize a luxurious lifestyle that was increasingly considered inappropriate during a time of war. During the U.S. occupation of Japan in the aftermath of the Second World War, kimonos were often

Overleaf
125 Infant's ceremonial robe (*omiyamairi*) with design of soldiers at war, *c.* 1940, paste-resist dyeing and painting on artificial silk.

126 Woman's kimono with design of a peacock perched amid peonies, 1930s, paste-resist dyeing on a figured silk ground.

bartered for food in the countryside or on the black market. The term 'bamboo shoot existence' (*takenoko seikatsu*) referred to the necessity of peeling off one's clothing, like the layers of a bamboo shoot, in order to trade these precious commodities for food and other necessities.[18] This revolutionary change in the symbolic and material value of the kimono marks the moment when its meaning was transformed from an everyday garment into a largely ceremonial costume. This shift, in turn, parallels the evolving role of the kimono designer from nameless artisan to celebrated artist. By the mid-1950s, the country's economic recovery and the establishment of government-sponsored programmes such as the Living National Treasure system created an ideal environment for emerging individual kimono designers. By the summer of 1964, when Japan played host to the Olympic Games in Tokyo, the kimono had become one of the country's national symbols.

The cachet of 'designer labels' – in the form of kimonos designed by recognized artists – continues a trend that dates back to the early eighteenth century in Japan. As previous chapters have discussed, while some painters designed directly on kimonos as if on a canvas, others created under-drawings, or patterns for kimonos. Following the lead of painters from the previous era, Nihonga painters working in the late nineteenth century produced kimono samples from which stencils were cut to realize the design in the newly developed *kata-yūzen* (stencilled paste-resist dyeing) process. Many artists of the modern era amassed personal collections of historical Japanese textiles to use as models for their paintings. These collections of historical textiles by painters and dyers from the beginning of the twentieth century, coupled with the publication of limited editions of new kimono designs in the 1930s, suggest the tension that emerged between preserving and revitalizing the kimono tradition.

It may seem counterintuitive that kimono production flourished in the 1920s and '30s given that during this period Japan was increasingly engaged in military conflicts beyond its borders, campaigns that would ultimately drain the national coffers and end in Japan's defeat in 1945. Extant examples, such as an obi with motifs of aeroplanes streaming diagonally across a background of golden clouds and gold-fret designs, suggest that luxurious fabrics were being produced throughout the 1930s (illus. 127, 128). The silver and gold bombs against a dark blue background, visible when the obi sash is opened, would have been hidden when properly tied around the wearer's body. This jarring juxtaposition of bombs on sumptuous textiles is specific to this moment in Japanese history, when military might was glorified.

From September 1939 and throughout 1940, the Japanese government targeted textile manufacturers, regulating their production.[19] In July 1940, the government issued a law curtailing the manufacture of luxury items –

Wartime Command Economy and Regulations Limiting Manufacture and Sale of Extravagant Goods, also known as the 7–7 Law, since it was issued on 7 July 1940.[20] Soon after, slogans declaring 'Luxury is the Enemy' began appearing on the streets. Fancy kimonos were one of many regulated luxury goods. In the same year Japanese subjects were encouraged to wear the 'clothing of the nation's people' (*kokuminfuku*), which consisted of trousers and a jacket for men; recommended 'standard attire' for women came in three styles: the most popular being a two-piece set comprising a simple top with trousers known as *monpe*.[21] The National Defence Women's Association posted women dressed in these simple two-piece sets on street corners, who entreated their female compatriots to shun luxurious clothes and expensive permanent waves for their hair to show support for the nation's war efforts. Some of the members of the association were reportedly so fervent that they cut the flowing kimono sleeves of non-complying women.[22]

While the efficacy of this campaign is debated, the fact that textile materials became so scarce that some Japanese were reduced to wearing fabrics made from cotton mixed with bark and wood pulp (*sufu*) is suggestive of the country's dire economic situation (illus. 129). In 1942, a member of the Welfare Ministry, Aoki Hideo, reflected on the relationship between clothing and nationalistic sentiment:

> Clothing and apparel are an expression of the rationale of the lives of citizens. With the nation on a war footing, the citizens' apparel must be appropriate for meeting head on and overcoming this time of emergency.[23]

In an article in the magazine 'Housewife's Companion' (*Shufu no tomo*) in 1941, the director of the Labour and Science Research Institute not only railed against luxurious garments, but singled out the kimono as inappropriate for the working women of Japan. He declared:

> Women who represent contemporary Japan are not forty-year-olds wearing only Japanese kimono and sitting on *tatami* mats, but young women at work, whether in cities or farming villages. For work, it's Western dress, not kimono, and there's no one working in a factory wearing kimono.[24]

How then, did kimono makers engaged in producing high-end, luxurious garments survive during these years of increasing deprivation, when kimonos were not only no longer affordable, but were seen by some Japanese as symbols of a level of luxury worthy of scorn? Some kimono-producing companies survived by emphasizing the need to preserve kimono-making techniques. Three

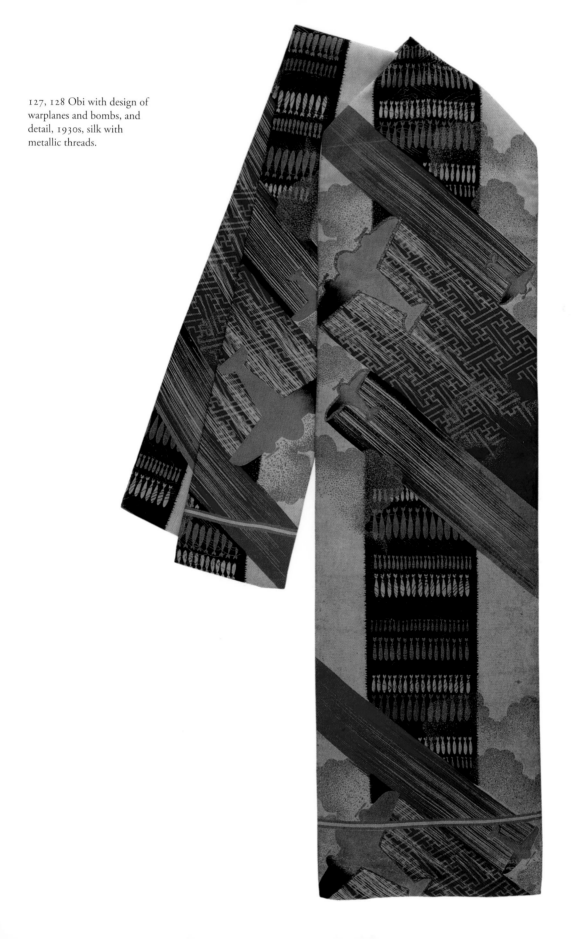

127, 128 Obi with design of warplanes and bombs, and detail, 1930s, silk with metallic threads.

129 Adult's under-kimono (*nagajuban*) with design of the Great Wall and aeroplanes, *c.* 1941, printed on fabric of cotton mixed with bark and wood pulp fibre known as *sufu*.

years after the anti-luxury proclamation by the government, the head of Chisō in Kyoto established the Nishimura Weaving and Dyeing Centre (Nishimura Sōsenshoku Kenkyūjō). That same year, the research centre applied for and was granted permission from the government to continue making *yūzen*-dyed silk kimonos in order to support weavers and dyers and ensure that their technical skills would be sustained for future generations. Department stores such as Matsuzakaya, which purchased kimonos from Chisō, continued to host 'invitation-only' events for its elite clientele. Remarkably, an invitation to one such event, dated 'Shōwa 15, third month' (March 1940), was produced with lavish gold- and silver-foil decorated paper (illus. 130). The Japanese government, already aware of the need to protect national treasures, recognized a need to preserve less tangible technical processes and craftsmanship as well.

130 Invitation to special clients of Matsuzakaya Department Store, March 1940, gold, silver foil and pigments on paper.

The genesis and evolution of the Japanese system for the protection of cultural properties, its designation of important cultural objects and, later, holders of intangible cultural properties was, in part, a response to the government's desire to revere and protect Japanese 'tradition'. As such, the system for designating national treasures is complex and has shifted with the political tide. Around 1897, a term originally used to refer to a treasured object from a feudal domain, *kokuhō*, came to refer specifically to a national treasure. With 'the recognition that traditional culture might serve as a tool in nation-building',

131 Imao Kazuo, woman's long-sleeved kimono (*furisode*) with design of boats in a Western-style landscape, 1936, pigment infused resist-dyeing and embroidery on silk.

survey teams set out to inventory the objects housed in temples, shrines and nobles' collections.[25] Museums were built to house and display the nation's cultural artefacts. At about the same time, certain painters and artisans were honoured with the title of 'Imperial Household or court-appointed artisan' (*teishitsu gigeiin*), in recognition of their craftsmanship.[26] Inaugurated in 1890, this institution lasted until 1944. Established artistic lineages may have contributed to the recognition of certain artist's contributions. In 1936, Imao Kazuo (1898–1973), grandson of the *teishitsu gigeiin* Imao Keinen (1845–1924), produced for Marubeni a kimono with a Western-style landscape utilizing a newly developed technique known as *ekigaki yūzen* in which dyes and pigments suspended in a rice-paste solution are painted directly onto the fabric (illus. 131).[27]

The honouring of individuals as court-appointed artists and the impulse to protect cultural property appears to have merged in what is today popularly referred to as the Living National Treasure system. The 1950 Law for the Protection of Cultural Properties was enacted in part to prevent the disappearance of skills in arts deemed to have historic or artistic value. The law was later revised to include all arts bearing significant historic or artistic value, endangered

or not.[28] While the selection criteria remained opaque, the laws were amended in 1955 to emphasize three basic tenets: 'artistic value, importance in craft history, and representative of a local tradition'.[29]

The tension between preserving Japanese 'tradition' while simultaneously appearing to be as modern and urbane as the citizens of Western nations intensified in the post-Second World War era as Japan recovered from the humiliation of defeat. The Cultural Properties Protection Committee established the first annual Japanese Traditional Craft Exhibition in 1955 in an effort to preserve traditional techniques of weaving and dyeing. Initially, kimono designers who were liberated from the constraints of the department store-based studio produced refreshingly innovative designs. Ironically, the struggle to protect and promote traditional crafts in an increasingly modernized, mechanized, urbanized and Westernized world may eventually have stifled their vitality and viability. As designers sought to both create 'one-of-a-kind' designs and preserve traditional techniques, the kimono evolved from an everyday garment into an expensive cultural relic.

The sections that follow focus on the biographies of individual kimono designers, beginning with recognized artists of the eighteenth century, then designers whose lives spanned the critical years when Japan was engaged in military conflict.

Named Designers of the Edo Period

While most of the identities of textile artisans active during the Edo period are lost to the historical record, there are a handful of exceptions. Famous artists such as Ogata Kōrin, Sakai Hōitsu, Gion Nankai and Matsumura Goshun engaged in the art of kimono design, applying their knowledge of ink painting on silk to great effect. The vogue for ink-painted kimonos that began in the early eighteenth century sparked one of the many evolutions in kimono design.

Ogata Kōrin (1658–1716), Sakai Hōitsu (1761–1828) and the Rinpa Brand

An ink-painted kimono commissioned by the wealthy timber merchant Fuyuki of Edo is so celebrated that it was designated an Important Cultural Property by the Japanese government. Although it is an unsigned work, it has been traditionally attributed to Ogata Kōrin based on a document written over 100 years after Kōrin's death. The document states: 'Fuyuki household possession, painted by Kōrin, white fabric . . . Tempō 9 (1838)'.[30] The kimono depicts autumn grasses, chrysanthemums, Chinese bellflowers, bush clover

and pampas grass in light and dark shades of green, yellow and pink, in India ink and other pigments painted on a white silk twill with gold pigment highlights for the veins of leaves. The harmoniously balanced motifs with heavier and denser elements around the hem area and lighter motifs around the neck and shoulder area reflect the distribution of design elements fashionable in the Genroku era (1688–1704). As noted in the Introduction, during this era the weight of the composition shifted from the shoulder area to the lower half of the kimono in response to the ever-widening obi sash. In the case of Kōrin's kimono, however, it is interesting to note that there is no clear break in design around the waist area for the placement of the obi. This garment appears to have been conceived as a *painting on a kimono*, rather than as simply as a kimono with a painted design.

Throughout his life, Kōrin distinguished himself from the anonymous craftsmen of his time. Kōrin's great-grandfather, Ogata Dōhaku, relinquished his samurai status to become a member of the weaving and dyeing profession.[31] Around 1560 he married Hon'ami Hoshu, sister of the celebrated calligrapher, potter, designer, tea master and sword connoisseur Hon'ami Kōetsu, and in 1590 established the textile business Kariganeya.[32] According to 'The Ledger for Dyeing at the Kariganeya' (*Kariganeya Senshoku Daichō*, 1602), elite patrons of the business included some of the highest-ranking members of Kyoto society.[33]

Indeed, Kōrin spent his childhood days as the son of an upper-class merchant whose patrons included some of the most prominent members of the military and imperial elite. When Kōrin's great-grandfather Dōhaku died, his son Sōhaku took over the family business. Ogata Sōken, Kōrin's father, was the second son of Sōhaku and became a textile merchant and owner of the Kariganeya in 1660.[34] In 1678, during Sōken's tenure as head of the business, the Kariganeya supplied 340 kimonos and other items to a single patron: the Empress Tōfukumon'in, daughter of Tokugawa Hidetada and consort of Emperor Gomizunoō.[35]

When Sōken died, Kōrin and his brother Kenzan were bequeathed money, land, furniture and textiles while, in keeping with cultural practices, their eldest brother Tōzaburō inherited the family business. By 1694, Kōrin was in dire financial straits and was forced to pawn some of his possessions.[36] Two years later, upon his brother Kenzan's request, Kōrin sold his father's inheritance in order to repay a loan from Kenzan. It was also around this time that Kōrin began to draw, upon request, designs on white satin, probably utilizing undyed materials that were left to him by his father. The erotic book 'A Chronicle of Love' (*Kōshokumon denjū*, 1699), states that Kōrin painted 'black pines on white satin' and the patron was highly pleased with the results.[37] By this time, Kōrin's painted kimonos were already highly prized. Kōrin constantly challenged himself with new formats for his decorative works,

132 Woman's kimono (*tomesode*) with design of stylized pine trees and gold mist, first half of the 20th century, paste-resist dyeing and painted gold accents on silk crepe ground.

which included folding screens, hanging scrolls, round fans, folding fans, incense-wrapping paper, lacquered writing boxes, medicine cases and textiles. In addition, Kōrin-inspired textile designs were compiled in a book known as 'Kōrin Pattern Book' (*Kōrin hiinagata*) with the first of such books appearing as early as 1706. There are many pattern books of Kōrin-inspired designs, collectively referred to as 'Kōrin patterns' (*Kōrin moyō*) that continued to be popular long after Kōrin's death in 1716. The legacy of Kōrin's work is memorialized in the artistic tradition known as Rinpa, derived from coupling the last character of Kōrin's name with the character '*ha*' meaning 'school of'.[38] A kimono with a Rinpa-style design appears on the previous spread (illus. 132).

One of Kōrin's followers, Sakai Hōitsu, also directed his artistic energy towards the kimono. Hōitsu painted a sprawling plum tree on the back of a *kosode* (illus. 133). Hōitsu's magnificent tree is painted with ink and colours on a white satin fabric. Although the kimono format requires the artist to conceptualize the design for use in a three-dimensional space, a hand-painted kimono, like a hanging scroll, is executed on a two-dimensional surface. Both require similar materials – brush, ink, pigments and silk – for their creation. The plum tree meanders across the entire kimono, including the neckband. Hōitsu appears to have perceived of this kimono as a painter's canvas, similar to his works in the hanging scroll format. Upon close inspection, the plum blossoms rendered in vermilion ink with gold pigment accents for centres become apparent. Around the base of the tree are dandelions and violets in yellow, blue and green with some gold pigment. The garment bears Hōitsu's round seal in vermilion ink on the right front panel, a precursor to the designer's logo (illus. 134). Although hidden from view when the garment was worn, Hōitsu's seal ensured that anyone privileged enough to view the garment at close range would know who created this stunning design.

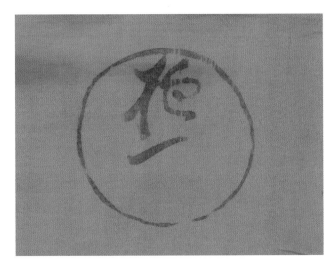

These two exceptional examples from pre-modern Japan highlight how designers who worked in other media also experimented with the kimono format. The example of well-known painters such as Kōrin and Hōitsu designing in various formats (including screens, fans and kimonos) set the stage for subsequent designers to establish brand recognition and sign their kimono productions.

Kimono Designers in Modern Times

Throughout the Edo period, most kimono designers continued to work in relative anonymity, involved in a system linking them to a producer who in turn procured the necessary materials and skilled labour to execute the design. By the early to mid-Meiji period, painters were commissioned by companies such as Chisō and Takashimaya to create sketches for kimonos. Kyoto-based artists such as Kishi Chikudō, Kōno Bairei, Imao Keinen, Kikuchi Hōbun and Takeuchi Seihō, and Tokyo-based artist Watanabe Settei, many of whom were later appointed *teishitsu gigeiin*, sketched designs for kimonos.[39] The second-generation of painters-cum-kimono-designers produced sketches that were often compiled into kimono design books, known today as *zuanchō*.[40] Some continued to paint screens and hanging scrolls, while simultaneously producing kimono *zuan*, while others, such as Furuya Kōrin, a disciple of Kamisaka Sekka, and Tsuda Seifu (illus. 135), a former student of the Western-style painter Asai Chū as well as a designer for the Takashimaya department store, rose to prominence as producers of kimono designs.[41]

The professionalization of designers evolved with the training available at educational institutions, the increased demand for novel kimono designs incited by department store and government-sponsored competitions, and the proliferation of venues to exhibit kimono patterns. In the late 1890s, design departments were established within some of the major universities, allowing incoming students to matriculate directly into design departments rather than approaching design through painting departments. These designers collaborated on publishing compilations of their designs, the most notable being *Seiei*, which was first published in 1903.[42] During the first two decades of the twentieth century, design competitions sponsored by department stores afforded these artisans an opportunity to distinguish themselves as kimono designers (illus. 136). The trading company Marubeni sponsored the Akane Kai group and gathered designs from renowned Nihonga and Yōga painters, such as Kitano Tsunetomi, Nakamura Daizaburō and Okada Saburōsuke, as well as illustrators, such as Takabatake Kashō, and designers (*zuanka*), such as Sugiura Hisui, in their efforts to promote the 'craftsman-ship of woven and dyed art' (*senshoku bijutsu no geijutsusei*).[43] Akane Kai drew inspiration from a competition established in 1927 known as the Biten, an exhibition featuring 'woven and dyed art'. As of 1927, textile artisans could also submit their work for possible inclusion in the 'crafts' (*kōgei*) section of the official government-sponsored 'salon' competition, Teiten (an abbrevia-tion of Teikoku Bijutsuin Tenrankai, or Exhibition of the Imperial Academy of Fine Arts). During the first half of the twentieth century, divergent profes-sional training opportunities for kimono designers expanded at the same

135 Tsuda Seifū, design of butterflies and stylized flowers, illustrated in *Kamonfu* (1900), published by Honda Ichijirō (Kyoto), polychrome woodblock-printed book, ink, colour and silver paint on paper.

拾弐号
雲一取花の丸

time as potential venues for selling their work and achieving individual public acclaim increased.

Tabata Kihachi III (1877–1956)

The biography of Tabata Kihachi III illuminates one route from anonymous artisan to celebrated dyer. The origins of the Tabata family of dyers in Kyoto can be traced to 1825, when they began dyeing textiles. During the late nineteenth century, the second head of the Tabata family began to amass a collection of kimonos.[44] This was due in part to the historical circumstance mentioned previously – namely, that during the social upheaval caused by the Meiji Restoration, many members of the samurai class suffered economically, but needed to maintain social appearances. When the daughters of samurai were to be wed, they needed to procure attire appropriate to their social position. According to family lore, Tabata Kihachi II, as a textile dyer, provided a recently impoverished samurai family with a design of his own. In exchange, he was presented with an heirloom kimono from the samurai family's collection. In this way, the Tabata collection, which now includes more than 10,000 objects, was born.[45]

At the age of sixteen, Tabata Kihachi III entered the Kyoto-fū Gagakkō (Kyoto Municipal Painting School) to study Japanese-style painting under the tutelage of Konō Bairei and later Takeuchi Seihō prior to becoming the head of the Tabata dye house. Kihachi III counted many painters among his friends: he was acquainted with painters who worked in the Japanese style of painting such as Uemura Shōen, Nishimura Goun, Irie Hakō and Kanashima Keika, as well as painters who worked in the Western style, such as the afore-mentioned Okada Saburōsuke, who also submitted kimono designs to the Akane Kai. All undoubtedly knew of Tabata's Japanese textile collection and likely studied and borrowed individual pieces to use in their paintings of historical figures. The artist Kikuchi Keigetsu once offered to trade any of his paintings for a particularly coveted garment in Tabata's collection. Kikuchi further offered to buy it for what was deemed an 'exorbitant sum', but Kihachi III declined the offer.[46] The treasures in the Tabata collection have increased in value because such exquisite examples are no longer produced. To some connoisseurs, the Tabata collection of historical textiles has gained more recognition than the kimonos designed by Tabata himself.

According to his son's recollections, Kihachi III 'never wanted to be treated as a mere dyer' and considered himself a 'dyer-painter'.[47] Nonetheless, painters came to Tabata to learn about the dyeing process. Similar to his pre-modern predecessors, such as Kōrin, for example, Kihachi III did not confine his artistic ability to a single medium.

136 Design (*zuan*) for kimono with flowers and butterflies amid clouds, awarded first prize in Mie prefecture, 1909, underdrawing, ink and colour on paper.

138 Tabata Kihachi, 'Cranes in a Pine Grove' design for woman's long-sleeved kimono (*furisode*), 1954, underdrawing, ink and colour on paper.

137 Tabata Kihachi, woman's long-sleeved kimono (*furisode*) of 'Cranes in a Pine Grove', May 1955, paste-resist dyeing and silk embroidery on silk.

In addition to assuming the leadership of the family business, Kihachi III developed the textile collection begun by his father. He conducted detailed analyses of his acquisitions, examining fibres, weave structures, dyeing techniques and compositions. After carefully classifying an object, he would store it in a specially constructed cabinet, sometimes cutting the object to conform to the size of his cataloguing system. Kihachi IV expressed regret that his father cut up garments or large fragments. He noted, however, that Kihachi III was primarily interested in design and technique, rather than the shape of the object.[48] Additionally, Kihachi III chose this mounting style for ease of transport when he went out to sketch from nature.

Kihachi III specialized in the resist-paste dyeing technique known as *yūzen*. In 1955, shortly before his death, Kihachi III was designated a Living National Treasure by the Japanese government for his *yūzen* technique.[49] His technique and dyeing process, from the drafting of the under-drawing to adding the final embroidered accents to the kimono, were documented. The finished kimono resulting from this process, together with the attendant documentation, is in the possession of the Agency for Cultural Affairs, and both were included in an exhibition of Kihachi's works in 2001 (illus. 137, 138).[50] Since the designation 'Living National Treasure' came so late in his career, it is difficult to discern the impact it had on Kihachi's productions, or those of his successors.

Kihachi III represents one of the last remnants of an apprenticeship system based on familial ties. The family's extensive collection of historical textiles, Kihachi III's practical training in the *yūzen* dyeing technique and his academic training in Japanese-style Nihonga painting immersed him in a world that embraced traditional Japanese practices, even as the country launched headlong into modernization. The Tabata family business as kimono makers, their renowned collection of historical Japanese textiles, and the kimono designs of the third-generation head of the Tabata family symbolize, for some, a traditional Japan.

Serizawa Keisuke (1895–1984) and Inagaki Toshijiro (1902–1963)

The kimono designs of the celebrated stencil-dyer Serizawa Keisuke represent only a small portion of his overall production, which included folding screens, shop entrance curtains (*noren*), calendars, book illustrations and bolts of cloth. His development as an artisan during the 1930s, '40s and '50s personifies the challenges faced by many artisans of this period. Serizawa possessed an intriguing artistic biography. As remembered in the cultural imagination, he represents an important transitional figure diverging from the anonymity of the *mingei* artisan of the mid-1930s and achieving the celebrated status of a Living National Treasure, as embodied in an individual craftsperson, in 1956.

With his vast personal collection of African masks, Korean paintings, Okinawan textiles and a plethora of Japanese crafted objects, Serizawa was a cultural translator who produced in a Japanese idiom.[51] His textile designs, though venerating Japanese precursors, drew from a visual repertoire that ranged beyond native cultural and temporal boundaries. Despite his eclectic approach, however, Serizawa has been both championed as a *mingei* artisan and designated as a Living National Treasure, thereby participating in two ideological Japanese systems that revere the preservation of distinct cultural practices and knowledge handed down from generation to generation – more commonly rendered as 'tradition'.

While it is difficult to discern precisely how knowledge of other cultural traditions affected Serizawa's productions or whether his creations are amalgams incorporating elements from multiple processes and practices, his works are often lauded today as 'traditionally' Japanese. In one of his early works in the traditional Japanese format of an obi sash, Serizawa elected to decorate the cloth with a repeated pattern of bamboo and peonies, a pairing of motifs adopted from the Chinese repertoire. The traditional design of peonies and bamboo is set against a background of scrolling vines. This obi sash is an example of Serizawa's early attempts to replicate Okinawa *bingata*, a stencil-dyeing technique with a colourful dye palette. By this point in his life, Serizawa had seen an example of Okinawan *bingata*, which was a transformative experience. But he had yet to actually travel to Okinawa, annexed by Japan in 1879, to learn the dyeing technique from local artisans.[52] To create and perfect his technique, he travelled to Okinawa in 1939 to study the *bingata* dyeing processes.

Although he trained as a graphic designer, Serizawa's chosen métier was dyeing, and more specifically stencil dyeing. Serizawa is known to have favoured the Okinawan practice of cutting stencils and dyeing fabrics himself, rather than relying on a division of labour between stencil cutter and dyer, the conventional practice in Japan. Some of Serizawa's compositions bear further visual and structural affinities with combinations of characters and motifs found on Korean screen paintings (*munjado*).[53]

Serizawa's interest in Korea and his association with one of the founders of the *mingei* movement, Yanagi Sōetsu, date from the late 1920s.[54] As originally defined by Yanagi, the now freighted term of *mingei*

> has the sense of 'the art of the common classes' . . . *Mingei* consequently have two characteristics: the first is functionality, the second is ordinariness. In other words, objects that are luxurious, expensive, and made in very small numbers do not belong to this category. The makers of *mingei* objects are not famous people but anonymous craftspeople.[55]

Yanagi later made an exception to this definition of *mingei* for the creations of the emerging individual artist-craftsperson, such as Serizawa.[56] Serizawa was a highly visible vanguard member of the *mingei* movement in the 1930s. In the early 1940s, his work was popularized in modern media through publications such as 'Ladies' Graphic' (*Fujin gahō*), a woman's magazine that devoted its entire 1941 issue to Serizawa's work and featured Serizawa as a 'lifestyle designer' (*seikatsu no dezainaa*).[57] Subsequently, he became a founding member of the 'Japan Art Crafts Association' (*Nihon Kōgei Kai*) in 1955 and the following year was designated a Living National Treasure by the Japanese government.[58]

The increasing syncretism of Serizawa's designs, which simultaneously venerated tradition and extolled innovation, becomes apparent when comparing some of his earliest recorded uses of combinations of written characters and motifs with his later works from the 1950s. One of Serizawa's signature themes is his rendition of the Japanese phonetic syllabary, known as *iroha*, named for the first three characters that begin a well-known poem.[59] The poem is taught to all Japanese school-aged children and can thus be considered quintessentially Japanese; yet Serizawa was the first to use it as the very subject-matter of his work. In his eight-leaf folding screen produced in 1940, Serizawa rendered individual sounds from the Japanese syllabary as stylized characters or motifs representing characters within circles, similar to formal Japanese family crests, or *mon*, albeit in a more playful form, approximating *hentaigana* (a historical variant and cursive style of *hiragana*). In Serizawa's 1960s rendition of the Japanese syllabary in the kimono format, however, he chose to render the characters in the more familiar and standardized *hiragana* form, and individual characters are no longer isolated and confined within circles but are interconnected and then abstracted to a level of pure graphic design (illus. 139).

Functional, yet exceptional in design, and more than ordinary – herein lies the tension epitomized by Serizawa's productions, which were promoted and marketed through department store exhibitions from the 1930s.[60] In keeping with *mingei* tenets that disavowed signatures and ciphers, Serizawa's works bore no emblazoned brand name.[61] His distinctive designs, however, became a signature of their own. Serizawa's subsequent acceptance of the Living National Treasure designation reinforced the elevated status of his works. Ultimately, Serizawa became a commercially successful artist producing recognizable and eminently marketable products, but they were neither ordinary nor 'made by the many for the many'.[62]

How then did Serizawa – whose later works were anything but anonymous, inexpensive or collectively produced – navigate the ideological terrain separating *mingei* objects from recognizable works produced by artists that attain government recognition and sponsorship?[63] The hoary debate juxtaposing the anonymous artisan and the individual artist began in the 1930s and became increasingly public when the government instituted a system for designating Living National Treasures.[64] Living National Treasures received government subsidies to perpetuate their craft by training successors. The government purchased their works, documented their processes and sponsored annual exhibitions.[65] Serizawa's designation was, in fact, exceptional. Government authorities coined a new term, *kataezome*, for his work.[66] The choice of this term *kataezome* valorizes the Japanese *katazome* stencil-dyeing process rather than the Okinawan *bingata* process that clearly inspired Serizawa. This neologism, moreover, effectively acknowledges Serizawa's innovative, even transcendent, dyeing practices.[67] Given his decision to cut his own stencils

139 Serizawa Keisuke, length of fabric with design of Japanese *iroha* syllabary, *c.* 1960s, stencil dyeing on raw silk.

and dye his own works, one wonders if Serizawa was following Okinawan precedents. Or perhaps Serizawa, in a fashion similar to the shift towards 'creative prints' among woodblock-print artists at the time, sought to elevate the dyeing profession from that of an artisan (*shokunin*) to one of an individual creator or producer (*kojin sakka* or *sōsakusha*) who was responsible for producing the entirety of a single work.[68]

Serizawa's acceptance of the designation as Living National Treasure contrasted with the *mingei* advocate and potter Kawai Kanjirō, who notably declined the designation.[69] Visitors to the Nihon Mingeikan (Japan Folk Crafts Museum) broached this issue with Yanagi, who felt compelled to respond in written form. In 1961 he penned *Sakka no hin to mingeihin* ('Works of the Artist and Mingei'). To sceptics who questioned how works by individual artists could also be classified as *mingei*, Yanagi responded: 'The characteristic of our Mingeikan artists circle such as Kawai [Kanjirō], Hamada [Shōji], Serizawa [Keisuke], and others we hold great respect for, have at their basis of creation the highest reverence toward the works of *Mingei*.'[70] Yanagi believed that more than one path existed to attaining beauty and that emphasizing 'conflicting contradictions' detracted from appreciating the sincerity and spirit of the maker, whose work is imbued with 'the highest reverence toward the works of *mingei*'.

While Serizawa's works reveal polarities between tradition and innovation, everyday and extraordinary, inexpensive and costly, regional and international, anonymity and identity, the attraction of his works may lie in their very ability to extract essential elements from the visual arts and technical processes of various cultural practices and transform them into works that appear fresh yet steeped in time-honoured conventions. His commercial success made it impossible for him to remain an 'unknown craftsman' and thereby adhere to the strict *mingei* ideal. Yet he ensured the longevity of certain motifs, techniques and formats by cultivating a taste among consumers for his deliberate selections of eclectic motifs and techniques. Later in life, he established a research institute to train apprentices in his 'paper-dyeing' technique.[71] In the guise of tradition, Serizawa's works have linked one generation of Japanese artisans to the next while simultaneously bridging cultural borders. Serizawa navigated the turbulent waters between 'tradition' and innovation, steering a new course for successive generations of Japan's artist-designers.[72]

Serizawa's eclectic choice of techniques, motifs and formats led one scholar to compare him to Ogata Kōrin:

The multifarious character of Serizawa's activities, which covered every aspect of daily life, could well have earned him the title of 'designer' or 'art director' and in this respect he invites comparison with an earlier artist Ogata Kōrin.[73]

The posthumous comparison of Serizawa to the celebrated Edo-period designer Kōrin suggests that designers whose work encompassed formats beyond the kimono were viewed as linking pre-modern practices with modern yet 'traditional' practices.

Like Serizawa, Inagaki Toshijiro received a designation as Living National Treasure for the technique known as *kataezome*. But the path that led to his designation was quite different from that of Serizawa. Inagaki Toshijiro was born in Kyoto and attended the Kyoto Bijutsu Kōgei Gakkō (Kyoto Art and Crafts School). He graduated in 1922 and entered the design department of the Matsuzakaya department store where he created kimono designs. He became an independent dyer in 1931, taught at Kyoto Bijutsu Daigaku (Kyoto University of Art) and was designated a Living National Treasure in 1962 (seven years after Serizawa received the designation for the same technique). Inagaki later went on to produce woodblock-printed designs for the Mikumo Mokuhansha shop in Kyoto.

Uno Chiyo (1897–1996)

Uno Chiyo was a maverick. She is described in her biography as a 'fashion ingénue, magazine editor, kimono designer and celebrated femme fatale'.[74] Narrative fiction and the realities of a modern Japanese woman's existence coalesce in her literary works. Her life – multiple divorces, financial independence and commercial success as a female writer – was atypical at a time when women were encouraged to lead a life modelled on the role of 'good wife, wise mother', a role which entrapped many.[75] Uno changed her persona as easily as she changed clothes.[76] As a young waitress working in a cafe frequented by writers, she was variously described 'as if she just stepped out of a Takehisa Yumeji painting' in a makeshift kimono and white apron; as the 'amorous wife of yesteryear' wearing a kimono with a black satin collar; or as a *modan gaaru* when she abandoned her kimono for Western dresses and bobbed hair.[77] In her twilight years, she often appeared in public wearing kimonos, long after Western-style clothing had become the norm in Japan. A fashion chameleon, comfortable in Japanese or Western-style clothes, Uno's mood seemed to dictate her mode of dress.

Uno's clothing selections further shaped her public identity. Her fashion taste, disseminated through her magazine 'Style' (*Sutairu*) and her kimono designs, offered models for women hoping to emulate her. In addition to her many literary accomplishments, Uno launched the women's magazine 'Style' in 1936 from a Corbusier-style house situated in the middle of Tokyo.[78]

Lauded as Japan's first fashion magazine, it was initially devoted to Western-style fashions, with articles that advised on such issues as the 'Proper Underwear – A Must for Western Dresses'. Aware of the growing anti-Western sentiment in Japan by 1941, Uno renamed the magazine 'Women's Life' (*Josei seikatsu*) and, rather than focusing articles on Western-style clothing, she featured the kimono. The privations of the war and efforts to conserve paper led to the government's closure of Uno's magazine in 1944. She successfully re-launched her magazine in 1946 and, despite the hardships imposed by the war, fashion-hungry readers lined up in the hopes of exchanging food for a copy of 'Style'.[79]

In 1949, at the age of 52, Uno established a kimono research project and began publication, as part of 'Style', of 'Kimono Primer' (*Kimono dokuhon*), which commissioned essays by female writers such as Yoshiya Nobuko, Enchi Fumiko, Ariyoshi Sawako and Shirasu Masako, as well as from the stencil-dyer Serizawa Keisuke, among others. Many of the kimonos featured in the magazine were modelled by famous actresses of the time.[80] Reflecting her cosmopolitan outlook, one double-page spread presented three Caucasian models dressed in kimonos with the headline: 'Kimono suits even foreigners quite well' (illus. 140). Her magazine promoted a line of kimonos Uno designed to be worn on a trip to Paris that she felt would convey the Japanese taste for understated elegance. Her name is prominently displayed as the 'designer', followed by the names of the 'maker' and the 'kimono dresser' of the models. Uno penned articles for the magazine with titles such as 'Kimono and Myself' and later in life wrote an entire book on the topic entitled *Watashi no kimono jinsei* (*My Kimono Life*, 1985).

The success of 'Style' afforded Uno the resources to travel to Paris with her friend Hayashi (Miyata) Fumiko in 1950, where Uno paraded along the Seine in her kimono, to the astonishment and appreciation of Parisians.[81] Recognizing the beauty of the kimono, she opened the Style Boutique (Sutairu no mise) in the Ginza, where she sold kimonos of her own design.[82] Uno's eponymous designs and delicate cherry blossom petal trademark – her favourite motif – were disseminated through her publications. Her kimono designs were featured on the covers of 'Style', her name was featured on many of the products sold in her shop, and kimonos bearing the Uno Chiyo name were sold in Daimaru department stores in the larger cities.[83]

Eventually her extravagant lifestyle, coupled with her lack of accounting oversight, jeopardized the solvency of 'Style'. She concentrated her efforts on kimono designs for her Style Boutique and successfully negotiated an American tour in April 1957, exhibiting her kimono designs at the International Exhibition, which was initially held in Seattle and then travelled to New York and Los Angeles.[84] Reflecting upon her double life as writer and kimono designer, Uno wrote: 'I have another occupation, one that is not as

140 'Kimono suits even
foreigners quite well',
double-page spread in
Kimono dokuhon magazine
(December 1952), ed. Uno
Chiyo, published by 'Style'.

constraining. It is easier, perhaps more enjoyable – kimono designing . . . If I
did not design kimonos, perhaps my energy for writing would wither.'[85]

In celebration of her 88th birthday in 1985, Uno wore a kimono of her
own design bearing her signature cherry blossom motif. She changed kimono
twice to maximize exposure of her creative talents. The event was attended by
many celebrities, including fashion designer Issey Miyake, by then a rising star
on the international fashion scene.[86]

Itchiku Kubota (1917–2003)

Like Uno, Itchiku Kubota was a novelty in the kimono design world. Inspired
by a sixteenth-century textile fragment viewed in a museum's display case,
Itchiku endeavoured to revive the aura and techniques of one of Japan's most
revered dyeing traditions – today commonly referred to as *tsujigahana*, and
poetically translated as 'flowers at the crossroads'. (*Tsujigahana* was briefly introduced in chapter Three.) Itchiku claimed that the memory of that piece of cloth,
first viewed in 1937 when he was twenty years old, both haunted and challenged
him to attempt to reproduce the sixteenth-century dyeing technique, the secrets
of which had been lost for generations.[87] His artistic aspirations challenged
established conventions in the kimono world on many fronts. In his most
ambitious production, the 'Symphony of Light' series, the kimono transcends
the traditional bounds of a wearable garment and emerges as an installation

141 Itchiku Kubota, *Symphony of Light*, displayed in 2009 at the Canton Museum of Art, Ohio, for the *Kimono As Art: The Landscape of Itchiku Kubota* exhibition.

work. In the series, a single kimono functions as one panel in a contiguous, panoramic view of the four seasons and the cosmos (illus. 141).

Domestically and internationally, Itchiku's work stirred admiration for his bold presentations and stunningly colourful designs. Having trained under Kobayashi Kiyoshi, a dyer who specialized in the paste-resist technique known as *yūzen*, Itchiku was already quite familiar with Japanese dyeing techniques. Itchiku's desire to learn more about *tsujigahana* was delayed for about 25 years from his initial encounter with it in 1937. After conscription into the Japanese army and detainment in Siberia, Itchiku returned to Japan in 1948. In 1961, he opened a studio and began to produce under the label Itchikuzome ('Itchiku Dyeing'), and a year later changed the name to the more controversial Itchiku Tsujigahana.

Within some circles, scepticism surrounded Itchiku's motivations for appropriating the word *tsujigahana* for his works. As noted in chapter Three, today *tsujigahana* is venerated as the apex of Japanese textile production, unmatched in its beauty and technical execution. The *tsujigahana* technique flourished in the fifteenth and sixteenth centuries and vanished at the turn of the seventeenth century, as other types of dyeing techniques became fashionable. The mystery surrounding the word *tsujigahana* and the techniques associated with producing it, as well as the scarcity of extant works, contributed to *tsujigahana*'s valorization as a hallmark of Japanese textiles. Ironically, little is known about the original meaning of the word *tsujigahana*.[88] The aesthetic value of sixteenth-century fragments today categorized as *tsujigahana* is uncontested, as evidenced by their inclusion in publications, exhibitions and collections that feature these textile fragments as prized works of art.[89] In the post-Second World War era, the promotion and popularization of *tsujigahana* inflated the market value of an already scarce supply of objects classified as such. In today's art market, fragments and garments labelled as *tsujigahana* command high prices.

The most securely dated whole garment of what is today termed *tsujigahana* bears an inscription from 1566. Extant paintings of the late sixteenth and early seventeenth centuries portray elite women of the military class wearing kimonos that appear to be of similar design to *tsujigahana* fragments. This observation has led some scholars to postulate that the prohibitive expense of producing *tsujigahana* fabric limited its consumption to the highest-ranking members of sixteenth-century society. The cachet of *tsujigahana* likely existed from the time of its production in the late sixteenth century.[90]

At the beginning of the twentieth century, as interest in historical textiles garnered the attention of Japanese painters, collectors, academics and curators, the meaning of the word *tsujigahana* evolved. Textile enthusiasts, enamoured with the textile fragments that had begun to circulate which incorporated a combination of stitch-resist dyeing and delicate ink-painted motifs often further embellished with gold-leaf imprinting and embroidery, searched for an appropriate term to describe this notable textile. Most of these fragments were obviously fifteenth- and sixteenth-century productions. Many bore visible similarities to the garments depicted in paintings of the period. Some time during the late nineteenth or early twentieth century, this particular group of exquisite, rare textiles was labelled *tsujigahana*. In today's common parlance, *tsujigahana* refers to a type of cloth executed in the stitch-resist dyeing and delicate ink-painting, often exhibiting motifs of flowers and geometric patterns.

When Itchiku's work is viewed retrospectively, some of the early works visually resemble the hallmark motifs of sixteenth-century productions (illus. 142). The delicate ink-painted floral motifs wafting diagonally across the back of his kimonos echo the style of ink-painting used in historical *tsujigahana*. Technically, Itchiku also employed in some pieces a resist-dyeing technique, as was used in sixteenth-century productions. Some of the underlying differences between Itchiku Tsujigahana and historical *tsujigahana*, however, are embedded in the materials he used, particularly in the ground fabric and the resisting material, the tie-dye technique and the dyestuff.

In some of his later works, Itchiku commissioned Kyoto weavers to create a fabric known as *kintōshi*, rather than the lightweight, crisp *nerinuki* fabric traditionally used as the base for *tsujigahana* designs. To produce *kintōshi*, gold threads – either flat or wrapped – are woven into the ground fabric, creating a shimmering effect where the gold thread appears on the fabric's surface.

142 Itchiku Kubota, 'Floral Illusion' (*Gen*) kimono, 1976, stitched-resist dyeing and ink painting on silk.

Itchiku selected ground fabrics that possess noticeable difference in their reflective ability from *nerinuki*. In contrast to the gold highlights woven into the fabric used by Itchiku, textiles of the sixteenth century were decorated with gold leaf by applying an adhesive substance to the fabric's surface and then rubbing gold leaf over the surface to create designs. Itchiku opted for contemporary materials: vinyl thread to outline his shapes and to cover areas to be resisted rather than the bast fibres used in sixteenth-century productions. Itchiku also relied on synthetic dyes rather than natural ones, which can be applied directly to the fabric with a brush and then set through a steaming process in order to achieve the desired effects of colourful patterning on his kimonos.

Like some of his high-profile, pre-modern predecessors – such as Hōitsu and Goshun – and many of his own contemporaries, Itchiku also placed his seal on the lower right front of his kimono productions, where it would be concealed when worn with the left front overlap over the right. Revivals and branding are not unique to Itchiku. In his claim to have revived the lost *tsujigahana* technique and in his very appropriation of *tsujigahana* as a label for his designs, he was following in a tradition established by designers who, similarly recognizing the value of Kōrin's designs, adopted and adapted the brand name for their own productions.

The inherited cultural memory of *tsujigahana* affects the perceived value of textiles bearing the *tsujigahana* label in our own time. Therein lies the controversy surrounding Itchiku's work: what some perceive as the misappropriation of the hallmark of Japanese textile 'traditions'. Given the material and technical discrepancies of historical *tsujigahana* and Itchiku's works, some Japanese textile historians question why he labelled his productions Itchiku Tsujigahana at all. Why not simply Itchikuzome ('Itchiku Dyeing'), a label he used in 1961? Detractors claim he intended to capitalize on the cachet of the term *tsujigahana*, a highly valued textile type that harkens back to Japan's golden age, the Momoyama era (1568–1615), and some of its most famous personalities. Supporters acknowledge the early inspiration for Itchiku's work based on historical *tsujigahana*, and his life-long endeavour to revive what many believed to be a lost tradition. According to Itchiku, historical *tsujigahana* was the catalyst for the works that today bear his name. The company's English- and French-language promotional brochures state: '[Itchiku] had devoted himself to modernizing the technique, not imitating the old method. It is the original "Tsujigahana" reflecting current tastes.' Putting aside quibbles over whether the use of the term *tsujigahana* is an appropriate label for his designs, when fairly viewed his work idealizes a centuries-old textile tradition and infuses it with a vitality reflective of Itchiku's personal tastes.

Itchiku has also been criticized for the presentation of his works, which distinguishes Itchiku's kimonos from those of both his predecessors and contemporaries. As seen with his 'Symphony of Light' series, Itchiku viewed the kimono as one panel in a panoramic view of a single season. Itchiku was celebrated in some circles, particularly outside Japan, for his efforts to break the boundaries of displaying kimonos. Yet within other circles in Japan, Itchiku was criticized for violating the conventional and some might argue rigid rules for wearing kimonos. His catwalk models, for example, wore high heels rather than Japanese split-toe socks (*tabi*) and sandals, with obi draped from the hips, rather than bound tightly around the waist, and donned flamboyant hairstyles and hair ornaments.

The world-renowned kimono designer Moriguchi Kunihiko, profiled below, believes that Itchiku's *Symphony of Light* series 'denies the function of the kimono and that Itchiku's adaptation of the technique has gone too far to be called *tsujigahana* and suggests the new term of Itchiku-some [Itchiku dyeing]'.[91] Moriguchi's comments on Itchiku's alleged transgressions are perhaps best understood in light of his family's own involvement in contemporary kimono design.

Moriguchi Kakō (1909–2008) and Moriguchi Kunihiko (*b.* 1941)

Moriguchi Kunihiko, designated a Living National Treasure in 2007, followed in the footsteps of his father Moriguchi Kakō, who was designated a Living National Treasure in 1967. Within the world of traditional Japanese craft, this is the first time both father and son have received the designation during their shared lifetimes; Kakō died shortly after his son received the designation. In 2009, the second exhibition of father and son's works were on display in the Shiga Prefectural Museum of Modern Art.[92]

Venerating tradition and expanding on the possibilities presented by it is a Moriguchi family trait. Moriguchi Kakō attributed his success to Ogata Kōrin, remarking that 'looking at earlier art helps me form modern ideas'.[93] Living National Treasures such as Kakō feel a responsibility to 'raise' apprentices based on their own experiences of being mentored. In an interview with art historian Michele Bambling, Kakō stated:

> I have a sense of gratitude for the past generations who preserved their work and passed down their skills to us. We must, in turn, pass down this feeling of appreciation to the people of the future. Everything begins and ends with thanks.[94]

Moriguchi Kakō, the third son in a family of five children, was given the name Heishichirō at birth. Through his mother's intervention when he was fifteen, Heishichirō apprenticed with the third-generation *yūzen* dyer Nakagawa Kason (1882–1967, illus. 143).[95] From the age of 25, Heishichirō created and took the artist's name Kakō by combining the first syllable of his master's name 'ka' (which could mean flower or gorgeous) and 'kō' (which means broad or wide). Kakō was fortunate in that in Kason's workshop most of the work was carried out under one roof, from the creation of the designs (*zuan*) through to the colouring in of minute details. The world of Kyoto *yūzen* dyeing can be very closed, even today, as workshops endeavour to protect the secrets they have developed over years of trial and error. There are many types of *yūzen* dyeing, which is fundamentally a very complicated process

143 Nakagawa Kason, woman's long-sleeved kimono (*furisode*) with design of spring and autumn landscapes, 1937, paste-resist dyeing and embroidery on silk.

requiring as many as 26 different steps and a variety of skills in order to complete one roll of cloth. Some workshops specialized in applying the colours to the cloth and contracted out the task of applying the paste resist. While under Kason's tutelage, Kakō was exposed to a variety of technical skills in the Nakagawa workshop and learned about all aspects of *yūzen*-dyeing until 1939, when he decided to establish his own studio.

When he was 30, Kakō decided to become an independent *yūzen* dyer; his timing could not have been worse. Japan was at war, and the government had just imposed anti-luxury laws restricting the production of luxury goods. It was not until 1948 that Kakō was able to re-establish himself as an independent *yūzen* artist. In 1950, the Agency for Cultural Affairs established the law for the protection of 'holders of intangible cultural properties'. In 1955, Kakō submitted three works to the Nihon Dentō Kōgei Kai exhibition, one avenue

144 Moriguchi Kakō, 'Fragrant Garden' (*Kun-en*) kimono, 1968, paste-resist dyeing on silk crepe.

that has typically set artists on a path towards possible designation as Living National Treasures. His work, entitled *Sōshun* ('Early Spring') was awarded third prize by the Asahi newspaper. Through participation in these exhibitions, Kakō became known for his *makinori* ('sprinkled rice paste') technique, and it was for his mastery of this technique that he was eventually designated a National Treasure in 1967.

Kakō's idea for developing his version of *makinori* is said to have been inspired by his studies of textiles and lacquers that were displayed in the permanent collection of the Tokyo National Museum.[96] With the idea of using the sprinkled lacquer technique on textiles, he returned to Kyoto to learn more about it. Lacquer makers, however, guarded their trade secrets as closely as *yūzen* dyers, and Kakō could not find a lacquer artisan to teach him the fundamentals of the process of applying sprinkled gold to a lacquered surface. Through trial and error, Kakō eventually developed a paste that not only allowed the sprinkled gold to adhere to the cloth's surface, but was also durable enough to ensure that the delicate gold on the textile's surface was stable, even with the repeated handling required of garments.

Among his many extant works, one of Kakō's favoured motifs is the chrysanthemum. Kakō painstakingly produced a work entitled 'Fragrant Garden' (*Kun-en*), which is his interpretation of a single, glorious chrysanthemum blossom (illus. 144). When animated by the wearer's movements, the blossom elegantly swirls and flows before the viewer's eyes. Yet this particular kimono has functioned primarily as an object for display rather than as a garment. While many of Kakō's other works were coveted and worn by wealthy patrons, this kimono remained in the Moriguchi family for over 30 years. 'Fragrant Garden' has since been exhibited in almost every major national and international exhibition of Kakō's work, attesting to its extraordinary artistry. In 1999, it was purchased by the Los Angeles County Museum of Art, where it continues to be revered as a work of art. Thus, although this work was created in the kimono format, its value as a hanging work of art was celebrated from the time of its making. Indeed, many of Kakō's kimonos are appreciated more for their technical and artistic qualities than as wearable garments.

Infusing the kimono tradition with new ideas and further expanding the horizons of the *makinori* technique is a goal for Kakō's second-born son, Moriguchi Kunihiko. Kunihiko studied in the Japanese-style painting department at the Kyoto Shiritsu Bijutsu Daigaku (Kyoto Prefectural University of Art). After graduating, he went to Paris to study at the Ecole Nationale Supérieure des Arts Décoratifs, where he specialized in graphic design. He worked as a graphic designer in Paris before returning to Japan in 1964. Three years after returning to Japan, Kunihiko entered his father's studio.[97] Unlike his father, who favoured abstracting motifs from nature, Kunihiko relies on his training in graphic design to guide his creative process. He drafts his designs on paper, each one painstakingly drawn by hand. His designs tend towards the geometric, and play with optical illusions, thereby infusing the kimono format with an entirely new genre of patterns (illus. 145).

As is true of many other prominent kimono designers of his generation, Kunihiko's kimonos are prized both as garments to be worn on very special occasions and as works to be displayed. The art critic Judith Thurman featured Kunihiko and his work in the October 2005 Arts and Architecture issue of the *New Yorker*. From Thurman's article, we learn that Kunihiko designed kimonos for female patrons of Japan's aristocratic families, including Madame Takako Shimazu, the Showa Emperor's youngest daughter, and that 10 per cent of Kunihiko's productions were 'designed for Western collectors and museums or for competitive annual exhibitions of traditional crafts sponsored by the Ministry of Culture'.[98] One art historian acknowledged that Kunihiko's father 'is one of the many artists who established their careers through the exhibition'.[99] In today's world, kimonos are displayed in exhibitions, both domestically and internationally, and purchased by museums worldwide as prized works of Japanese art and craftsmanship.

At the time the *New Yorker* article was published, Kunihiko reportedly worked for six to eight weeks on a single kimono, producing about two kimonos a month with the help of assistants. The kimonos sold for $40,000–$80,000 each.[100] In her interview with Kunihiko, Thurman reported that 'at this stage of his career . . . [Kunihiko] is more interested in the kimono as a work of art than as a wearable object'.[101] But later, Kunihiko himself mused and posed a startling, contradictory question: 'I admire the Japanese avant-garde . . . We have to answer the challenge of modernity: what is a kimono, or what will it become, if it ceases to be a thing worn?'[102]

In my interview with Kunihiko in May 2009, he recounted the biography of one of his creations and its transformation from a 'thing to be worn' into an 'art object'. One of his kimonos, exhibited in 1968 at the Fifteenth Japan Traditional Craft Exhibition, was purchased by a woman from Osaka whom Kunihiko had never met. She wore it twice, on two very special occasions. Approximately 30 years later, the woman went to Moriguchi's home with the kimono, stating that she wanted to return it to him since she felt it belonged in their collection. Kunihiko did not feel it would be appropriate to accept this offer, yet he realized it was an important example of one of his earlier works. To resolve the dilemma, a curator from the National Museum of Modern Art offered to accept the kimono as a donation to the museum, where it is kept today.

When designing a kimono, Kunihiko envisions how his composition will change with the movement of the wearer. He views his artistic expression

145 Moriguchi Kunihiko, woman's kimono with design of gradated bamboo net, 1968, paste-resist dyeing on silk.

and designs as multi-dimensional. The first artistic expression is his design in the two-dimensional format of ink and colours on paper. When made into a kimono and exhibited in a museum, his designs often appear as two-dimensional objects, draped on T-stands. When worn as a garment however, the kimono takes on a third dimension. Time (or the context in which a person wears the kimono) creates a fourth dimension. Some believe that the kimono is out of place in the contemporary world, thus it is crucial to match it properly with the place and occasion for which it is worn. Kunihiko, however, is evolving with the times and understands that his works today are valued both as kimonos ('things to wear') and as expressions of his artistic sensibility and technical achievements. He has extended his repertoire to include two-panel folding screens used in tea ceremony rooms, while continuing to extend his range of kimono motifs and techniques.

Tradition in Transition

Kimonos today are still viewed as a symbol of a 'traditional' Japan, and many kimono makers are lauded as 'traditional craftspeople'. Some have garnered the esteemed designation of Living National Treasure conferred by the Japanese government. Various avenues exist to attain this designation. Some, like Tabata Kihachi III, come from long-established kimono-making families, firmly rooted in nineteenth-century practices but developing new techniques and bold designs. Others, such as Serizawa Keisuke, adherents of the *mingei* movement, have been recognized as preserving traditional techniques. Still others, like Moriguchi Kakō and later his son Kunihiko, broke with previous family tradition, learned the trade and then rose to prominence by garnering awards that lauded their innovative technical advancements on traditional techniques.

But what, exactly, does 'tradition' mean? As the historian Stephen Vlastos notes:

> tradition is not the sum of *actual* past practices that have perdured into the present; rather, tradition is as a modern trope, a prescriptive representation of socially desirable (or sometimes undesirable) institutions and ideas thought to have been handed down from generation to generation.[103]

Yet the transmission of 'traditional' practices, techniques and ideas does not take place in stasis or isolation. New technologies are invented. Consumer culture evolves. Shifting tastes dictate new trends. Producers respond to, and attempt to shape, current demand. Thus the world of kimono design is dynamic, and the kimono designer responds to multiple stimuli.

In the 1910s, many artisans began to grapple with circumstances of anonymity and individuality, and engaged in debates about the distinguishing features of 'craft' and 'art'.[104] Given that concepts such as 'fine art' and 'decorative art' were imported into Japan beginning in the 1870s, and that distinctions among concepts such as 'folk craft or people's crafts' and 'commercial art' emerged only in the mid-1920s, the terrain through which artists, designers and craftspeople formulated their 'designs' was fraught with issues of how to self-identify in an increasingly complex artistic environment. Kimono producers, some formerly anonymous craftspeople, continued to toil at their given speciality in relative obscurity, but increasingly, emergent kimono designers were marketed as individual makers whose products were sold under specific brands, or eventually under the designer's name. In contrast, companies such as Chisō sell only under the Chisō company label, regardless of how talented or famous their in-house designers may be.

Concurrent shifts in consumer culture, particularly evident from the 1920s, affected kimono production and marketing strategies. Urban shoppers perused displays of kimono fabrics rather than waiting for shop boys to fetch rolls from the storeroom. In an effort to stimulate desire for the most up-to-date patterns and fabrics, marketers designed posters and magazine advertisements that featured celebrated women wearing the latest fashions. Kimono designers packaged their merchandise under their own labels, giving birth to brand-name recognition.

In the post-Second World War era, government sponsorship of 'traditional' craftspeople, many of whom engaged in kimono production, buttressed an industry that was in decline. Kimonos produced by Living National Treasures are highly coveted by museums and private collectors as objects for veneration and display, and less so as clothing to wear.

Kunihiko's question is apt: what, then, is the kimono's destiny 'if it ceases to be a thing worn?'

SIX

EVERYDAY AND EXTRAORDINARY, THEN AND NOW

The real reason why traditional kimono culture is about to [become] extinct is because of its tendency to aspire to 'perfection' as a style that does not allow any other foreign items to be added to it. My advice for anyone wearing kimono is . . . to challenge this rigidity; let's forget about attending kimono lessons . . . let's just wear [kimono] the way you want to, it's only a kimono (meaning 'material for wearing'), do it your way . . . make it your own style. Be cool.

Yohji Yamamoto[1]

In the first decade of the twenty-first century, the fashion designer Yohji Yamamoto (*b.* 1943) based his ideas about liberating kimonos on his observations of Japanese fashions that were popular a century earlier. Yohji professed admiration for the Japanese of the Meiji and Taishō eras who were 'very good at blending the Western and the Traditional'. He romanticized, in particular, a political leader of the Meiji Restoration who returned from America wearing 'a pistol on his *hakama* pants, his hair in a pony tail, his feet clad in leather boots'.[2] As previously discussed, some women in late nineteenth-century Japan who possessed the economic means also opted for Western-style finery, which was still largely imported and rather expensive, but the majority of women continued to wear kimonos. Even so, as Yohji observed of men's fashion of that time, the kimono ensemble might include Western-style accessories such as leather boots or, for women, possibly a parasol, gloves or a handbag. The kimono might further incorporate Western-style motifs in its decorative patterning such as yachts, tulips or roses.

At the turn of the twentieth century, modernization and Westernization referred not only to a Japanese kimono decorated with imported chemical dyes of the most up-to-date colours and Western-style motifs. These terms also encompassed the appropriation of Western elements or accessories when used in combination with Japanese-style garments. A *sugoroku* game sheet of 1914, published in the magazine 'Young Girls' Companion' (*Shōjo no tomo*) and based on the layout of the Mitsukoshi store in Nihonbashi, reveals

146 Kawabata Ryūshi, 'Shopping *Sugoroku*: Department Store' (*Kaimono sugoroku: ichimei depaatomento sutoa*), supplement to 'Young Girls' Companion' (*Shōjo no tomo*) magazine (January 1914), published by Jitsugyo no Nihon sha, Tokyo.

a floor-by-floor interior view of a department store and depicts all types of
people in various combinations of Japanese and Western-style dress shopping,
viewing displays and engaging in an array of other activities (illus. 146).[3]
As prints, posters and photographs of those times demonstrate, fashions were
eclectic fusions of Japanese and Western elements, both traditional and modern.
Indeed, delineating 'modern dress' as exclusively Western and 'traditional
dress' as exclusively Japanese is a later mischaracterization of the fashions of
that period. Moreover, the fashions created in Japan in the early twentieth
century might be viewed as one way in which the global (parasols, boots,
Western motifs) were incorporated into the local (kimonos and *hakama*) to
produce a cosmopolitan look.

Department stores and their in-store design sections, then and now,
have played a major role in the production and dissemination of fashionable
attire. Not only did the stores sell the latest imported European, British and
American goods in the first few decades of the twentieth century, department
store staff also assumed the responsibility of educating and helping Japanese
to acclimatize to such unfamiliar items. At the same time, department stores
stood at the forefront of producing new kimono styles and stimulating desire
for their latest kimono fashions. As demonstrated in chapter Three, during the
first three decades of the twentieth century, Japanese women, men and children
continued to wear combinations of Japanese and Western-style clothing.
With the diversification of clothing choices, gender and age distinctions became
ever more apparent. Most men opted for Western-style suits and uniforms,
especially when appearing in public or on official business. Kimonos were
preferred by men of certain occupations, such as shopkeepers and craftsmen,
or as leisure garments in the private sphere. Most women, on the other hand,
continued to wear Japanese-style clothing both as everyday attire and for
special occasions. With the exception of women engaged in certain civic
occupations, such as teachers, nurses, telephone operators and bus conductors,
for example, most women, according to Kon Wajirō's survey of people strolling
the Ginza in 1925, wore kimonos.[4] When children were required to attend
school, with the initiation of mandatory school attendance in the 1890s, many
were introduced to Western-style uniforms from a very young age. By the
1920s, both young boys and girls could be seen wearing uniforms to school
and it was common to see a child in Western-style clothing, often a sailor-suit-
style school uniform, while holding hands with his or her mother, who was
likely wearing a kimono.

Since the second half of the nineteenth century, major shifts in the
design and use of Japanese-style clothing, particularly the kimono, have been
inextricably linked to Japan's evolving status in a dynamic international setting.
Increased cultural interaction between Japan and the outside world from the

147 Woman's over-robe
(*uchikake*) with design of
phoenixes, 19th century,
resist-dyeing and painting
on plain weave silk with
embroidered details.

148, 149 Woman's kimono gown and sash for the Western market with design of wisteria, also shown on mannequin, *c.* 1930, silk embroidery on plain-weave silk.

1850s onwards brought non-Japanese into the realm of kimono marketing and consumption. Their participation and engagement, in turn, affected the nation's attitudes towards what was increasingly perceived as the Japanese national costume. As revealed in chapter Four, women in kimonos appeared in visual media of all types produced by and for both Japanese and Westerners, including paintings by European, American and Japanese artists, advertisements for Japanese theatre productions travelling in other countries and photographs of American actresses and dancers. The kimono became a collectible item, and well-known figures such as Abby Aldrich Rockefeller acquired kimono ensembles, which she later donated to the Metropolitan Museum of Art (illus. 147). Modified versions of the T-shaped kimono produced exclusively for export by American, British, Chinese and Japanese companies altered the kimono's shape, meaning and function. The garment worn in Japan as an everyday or formal garment was increasingly transformed in new markets into loungewear in the form of 'dressing gowns' or 'tea gowns' (illus. 148, 149). Outside Japan, the kimono became a symbol of an exotic, and often erotic, country. In turn, the Japanese capitalized on this international trend by auto-exoticizing the kimono.

The 1940s and '50s marked a pivotal moment in the history of the kimono, and trends evident in that period further complicated its expressive meanings. During the early 1940s, the Japanese government made efforts to mandate a form of dress in order to economize on the use of already scarce fabric as well as to promote a more practical form of clothing that allowed greater physical mobility. Some scholars speculate that there was an additional incentive for the government to redesign the 'clothing of the nation's people' (*kokuminfuku*).[5] Amidst battles among nations for supremacy, the Japanese government felt some urgency to preserve a distinct native standard of dress in the wake of Westernizing trends. As the Japanese began to regard Western-style garments as more suitable for an active lifestyle, the kimono of the early 1940s came to symbolize an ostentatious and luxurious way of life that was frowned upon during times of deprivation. Faced with the conundrum of how to dress more appropriately in a country at war and yet not adopt the clothing worn by the enemy, the Japanese refashioned a style of clothing then still popular in rural areas of Japan (illus. 150). For women, a short jacket with tight-fitting sleeves wrapped around the upper body and tied at the waist was paired with loose trousers cinched at the ankles, known as *monpe*. Luxurious silk kimonos for women, which had been a mainstay for kimono producers throughout the first three decades of the twentieth century, all but disappeared from the cityscape during the Pacific War years. During the Allied Occupation of Japan, when the production and availability of cloth was severely limited, the Japanese learned to unstitch their kimonos and remake them into 'Western-style' clothing that optimized the narrow 14-inch-wide

150 'Protective Gear' featured in *Yomiuri Shinbun* newspaper, 1943. The text under the photo reads: 'This uniform, which meets wartime standards, while retaining feminine beauty, can be changed instantly into protective gear against air raids with just two strings of *hirahimo* [shoelace-type cords] as a substitute for gaiters.'

pieces of fabric. With minimal tailoring, kimonos were remade into garments that more closely mimicked 'Western-style' clothing while still retaining a Japanese flavour in their simple construction and fabric designs (illus. 151). For Japanese born and raised in the immediate post-Second World War era, this notion of 'Western-style clothing' became the norm. As they had done after Commodore Matthew Perry's opening of Japanese ports in the 1850s, many Japanese a century later again opted for clothing styles similar to those worn by the American forces.

Kimono designers whose lives spanned this tumultuous period took divergent paths in navigating the road from anonymous craftsperson to celebrated designer. Their biographies, outlined in chapter Five, reveal their search for ways to continue the practice of making kimonos despite shrinking market demand. The transmutation of 'kimono as wearable garment' to 'kimono as craft', 'kimono as art' or 'kimono as national costume' shaped what these designers produced and how they marketed their productions. Systems of government support, such as the Living National Treasure designations and the annual Japan Traditional Crafts Exhibition, buttressed the kimono industry

151 Trade sample book for *yukata* fabrics (*Ōhana yukata*), *c.* 1940s, fabric samples and ink on paper.

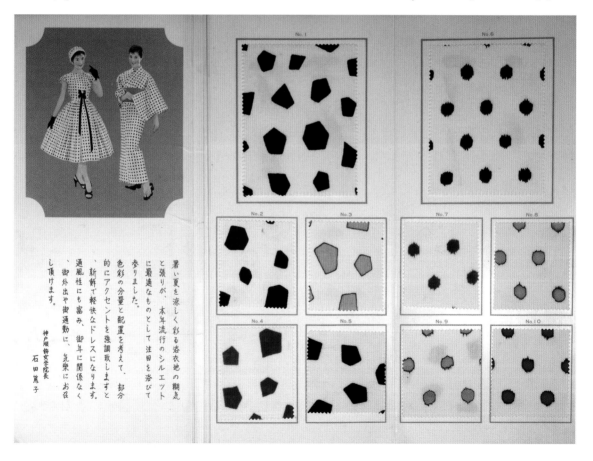

and temporarily secured new markets for kimonos among collectors and connoisseurs in Japan and abroad. While government efforts failed to stimulate a large enough consumer base for new kimono purchases to sustain the struggling industry, their promotion of the kimono as a traditional Japanese craft and the designation of kimono makers as Living National Treasures resulted in an increasingly permeable border between the realms of 'kimono as garment' and 'kimono as art'.

The shift in the kimono's function from its original use as an everyday garment to its new status as an object of veneration – not only revered as a national costume but also elevated as a 'traditional' Japanese art – is closely tied to the activities of artists, collectors and dealers active in Japan and abroad throughout the twentieth century. As discussed in chapters Three, Four and Five, kimono designers supported this trend. Tabata Kihachi treasured old Japanese silk fragments, often cutting them up and sharing them with fellow painters to be used as models in historical paintings. Many garments preserved in the Tabata collection, originally worn as everyday wear by elite families and later bartered by impoverished families for new robes, are today displayed in museums as works of art.[6] Likewise, the collector and dealer Nomura Shōjirō, an acquaintance of Tabata's, not only bought and sold kimonos and Japanese textiles for major collectors and museums outside of Japan, but his own world-renowned collection of historical textiles has been exhibited at the Kyoto National Museum in 1934, at the Metropolitan Museum of Art in New York in 1956 and 1959, in Toronto in 1958, at the Tokyo National Museum in 1973, the Japan Society in New York in 1984, and on numerous occasions at other venues since then. Today, institutional and private collectors of Japanese textiles active both within and outside Japan contribute to a heightened appreciation of Japanese garments. Thus the kimono enjoys an elevated status, not simply as a garment, or even a national costume, but also as an object of Japanese artistry and craftsmanship worthy of museum display.

Throughout the 1950s and '60s, the kimono's rising status as a luxury garment reflected Japan's rising economic status, domestically and internationally. Discouraged from wearing or unable to afford silk kimonos during the war years, many Japanese families spared no expense to acquire kimonos and revelled in this newly regained luxury. Brides were bedecked with expensive layers of silk garments on their wedding day. Those of Japanese ancestry residing abroad donned similarly lavish garments for formal wedding portraits (illus. 152). Parents exhibited their family's wealth by adorning their children in the finest attire they could afford for coming-of-age celebrations. In 1953, when Itō Kinoko won third prize in the international Miss Universe competition, a kimono style that accentuated a curvaceous, long-legged silhouette, known as

the *hattō shin bijin*, became all the rage in Japan among women of a similar age. The renewed and escalating Japanese pride elevated the kimono's status from quotidian to ceremonial.

From the late 1950s through the '60s, the kimono was used as an icon of Japan in several major orchestrated appearances. The excitement and publicity generated by the 1959 imperial wedding of then Crown Prince Akihito to the commoner Shoda Michiko included many photographs of the bride-to-be dressed in kimonos, thereby visually tying the kimono to a female associated with one of the most symbolically charged households of Japan.[7] Advertisements for the government-sponsored Japan Airlines, which launched international flights in 1954, featured female flight attendants wearing kimonos in their first-class cabins, catering to international businessmen and presumably also to a new type of visitor on their sojourn to experience a post-war Japan. (As one such advertisement purred, the kimono, 'the world's oldest "flight uniform," sets the mood for your silken flight'.) In 1959, Kojima Akiko won international acclaim when she was crowned Miss Universe – the first woman from Asia to achieve this title. Several pictures from her reign show Kojima dressed in formal kimonos, sometimes while wearing her crown.

Ironically, the 1960s also witnessed the birth of kimono dressing schools that sprang up around the country in order to capitalize on the younger generation's diminished knowledge of how to wear a kimono properly. Yamanaka Norio (*b.* 1928) purportedly opened the 'first institute of its kind to encourage the wearing of Japan's national dress in everyday life'.[8] Yamanaka founded the Sōdō Kimono Academy in 1964. He later published his English-language title, *The Book of Kimono*, and 'since 1970 he has annually led delegations of more than 100 members each, traveling to 45 countries in Asia, Europe and North and South America to promote international understanding of the kimono.'[9]

Academies such as Yamanaka's established rules for how to put on a kimono and how to incorporate the complex array of accessories and padding.[10] In essence, a particular way of wearing a kimono was codified by these kimono-dressing schools. What had once been a simple robe-like garment worn with a narrow belt in the seventeenth century had become so cumbersome that the average Japanese woman required assistance and instruction in order to wear a kimono. Everyday wear had become extraordinary.

Consider the factors that potentially contributed to the transformation of the T-shaped kimono into an emblem of Japan. The early 1940s attack on the kimono as a 'luxury item' may have inadvertently laid a path for the garment's resurrection as the country's national form of dress.[11] Wartime deprivations in the 1940s and '50s, when treasured kimonos were traded as commodities and bartered for sustenance, directly affected the ways in which the kimono later came to be perceived as a symbol of a family's, and by association the nation's, hard-won affluence. This experience may also have reinforced the notion that a kimono could be a work of art in its own right. Alternatively, might the revival and recognition of the kimono as a national costume have occurred naturally? Young girls brought up wearing Western-style clothing in all aspects of life in the post-Second World War era may have eventually discovered the temporal distance yet cultural proximity of the kimono to be both 'alien' and alluring, at once foreign and familiar. Did nostalgia for a mythical, 'traditional' Japan propel the kimono into the role of a national costume and beyond, into a lauded example of a form of Japanese craft or art?

If so, we might further consider the historical circumstances that account for the kimono's continued survival in all its variant uses in today's globalized world.

When viewed retrospectively, how and why the kimono, from among the numerous types of Japanese-style garments, became emblematic of Japan's national dress is no mystery. Whereas the entire population – men, women and children of all classes – wore kimonos as daily wear, formal dress and for ceremonial occasions through the mid-nineteenth century, the numbers of kimono wearers decreased dramatically beginning in the 1870s when men opted for Western-style garments. By the 1920s, many children were wearing Western-style uniforms for school, further eroding the number of kimono consumers.[12] In 1937, the ethnographer Kon Wajirō noted that Western fashions had become 'relatively static', and that in contrast, Japanese fashions were 'creative and innovative'.[13] A 'reactionary revival of kimono' was noted around 1948, and in the summer of 1950 demand for *yukata* reportedly over-whelmed department store supplies.[14] Yet, in the immediate post-Second World War era of the Allied Occupation of Japan, and certainly since the 1960s, increasing numbers of Japanese opted for 'Western-style' clothing. Even women no longer wore the kimono as everyday wear, reserving it primarily for special events. As 'Western-style' clothing was domesticated and became normalized simply as 'clothing' among younger Japanese, the 'way of wearing' the kimono became less familiar.

The type of kimono that survived primarily as a 'thing to wear' in the post-Second World War era was the more formal silk kimono. Increasingly donned by women and children for ceremonial occasions, or by practitioners of 'traditional Japanese arts', it was the highly decorated, formal silk kimono that became a national symbol of a 'traditional Japan'. At the same time, however, the kimono had also become an enchanting anachronism that has continued to exist – partly with the help of the Japanese – in the fantasies of foreigners along with other steadfast cultural icons such as Mount Fuji and cherry blossoms.

As cultural icons, women in kimonos have long been appropriated to market tourism in Japan. The book *Kimono: Japanese Dress*, published by the Board of Tourist Industry and the Japanese Government Railways in 1936, promoted the allure of the kimono to an English-speaking audience through the guise of a Parisian painter. The Japan Airlines advertisements with kimono-clad flight attendants in the 1960s are a post-war example. More recently, a tourism poster issued in 2006 represents the Japanese government's 'soft' campaign for a 'Cool Japan', deliberately co-opting appealing icons of both traditional and contemporary Japan (illus. 153).

This contemporary, more nuanced melding of the kimono and Japan looks beyond trusted icons of the past by updating them with pop culture

153 Japan Travel Bureau, 'Cool Japan' campaign poster with pop stars Puffy AmiYumi, 2006.

appeal and cultural immediacy. The poster depicts the
Japanese pop stars Ami Onuki and Yumi Yoshimura,
known by their stage name Puffy AmiYumi. The duo is
dressed in boldly patterned red and pink kimonos and
1960s-style boots. They stand in front of a backdrop of
a blown-up image of the internationally recognizable
woodblock print by Katsushika Hokusai (1760–1849),
'Great Wave at Kanagawa' from the series *Thirty-six
Views of Mount Fuji* (c. 1831–3). One of the pop star
figures holds up a ripe aubergine while the other allows
a hawk with outstretched wings to perch on her hand.
Together, the hawk, aubergine and Mount Fuji are
auspicious symbols when appearing in one's first dream
(*hatsuyume*) of the New Year. Compared with Isoda
Koryūsai's (1735–1790) pair of woodblock-printed
images of the same theme (illus. 154), the imaginatively
updated poster targets a global audience. The multi-
valent Japan–global appeal extends to the Cartoon
Network's animated version of the Puffy AmiYumi
characters that appear in the poster's lower left corner.
The Japanese pop stars, in contemporary synchrony
with their animated avatars, are touted in English as
the 'Goodwill Ambassador [*sic*] for the Visit Japan
Campaign in the U.S.'. The kimono is positioned at
the centre of this juxtaposition of then and now, real
and imagined.

Judging from the manner in which the kimono
is worn by the pop stars in this poster, they, or the
tourism campaign promoters, seem to have heeded
Yohji's advice to challenge rigid rules dictating how to
'properly' wear a kimono. Yohji's exhortations to 'do it
your own way', 'be brave', 'be cool' and break through
the rigid rules for wearing kimonos may reflect
contemporary attitudes towards this once classical
garment. Yohji's thoughts on the kimono and its
impending demise, and his ideas on how to revive the kimono-wearing tradition, appeared in the introduction of a two-volume set that reproduced select
yūzen designs from the historical textile collection of the kimono design house
Chisō. This kimono design company survived the war and its aftermath, gaining
exemption from the anti-luxury laws of 1940 by establishing a research centre
in order to preserve traditional techniques and craftsmanship. Published to

154 Isoda Koryūsai, young
couple with Mount Fuji,
hawk and aubergines – a
lucky first dream of the New
Year, *c.* 1775, diptych of
polychrome woodblock
prints (*hashira-e*), ink and
colour on paper.

celebrate Chisō's 450th anniversary, the catalogue promoted traditional and modern Japanese and Western-style motifs designed in the quintessentially Japanese decorative technique of *yūzen* paste-resist dyeing. Binary tropes such as traditional and modern, East and West, local and global, no longer capture the complexity of today's interconnected environment in which the world-renowned fashion designer Yohji Yamamoto promotes the designs of the 450-year-old kimono production company Chisō in a bilingual English and Japanese catalogue.

Yohji's ability to transcend the cultural limitations that equated Japan and the kimono helped him to distinguish himself as a global fashion designer. In 2004, Yohji's designs were exhibited at the Palazzo Pitti in Florence, at the Musée de la Mode et du Textile in Paris and at the ModeMuseum in Antwerp.[15] That a living Japanese designer was given major retrospectives in some of the most fashionable cities in the world could not have been predicted when Yohji's designs first arrived on the catwalks in the early 1980s. By reviewing how Yohji's work was initially received by non-Japanese audiences and how his work is positioned today, we might better understand how the kimono is moving beyond the narrow role of national costume and into another realm.

Yohji was born in Tokyo in 1943 as Japan was embroiled in the Second World War. His mother, widowed during the war, supported herself and her son by working as a dressmaker. Yohji came of age during the occupation of Japan. His mother dreamed he would become a lawyer, so he proceeded to study law at Keio University, receiving his degree in 1966. Ultimately, however, Yohji decided he preferred to work in his mother's shop, where she set one condition: that he acquire a basic knowledge of the craft of dressmaking.

Yohji attended the Bunka Fashion College and graduated in 1969. He subsequently entered a competition, won a trip to Paris and, although he spoke no French and had little money, remained there for eight months. He returned to Tokyo, and thereafter founded his first business in 1972. By 1981, he was back in Paris, showing his own collection. That same year, Rei Kawakubo (*b.* 1942), who designed under the label Comme des Garçons ('Like the Boys'), also displayed her collection in Paris. Some fashion critics lauded their work as visionary. Others criticized the works of Yohji and Kawakubo, 'dismiss[ing] the new styles as the Hiroshima bag-lady look, too avant-garde and depressing to be a serious competitor for global markets'.[16] More significantly, the debut of these designers on the Paris catwalks forced Paris and New York to acknowledge both them and Japan's fashion industry as a creative presence on an international scale, not merely as a site of production – the stereotypical role played by Asian nations in the globalizing fashion industry.[17]

While Yohji is Japanese by birth, he refuses to identify himself in terms of his Japanese origins.[18] When questioned by a reporter about the effect of

Japanese aesthetics on his work, Yohji responded: 'Why am I Japanese, why? I never caused it. There was never any choice. I just happened to be born in Tokyo.'[19] And yet in some ways Yohji's work has been essentialized as 'Japanese'.[20] Despite how the overall silhouettes of some of Yohji's designs appear to share affinities with Western-style dress, some critics see in their underlying construction oblique references to kimono construction based on the use of straight-line cutting and minimal tailoring. Nonetheless, in Yohji's work, as with Issey Miyake's (*b*. 1938), the design's emphasis is on the space between the material and the body. Many view the creations of Yohji Yamamoto, Issey Miyake and Rei Kawakubo as meldings of Eastern and Western aesthetic traditions. But it is also possible that their work transcends such static categories.

Eastern and Western distinctions encouraged by expressions such as 'Western-style' and 'Japanese-style' were naturally more significant in the 1860s when 'Western-style' clothing initially became a sartorial choice for the Japanese. When Yohji came of age a century later, however, most Japanese were more familiar with 'Western-style' clothing than with the kimono.[21] In fact, so complete was the transformation to 'Western-style' dress that Japanese, unfamiliar with how to don a kimono correctly, sought advice from experts. Department stores continued to play a role as arbiters of taste and disseminators of fashion advice. In a reversal of their previous role of introducing and promoting 'Western-style' dress to the Japanese, department stores now assumed the responsibility of teaching Japanese consumers how to properly wear their kimonos.[22]

Department stores might also be credited with generating a yearning for 'what retailers called the "retro boom" in the 1980s and 90s – a thirst for neo-nostalgic products and consumer events tied to the rhythm of agricultural and village-based life, even inventing some new traditions in the process.'[23] This nostalgia for agricultural life echoes the aspiration of the 1920s and '30s, discussed in chapter Three, that the pastoral not be abandoned for the urban.

Indeed, growing interest in the kimono may have ties to a longing for a slower, more 'traditional' way of life that was no longer sustainable in the high-growth, bubble economy of the 1980s, which abruptly burst at the start of the 1990s. Given this nostalgic trend, perhaps the comfortable, easy-care *yukata*, worn by males and females of all ages and appealing to natives of and visitors to Japan, may be Japan's answer to reviving interest in the T-shaped garment that is broadly encapsulated by the term *kimono*.[24]

A foreign visitor to a summer festival in Japan might refer to a *yukata* as a cotton kimono, or more generally, a summer kimono. But to a Japanese, this festive, unlined, cotton garment is deemed a *yukata*, a category distinct from kimono. The term *yukata* is an abbreviation of *yukatabira*, a garment

usually made of bast fibres that was worn as early as the Muromachi era
(1392–1573). As cotton became more readily available and affordable in the
eighteenth century, *yukata* were made of cotton, as well as a crepe-like fabric
from the regions of Echigo and Akashi. In the Meiji era, the *yukata* emerged
as a casual form of dress for summer evenings. The Chinese characters now
used for the term *yukata* are *abiru* ('to bathe') and *koromo* ('clothing'). For
women who came of age during the early twentieth century, *yukata* were worn
upon emerging from a steamy bath – taking advantage of the absorbent, cool
cotton fibres. Today, *yukata* again appeal to young women as festive dress for
summer events.[25] The easy-to-wear blue and white cotton *yukata* laid out for
guest use at Japanese-style inns and upscale hotels afford visitors a chance to
wear this kimono-shaped garment in relative privacy.

Generations and cultures are divided on the appropriateness of *yukata* for
private or public dress. As the roots of its name reveal, the *yukata* was traditionally worn after the bath, so some feel it is inappropriate for wear during the
day, even in its designer-version form. Others feel that the comfort of the
yukata and the ease with which one can dress oneself in it make it a perfect
choice for Japan's notoriously hot and humid summers. The gaily coloured
yukata is now a familiar sight during summer festivals such as the observance
of Obon (Festival of the Dead) when individuals return to their hometowns
to honour their ancestors. Media tools such as magazines and television in
Japan anticipate the annual festival and the practice of *yukata* wearing in the
summer months by advertising the upcoming season's fashionable *yukata*
patterns. Attesting to a broad interest in *yukata* among Japanese youth today,
Uniqlo, Japan's popular version of a Gap-style clothing producer, manufactures *yukata* and sells them pre-packaged with a matching obi. In 2002, the
Japanese textile production company Kawashima Orimono collaborated with
the British design firm Bentley & Spens to produce a line of designer *yukata*
for the global market. The designs are often British, the fabric is produced
in Japan, the garment is sewn in China and the finished product is distributed
in Japan and England.

In addition to the *yukata* market and the burgeoning interest in antique
kimonos as an alternative to everyday clothing, members of the traditional
kimono industry are attempting to regain the attention of a lost audience: men.
Yamaguchi Genbei (*b.* 1949), the tenth-generation head of the centuries-old
obi wholesaler Kondaya, is striving to revolutionize the world of kimono
design.[26] For his spring 2008 show, male models whipped *haori* coats off their
tattooed bodies to reveal the latest underwear fashions for men. Before swag-
gering back to their curtained enclave, the models mimicked a practice of
Edo-period firemen who, after extinguishing a fire, removed their reversible
jackets and slipped them back on, lining side out, to display the bold designs

hidden within. Yamaguchi's designs reflect the achievements of a designer who aspires to invigorate traditional craftsmanship with new materials and technological advances while remaining steeped in family traditions rooted in the Edo period. His recent forays into the kimono design world have reverberated across the Internet. Recorded and disseminated via podcasts, Kondaya's marketing strategies are definitely attuned to the savvy, young kimono fashionistas around the world. In a country where it is rare to spot a man in a kimono on the street, and where few men today own a single kimono, the impact of Yamaguchi's bold vision remains to be seen.

Creating new occasions for wearing kimonos may also revitalize consumer interest. *Ginbura*, or 'strolling the Ginza', popularized in the early part of the twentieth century, has today been recast as 'Kimono de Ginza'. Since the early 2000s, men and women, young and old, Japanese and foreign, dressed in kimonos have congregated on certain Saturday afternoons when the Ginza is reserved for pedestrian traffic.[27] They parade through the street adorned in their kimonos, whether vintage, new or a combination of both. Abstaining from criticizing the way others dress is a golden rule, and anyone who enjoys wearing a kimono is welcome to participate. Other incentives to wear kimonos have included free rides on Kyoto public transportation and free museum entrance to major kimono exhibitions to anyone wearing one. In 2010, eleven kimono enthusiasts in Kyoto organized an event, via Twitter, known as 'Kimono de Jack'. Participants, regardless of nationality, arrive at a designated time and place wearing a kimono. The event has attracted a following within Japan (illus. 155), and more recently, Kimono de Jack events have been held in England, the United States and other countries. These events suggest a commitment on the part of select groups to ensuring that kimono culture endures and is not limited only to Japanese wearers, but extends the wearing of kimonos to citizens of the world.

155 'Kimono de Jack' participants in Kyoto, 2014.

References

Introduction

1 Kawamura claims that 'fashion is not created by a single individual but by everyone involved in the production of fashion, and thus fashion is a collective activity'. Yuniya Kawamura, *Fashion-ology: An Introduction to Fashion Studies* (Oxford and New York, 2005), p. 1.

2 Michael Zielenziger, *Shutting Out the Sun: How Japan Created its Own Lost Generation* (New York, 2007), pp. 154–5.

3 Shadan Hōjin Zen Nihon Kimono Shinkōkai, ed., *Kimono no kihon – kimono bunka kentei kōshiki kyōbon I* (Tokyo, 2006).

4 Dōmyō Mihoko, *Sugu wakaru kimono no bi: kamikazari kara hakimono made* (Tokyo, 2005).

5 Maïa Maniglier, *Parijiennu no kimono hajime* (Tokyo, 2005).

6 Hirano Eriko, *Kimono, Kiyō, yo!* (Tokyo, 2008).

7 *Momi: Kimono kimawashi kōdinēto*, vol. II (Fukuoka, 2009), pp. 4–17.

8 Aida Shōko, 'Kimono shūgyō' (Tokyo, 2009).

9 CLAMP Mokona, *CLAMP Mokona no okimono kimono* (Tokyo, 2007); CLAMP Mokona, *CLAMP Mokona's Okimono Kimono* (Milwaukie, OR, 2010).

10 Kimono pattern books produced from the 1890s to the 1940s are referred to as *zuanchō* (design books). Yokoya Kenichirō, 'Kimono Zuanchō in Kyoto', in *Zuanchō in Kyoto: Textile Design Books for the Kimono Trade*, exh. cat., Peterson Gallery and Munger Rotunda Green Library, Stanford University (Stanford, CA, 2008).

11 Recently, sociologists as well as economic and business historians have analysed the major agents involved in the networked systems responsible for producing fashion. Regina Lee Blaszczyk, ed., *Producing Fashion: Commerce, Culture, and Consumers* (Philadelphia, PA, 2008), pp. 1–18.

12 For a discussion of 'modern' Japan that emphasizes Japan's 'connectivity' to other nations rather than its isolation, see Andrew Gordon, *A Modern History of Japan from Tokugawa Times to Present* (New York and Oxford, 2003), pp. xi–xiii. For an outline of how the concepts and ideals of 'modern' Japan, broadly defined, might eventually be interwoven with discussions of 'modernism' writ large, see Andreas Huyssen, 'Geographies of Modernism in a Globalizing World', in *Geographies of Modernism*, ed. Peter Brooker and Andrew Thacker (London, 2005), pp. 6–18.

13 Okakura Kakuzō, *The Ideals of the East: With Special Reference to the Art of Japan* (New York, Tokyo, Osaka, London, 2000, originally published in 1904), pp. 218–19.

14 The empress's proclamation was published in *Chōya shinbun*, 19 January 1887. Translated in Julia Meech-Pekarik, *The World of the Meiji Print: Impressions of a New Civilization* (New York and Tokyo, 1986), pp. 128–30.

15 Nagasaki Iwao, 'Kosode kara kimono he' (From Kosode to Kimono), *Nihon no bijutsu*, CDXXXV (2002), pp. 22–3.

16 Stephen Vlastos provides two general meanings for the term 'tradition': 'First, tradition designates a temporal frame (with no clear beginning), which marks off the historical

period preceding modernity. Used in this way tradition aggregates and homogenizes premodern culture and posits a historical past against which the modern human condition can be measured . . . Tradition in the second and more frequent usage represents a continuous cultural transmission in the form of discrete cultural practices of "the past" that remain vital in the present.' See Stephen Vlastos, 'Tradition: Past/Present Culture and Modern Japanese History', in *Mirror of Modernity: Invented Traditions in Modern Japan*, ed. Stephen Vlastos (Berkeley, CA, Los Angeles, London, 1998), p. 3.

17 Kawamura, *Fashion-ology*, pp. 3–6.

18 For comments on the question of fashion in China, see Antonia Finnane, *Changing Clothes in China: Fashion, History, Nation* (New York, 2008), pp. 6–14.

19 Kawamura, *Fashion-ology*, p. 27.

20 Lars Svendsen, *Fashion: A Philosophy*, trans. John Irons (London, 2006), p. 23.

21 Kawamura states, 'no matter which time period in history one is talking about, the definite essence of fashion is change.' Kawamura, *Fashion-ology*, p. 5.

22 Ibid., p. 2.

23 Japanese art historian Reiko Tomii's outlook on the study of 'contemporary art' and its history serves as a new way of envisioning Japanese textiles, clothing and fashion in the modern era and beyond. In the introduction to her essay on 1960s art discourse in Japan, Tomii noted, 'more than a compendium of local and/or national art histories, "world art history" in [this] definition is a networked whole of local/national histories linked through resonances and connections. The connectedness is both explicit and implicit, underscored by the idea of "international contemporaneity".' Tomii points out that 'ultimately, the study of "contemporaneity" helps us to suspend – if not outright dismantle – the omniscient single perspective (which is more often than not Eurocentric) that we, art historians or not, are consciously or unconsciously accustomed to assume. Only by doing so, can "multiplicity" – or more precisely, "multiple perspectives" – be injected into art-historical discourses, and the horizon of world art history expanded.' Reiko Tomii, '"International Contemporaneity" in the 1960s: Discoursing on Japan and Beyond', *Japan Review*, XXI (2009), pp. 123–5.

24 On the wearing of kimonos in Korea, see Mori Rie, 'Perceptions of Kimono in Literature, Film, and Other Forms of Visual Media During Japan's Colonization of Korea', *Journal of the International Association of Costume*, XXXVIII (2010), pp. 27–32, and 'Kimono and Colony: From Testimonies and Literatures', *Voices from Japan*, XXV (March 2011), pp. 17–20. On the wearing of kimonos in Taiwan, see Dean Brink, 'Pygmalion Colonialism: How to Become a Japanese Woman in Late Occupied Taiwan', *Sungkyun Journal of East Asian Studies*, XII/1 (2012), pp. 41–63.

ONE: The Foundations of a Kimono Fashion Industry

1 From 'The Japanese Family Storehouse' (*Nihon eitaigura*, 1688), as trans. in Donald H. Shively, 'Sumptuary Regulation and Status in Early Tokugawa Japan', *Harvard Journal of Asiatic Studies,* XXV (1964–5), pp. 124–5.

2 The historian Mary Elizabeth Berry argues that the concept of Japan as a nation emerges from formulations beginning in the seventeenth century. See Mary Elizabeth Berry, *Japan in Print: Information and Nation in the Early Modern Period* (Berkeley, CA, Los Angeles, London, 2006), p. 211.

3 Maruyama Nobuhiko, 'Kosode hinagatabon kenkyū joshō: kinsei no ryūkō ni okeru shuppan no yakuwari o chūshin ni', in *Nihon bijutsushi no suimyaku (Currents in Japanese Art History)*, ed. Hashimoto Aiki (Tokyo, 1993), pp. 728–36 and Maruyama Nobuhiko, ed., *Edo no kimono to iseikatsu: Nihon bizuaru seikatsushi* (Tokyo, 2007), pp. 80–81, 103–17.

4   Allen Hockley, *The Prints of Isoda Koryūsai: Floating World Culture and Its Consumers in Eighteenth-century Japan* (Seattle, WA, 2003), p. 124. Hockley notes: 'Some of the garments worn by the courtesans in the *Hinagata* prints have *mon* (crests) that bear no relationship to the woman or her brothel. These may belong to the fabric or garment merchants.' A comparison of these *mon* to the crests of kimono purveyors listed in *Edo kaimono hitori annai* (1824) may reveal conclusive connections.

5   David Pollack's research situates what he terms the 'economy of desire' within the larger domain of advertising, which he uses 'in its broadest sense, meaning all representation employed for the purpose of stimulating desire'. David Pollack, 'Marketing Desire: Advertising and Sexuality in Edo Literature, Drama, and Art', in *Gender and Power in the Japanese Visual Field*, ed. Joshua S. Mostow, Norman Bryson and Maribeth Graybill (Honolulu, HI, 2003), p. 72.

6   Around the time Utamaro produced his 'Contemporary Beauties' series, a landmark event occurred in women's magazine publishing in England. In 1806, the businessman and publisher John Bell recognized the growing importance of the ladies' magazine market, and distinguished his magazine, *La Belle Assemblée*, from others by 'the quality of its production and its coverage of "fashion." It was beautifully produced, in a large size (royal octavo), with a high quality engraved portrait and a double-page engraving of the latest fashions, which were also available coloured (which meant by hand).' Margaret Beetham, *A Magazine of Her Own? Domesticity and Desire in the Woman's Magazine, 1800–1914* (London and New York, 1996), p. 32.

7   In addition to functioning as souvenirs, might prints such as these have been available to travellers entering the city with an interest in locating the most up-to-date urban fashions? The publisher of Utamaro's 'Contemporary Beauties' series was Izumiya Ichibei, based in Shiba in the south of Edo. As the print scholar Matthi Forrer points out, 'anyone leaving the city to travel west along the Tōkaidō Highway would have passed through [Shiba]. From their shops at the entrance to the city, in Shiba Shinmei-mae, publishers may have aimed at the tourist market, catering to those who wished to take home a souvenir in the form of the famous *Azuma nishiki-e* ("brocade pictures from the Eastern capital").' Matthi Forrer, 'The Relationship Between Publishers and Print Formats in the Edo Period', in *The Commercial and Cultural Climate of Japanese Printmaking*, ed. Amy Reigle Newland (Amsterdam, 2004), p. 181.

8   In his essay 'Marketing Desire', Pollack points out that 'entire works of fiction often consist of little more than entertaining advertisements for particular shops and goods'. One notable example is the story that 'accounts in legendary form the founding of three great Edo kimono shops' – Echigoya, Kameya and Ebisuya. Pollack, 'Marketing Desire', pp. 81–2. Two of these shops are featured in Utamaro's 'Contemporary Beauties' series.

9   Shopping guides, such as 'The List of Kimono Shops in Edo' (*Edo gokufuten nayose*, 1735), counted 63 major clothiers, almost a four-fold increase from the seventeen major stores that appeared in a list of Edo kimono retailers published in 1697, reflecting a maturation of the popular commercial clothing market. Eiko Ikegami, 'Categorical Protest from the Floating World: Fashion, State, and Gender', in *Bonds of Civility: Aesthetic Networks and the Political Origins of Japanese Culture* (New York, 2005), p. 272. The 'Self-guided Shopping in Edo' (*Edo kaimono hitori annai*, 1824) served as a kind of yellow-pages guide to Edo shopping. Listed in David Waterhouse, 'The Cultural Milieu of Suzuki Harunobu', in *The Commercial and Cultural Climate of Japanese Printmaking*, ed. Newland, p. 61.

10   These four roles were designated the '*ukiyo-e* quartet' by T. Volker. See T. Volker, *Ukiyo-e Quartet: Publisher, Designer, Engraver and Printer* (Leiden, 1949).

11   In his discussion of the process that led to the production of a print, Chris Uhlenbeck suggests 'one typical route whereby a group, a shop or a person commissioned a print

from a publisher with or without specifying the artist'. A second is 'the publisher who, as a trend-spotter, speculated on what types of prints would become fashionable and what therefore would be easy to sell'. Uhlenbeck believes 'that this second method was the one most frequently used. However, the only documented case is . . . from the 20th century.' Chris Uhlenbeck, 'Production Constraints in the World of Ukiyo-e: An Introduction to the Commercial Climate of Japanese Printmaking', in *The Commercial and Cultural Climate of Japanese Printmaking*, ed. Newland, p. 18.

12 Pollack, 'Marketing Desire', p. 83.

13 Initially referred to as a *yukatabira*, this garment is the forerunner of the *yukata*.

14 Lars Svendsen, *Fashion: A Philosophy*, trans. John Irons (London, 2006), p. 19.

15 Shively, 'Sumptuary Regulation', pp. 126–31.

16 According to Svendsen, 'these laws served precisely to strengthen the role of clothes as an important social marker as they created relatively clear criteria for the social status of various objects. With the increasing weakening of class divisions and great social mobility, however, the battle to maintain such rules was lost.' Svendsen, *Fashion*, p. 37.

17 Yamakawa Kikue, *Women of the Mito Domain: Recollections of Samurai Family Life*, trans. Kate Wildman Nakai (Stanford, CA, 2001), p. 40.

18 Shively, 'Sumptuary Regulation', p. 132.

19 Ibid., p. 129

20 Ibid., pp. 144–5. Shively infers from these orders that a rivalry existed among the *daimyo* in the dress of their wives and female attendants, and that perhaps also the quality of their dress was difficult to distinguish from that worn at the shogun's castle.

21 Ibid., p. 145.

22 English versions of this story appear in Jill Liddell, *The Story of the Kimono* (New York, 1989) p. 147; Ichida Hiromi, 'A Brief History of Kimono', *Chanoyū Quarterly*, XXI (1978), p. 29; Shively, 'Sumptuary Regulation', p. 128; Helen Benton Minnich, in collaboration with Nomura Shōjirō, *Japanese Costume and the Makers of its Elegant Tradition* (Rutland, VT, and Tokyo, 1963) pp. 206–7; and Alan Kennedy, *Japanese Costume: History and Tradition* (Paris, 1990), p. 19.

23 Liddell, '*The Story of the Kimono*', p. 147. Ichida's account gives Rokubei's surname as Ishii. There are other discrepancies among versions regarding participants' names and the identity of the contestant wearing the kimono designed by Ogata Kōrin. Nevertheless, in every version of the story, the Kōrin-designed kimono is the winner, illustrating the high regard accorded to his designs in his own time.

24 Richard L. Wilson, 'Motifs and Meanings', in *Carved Paper: The Art of the Japanese Stencil*, ed. Susan Shin-Tsu-Tai, exh. cat., Santa Barbara Museum of Art; Museum of Art, Rhode Island School of Design; Mingei International Museum, San Diego (New York and Tokyo, 1998), p. 126.

25 The preface to this pattern book was written by Asai Ryōi, who is credited with establishing the classic definition of the term *ukiyo* to suggest the floating world in which people celebrate by 'living only for the moment . . . diverting ourselves in just floating, floating'. See Timothy Clark, *Ukiyo-e Paintings in the British Museum* (Washington, DC, 1992), p. 9. The pattern book was published by Yamada Ichirōbei of Kyoto, located on Teramachi Street, who also published Ryōi's *Kyō suzume*, a guidebook to Kyoto. Ryōi's work was also published by Imada Yōsan, so he did not have an exclusive relationship with Yamada. See Maruyama, 'Kosode', pp. 715, 719.

26 Yamanobe Tomoyuki and Ueno Saeko, *Kosode moyō hinagata bon shūsei* (Compendium of *Kosode* Pattern Books), 4 vols (Tokyo, 1974). For a listing and brief description of many kimono pattern books, see the entry for '*hiinagata*' in *Genshoku senshoku daijiten* (Illustrated Textile Dictionary), ed. Itakura Toshirō et al. (Kyoto, 1977), pp. 874–95.

27 As the sociologist Eiko Ikegami notes, 'Tokugawa fashion differed from that of previous eras because it was conspicuously linked to the operations of a large scale market

economy.' Ikegami, 'Categorical Protest', p. 245. As the *ukiyo-e* painting and print scholar Timothy Clark points out: 'Coiffures, length of *kosode* sleeves, textile patterns, manners of tying the obi – all were subject to increasingly rapid changes of fashion, encouraged by clothing manufacturers, *abetted by the publishing industry* and to be paid for in cash in what surely marks the beginnings of advanced urban consumerism in Japan.' (Emphasis added.) Timothy Clark, 'Image and Style in the Floating World: The Origins and Development of Ukiyo-e', in *The Dawn of the Floating World, 1650–1765: Early Ukiyo-e Treasures from the Museum of Fine Arts, Boston*, ed. Timothy Clark, Anne Nishimura Morse, Louise E. Virgin with Allen Hockley, exh. cat., Museum of Fine Arts, Boston (Boston, 2000–01), p. 11.

28 Maruyama, 'Kosode', p. 722. Maruyama goes on to suggest that by 1692–3, *hinagatabon* were no longer used simply as illustrations of under-drawings for garments. Consumers enjoyed pattern books for the sheer pleasure of looking, much like 'picture books' (*ehon*). Maruyama, 'Kosode', p. 727.

29 *Nishikawa Sukenobu shū jōkan* (Osaka, 1999), vol. 1, p. 123.

30 Maruyama Nobuhiko, *Edo mōdo no tanjō: monyō no ryūkō to sutaa-eshi* (Tokyo, 2008), pp. 137–9, and Maruyama, 'Kosode', p. 729.

31 Nagasaki Iwao, 'Designs for a Thousand Ages: Printed Pattern Books and *Kosode*', in *When Art Became Fashion: Kosode in Edo-period Japan*, ed. Dale Carolyn Gluckman and Sharon Sadako Takeda, exh. cat., Los Angeles County Museum of Art (Los Angeles, 1992), pp. 100–01.

32 On the problems of profiling the consumer and calculating the popularity of printed material such as woodblock prints, and in the case studied here, pattern books, Hockley surmises that 'we may never know the precise demographics of the print market. We may never know exactly who consumed *ukiyo-e*, but it is possible to retrieve a trace of their sensibilities through less direct means.' Hockley, *The Prints of Isoda Koryūsai*, p. 8.

33 As the historian Henry Smith notes, 'Commercial woodblock printing in Japan grew rapidly in the seventeenth century, first in Kyoto from the 1630s and then in Osaka from the 1660s. Publishing in Edo, which in the seventeenth century was little more than a market for books produced in the Kamigata region, expanded dramatically from the mid-eighteenth century, surpassing both Kyoto and Osaka by 1800.' See Henry D. Smith II, 'The Floating World in Its Edo Locale, 1750–1850', in *The Floating World Revisited*, ed. Donald Jenkins, exh. cat., Portland Art Museum (Portland, OR, and Honolulu, HI, 1993), p. 38.

34 Imura Katsukichi is listed in 'Compendium of Patterns of Our Country' (*Wakoku hiinagata taizen*, 1698), 'Patterns of Large Clothing' (*Tanzen hiinagata*, 1704) and 'Successfully Elegant Patterns' (*Fūryū hiinagata taisei*, 1712). The preface to the 'Pattern Book for Order Selections' (*Chūmon hinagata*, 1716) was written by Imura Katsukichi, the same person who identified his drawings in other pattern books with the imprimatur 'pictures by the Kyoto dyer–painter Imura Katsukichi'.

35 Maruyama, *Edo mōdo no tanjō,* pp. 140–42.

36 Jack Hillier, *The Art of the Japanese Book*, 2 vols (New York, 1987), vol. 1, pl. 64.

37 David Waterhouse, 'Hishikawa Moronobu: Tracking Down an Elusive Master', in *Designed for Pleasure: The World of Edo Japan in Prints and Paintings, 1680–1860*, ed. Julia Meech and Jane Oliver, exh. cat., Asia Society, New York (Seattle, WA, and London, 2008), p. 34.

38 Among them 'Kosode in a Full-length Mirror' (*Kosode no sugatami*, 1682), 'Designs Fitting for Our Age' (*Tōsei sōryū hinagata*, 1684), 'Newly Published Kosode Patterns' (*Shinpan kosode onhiinagata*, n.d.) and 'Newly Published Up-to-date Designs' (*Shinpan tōfū onhiinagata*, n.d.).

39 Liza Dalby, *Kimono: Fashioning Culture* (New Haven, CT, and London, 1993), p. 279.

40 Nishikawa Sukenobu's 'One Hundred Women Classified by Rank' (*Hyakunin jorō shina sadame*, 1723) depicts women of various ranks from peasant to empress. Some scholars see this as a burgeoning of interest in the female form, beyond the stereotypical courtesan and 'beauties' (*bijinga*) genre. Hockley, *The Prints of Isoda Koryūsai*, p. 121. Hockley further notes that Nishikawa's publication coincided with the release of a new format: a set of three images on one sheet of paper (*sanpuku-tsui*), often used to compare courtesans of the three major cities: Kyoto, Osaka and Edo.

41 Nagasaki, 'Designs for a Thousand Ages', p. 99.

42 Another extant copy of 'Nishikawa's Book of Patterns' is in the Kawashima Textile Museum in Kyoto. Titles of kimono pattern books represent designations used in the various secondary sources on the genre. In some cases, the titles derive from title slips affixed to the front of the book or the title listed in the foreword or end page. Some titles may represent later designations by publishers who reissued a group of illustrations under a new title. In a few cases the book bears no title at all, and later collectors and scholars refer to them simply as *hinagata*, *hiinagata* or *hinakata*. These three terms, all translated as 'pattern book', derive from the various ways of romanizing Chinese characters. It is important to recognize that titles may have been ascribed to the book when it was first distributed or may represent later editions.

43 This pattern book was published by Hishiya Shizoemonbei based on a recompilation of images originally published under the previously discussed title *Wakoku hinagata taizen* by Imura Katsukichi. See Itakura, ed., *Genshoku senshoku daijiten*, p. 895.

44 The term here translated as 'order books' is *chūmon chō* in the original.

45 Early European examples of how magazines disseminated information about fashion are discussed in Beetham, *A Magazine of Her Own?*, p. 31: 'In the 1790s a number of publications devoted to fashion began to appear, including the *Gallery of Fashion* in 1794 and the *Magazine of Female Fashions of London and Paris* in 1798.'

46 Monica Bethe, 'Color: Dyes and Pigments', in Amanda Mayer Stinchecum, *Kosode: 16th–19th Century Textiles from the Nomura Collection*, ed. Naomi Noble Richard and Margot Paul, exh. cat., Japan Society, New York (New York and Tokyo, 1984), pp. 61–2.

47 Yoshioka Sachio, *Nihon no iro jiten* (Dictionary of the Colours of Japan) (Kyoto, 2000), p. 225.

48 Indeed, the Kabuki scholar C. Andrew Gerstle notes that 'famous actors were greatly influential in ladies' fashion – in coiffure, kimono design, walking style, and a general sense of "femininity", extending from commoner homes through samurai residences all the way to the shogun's castle.' C. Andrew Gerstle, 'Flowers of Edo: Eighteenth-century Kabuki and Its Patrons', *Asian Theater Journal*, IV/1 (Spring 1987), p. 61.

49 David Pollack dates the popularity of *Rokō-cha* (dark yellow-brown) from 1766. David Pollack, 'Designed for Pleasure: *Ukiyo-e* as Material Culture', in *Designed for Pleasure: The World of Edo Japan in Prints and Paintings, 1680–1860*, ed. Julia Meech and Jane Oliver, exh. cat., Asia Society, New York (Seattle, WA, and London, 2008), p. 173.

50 Extant copies can be found in the British Museum, London and the Museum of Fine Arts, Boston collections.

51 See Itakura, ed., *Genshoku senshoku daijiten*, p. 895. *Toshi no hana* is also known under the title *Yarō hinagata*. For illustrations of pages from this book, with English translations of the text, see Dalby, *Kimono*, pp. 305–8.

52 Many scholars have discussed the possible function of pattern books. For their various interpretations see Nagasaki, 'Designs for a Thousand Ages', pp. 95–113; Yamanobe and Ueno, *Kosode moyō*, pp. 6–7, 12; and Maruyama, 'Kosode', pp. 714–36.

53 The term used in this preface to refer to the woodblock printed pattern books is *kosode moyō hinagata bon*. In his study of kimono pattern books, Nagasaki Iwao noted that the preface to the 'Collection of Ten Thousand Women' pattern book includes one of the

earliest descriptions of pattern books and includes the phrase *kosode moyō hinagatabon*. *Kosode*, literally 'small sleeves', refers to the garment itself, the forerunner of the kimono. *Moyō* is generally translated as 'motif', *hinagata* as 'pattern' or 'model', and *hon* as 'book'. Nagasaki, 'Designs for a Thousand Ages', pp. 96–7.

54 For a historical overview of Japanese consumption patterns from the Edo period through to modern times, see Penelope Francks, *The Japanese Consumer: An Alternative Economic History of Modern Japan* (New York, 2009).

55 For more detailed information and an example of the *Shōtoku hinagata* in the Museum of Fine Arts, Boston collection, see Clark et al., *Dawn of the Floating World*, p. 203.

56 From 'Tales of Olden Days' (*Mukashi mukashi monogatari*, Kyōhō era [1716–36]), as translated in Maruyama Nobuhiko, 'Fashion and the Floating World: The *Kosode* in Art', in *When Art Became Fashion: Kosode in Edo-Period Japan*, ed. Dale Carolyn Gluckman and Sharon Sadako Takeda, exh. cat., Los Angeles County Museum of Art (Los Angeles, 1992), p. 211.

57 As Pollack points out, 'One way to promote an understanding of a general economy of desire is to consider art, fiction, and drama – that is, the various genres used to represent desire – as more narrowly focused modalities of the comprehensive set of practices of what we have come to think of as the more specialized domain of advertising.' Pollack, 'Marketing Desire', p. 72.

58 For another example, see Pollack's 'Marketing Desire', in which he notes that Jippensha Ikku's 'Sexy Prints in Newly Dyed Patterns' (*Irozuri shinsomegata*) was composed for the Tokiwaya kimono shop's winter sale. See Pollack, 'Marketing Desire', p. 81.

TWO: Modernizing the Kimono

1 As translated in Julia Meech-Pekarik, *The World of the Meiji Print: Impressions of a New Civilization* (New York and Tokyo, 1986), pp. 128–30.

2 Shōken was the posthumous name of the Meiji empress, whose given name was Haruko.

3 On Japanese women's preference for hand-stitched kimonos and their seeming reluctance to use sewing machines to produce them, see Andrew Gordon, *Fabricating Consumers: The Sewing Machine in Modern Japan* (Berkeley, CA, 2012), pp. 13–17, 84.

4 Julia Meech, 'For the Good of the Nation', *Asian Art*, VI/1 (Winter 1993), pp. 2–6.

5 Hanafusa Miki, 'Empress Tōfukumon'in and Empress Shōken', in *Amamonzeki – A Hidden Heritage: Treasures of the Japanese Imperial Convents*, ed. Medieval Japanese Studies Institute et al., exh. cat., University Art Museum, Tokyo University of the Arts (Osaka and Tokyo, 2009), pp. 268–9.

6 Sally A. Hastings, 'The Empress' New Clothes and Japanese Women, 1868–1912', *Historian*, XXXIII/4 (Summer 1993), p. 678.

7 Meech-Pekarik, *World of the Meiji Print*, pp. 145–7.

8 Carol Gluck, *Japan's Modern Myths: Ideology in the Late Meiji Period* (Princeton, NJ, 1985), p. 42–3.

9 For a more nuanced assessment of the incorporation of Western dress styles into Japanese clothing practices during the Meiji era, see Hirano Ken'ichiro, 'The Westernization of Clothes and the State in Meiji Japan', in *The State and Cultural Transformation: Perspectives from East Asia*, ed. Hirano Ken'ichiro (Tokyo, New York, Paris, 1993), pp. 121–31.

10 For a discussion of historical transformations in Japanese menswear, see Toby Slade, *Japanese Fashion: A Cultural History* (Oxford and New York, 2009), pp. 65–97.

11 Mori Rie, 'Kimono no joseika, fuasshonka to minzoku ishōka', in *Tokimeku fuasshon: Komachi musume kara modan ga-ru made*, ed. Ehimeken Rekishi Bunka Hakubutsukan, exh. cat., Ehimeken Rekishi Bunka Hakubutsukan (Ehime, Japan, 2007), pp. 114–18.

12 Hanna Papanek, 'Development Planning for Women', in *Women and National Development: The Complexities of Change*, ed. Wellesley Editorial Committee (Chicago, 1977), p. 15, as quoted in Sharon L. Sievers, *Flowers in Salt: The Beginnings of Feminist Consciousness in Modern Japan* (Stanford, CA, 1983), p. 15.

13 T. Fujitani, *Splendid Monarchy: Power and Pageantry in Modern Japan* (Berkeley, CA, Los Angeles, London, 1996), p. 49.

14 Ibid., pp. 1–28. See also Gluck, *Japan's Modern Myths*, pp. 32–5.

15 Chang-Su Houchins, *Artifacts of Diplomacy: Smithsonian Collections from Commodore Matthew Perry's Japan Exhibition (1853–1854)*, exh. cat., Smithsonian Institution (Washington, DC, 1995), pp. 136–7.

16 Roger Pineau, ed., *The Japan Expedition, 1852–1854: The Personal Journal of Commodore Matthew C. Perry* (Washington, DC, 1968), pp. 194–6.

17 Similar biases emerged during the exchange of gifts between the Japanese embassy and the Americans during travels to Washington in 1860. Masao Miyoshi, *As We Saw Them: The First Japanese Embassy to the United States* (New York, Tokyo, London, 1979, reprinted in 1994), pp. 49–51.

18 Pineau, *Japan Expedition,* pp. 233–4; Houchins, *Artifacts,* p. 149.

19 Miyoshi, *As We Saw Them,* p. 35.

20 Debin Ma, 'The Modern Silk Road: The Global Raw-silk Market, 1850–1930', *Journal of Economic History*, LVI/2 (1996), pp. 332–5.

21 Sievers, *Flowers in Salt,* p. 56.

22 William B. Hauser, 'A New Society: Japan under Tokugawa Rule', *When Art Became Fashion: Kosode in Edo-Period Japan*, ed. Dale Carolyn Gluckman and Sharon Sadako Takeda, exh. cat., Los Angeles County Museum of Art (Los Angeles, 1992), p. 53.

23 For a comprehensive study of the silk-reeling, cotton-spinning, and weaving industries from the 1880s to the 1930s, see Janet Hunter, *Women and the Labour Market in Japan's Industrialising Economy: The Textile Industry before the Pacific War* (London and New York, 2003). For a discussion of how these two areas differed in their incorporation of Western silk-reeling technology into daily practice see Furuta Kazuko, 'Cultural Transformation in Japan's Industrialization: Local Adaptation to Foreign Silk Technology', in *The State and Cultural Transformation: Perspectives from East Asia*, ed. Hirano Ken'ichiro (Tokyo, New York, Paris, 1993), pp. 142–60.

24 Kären Wigen, *The Making of a Japanese Periphery* (Berkeley, CA, Los Angeles, London, 1995), pp. 139–79.

25 Ibid., p. 265.

26 For a discussion of the shifting value of fabrics in Europe at the turn of the eighteenth century, see Lou Taylor, 'De-coding the Hierarchy of Fashion Textiles', in *Disentangling Textiles: Techniques for the Study of Designed Objects*, ed. Christine Boydell and Mary Schoeser (London, 2002), pp. 68–70.

27 Ma, 'Modern Silk Road', pp. 333–4.

28 Ibid., p. 334.

29 Ibid., pp. 337–9. The demand was mainly for fabrics listed as *habutae* and *pongee* in the U.S. Tariff Commission's *Broad-Silk Manufacture.*

30 Ibid., p. 341.

31 Ibid., pp. 341–2.

32 Shinya Sugiyama, 'Textile Marketing in East Asia, 1860–1914', *Textile History*, XIX/2 (1988), pp. 287–9.

33 William B. Hauser, *Economic Institutional Change in Tokugawa Japan: Ōsaka and the Kinai Cotton Trade* (London, 1974), p. 2.

34 Ibid., pp. 21, 59–60.

35 Ibid., p. 53.

36 Ibid., pp. 138–9.

37 Thomas C. Smith, *Native Sources of Japanese Industrialization, 1750–1920* (Berkeley, CA, Los Angeles, London, 1988), pp. 74–5.

38 Tessa Morris-Suzuki, *The Technological Transformation of Japan from the Seventeenth to the Twenty-first Century* (Cambridge, New York, Melbourne, 1994), p. 42.

39 Wigen, *Making of a Japanese Periphery*, p. 144; Sievers, *Flowers in Salt*, p. 56.

40 Peter Duus, 'Zaikabō: Japanese Cotton Mills in China, 1895–1937', in *The Textile Industry and the Rise of the Japanese Economy*, ed. Michael Smitka (New York and London, 1998), pp. 29–30, 37–8.

41 Ibid., pp. 27–9. A 1930 report on 'The Textile Industry of China' revealed that 'in 1928, there were only three British-owned mills to seventy-four Chinese, but there were forty-three Japanese mills, and the number of Japanese looms (13,981) actually exceeded Chinese (13,907)'. See Antonia Finnane, *Changing Clothes in China: Fashion, History, Nation* (New York, 2008), p. 108, quoting Evan B. Alderfer, 'The Textile Industry of China', *Annals of the American Academy of Political and Social Science, 152, China* (November 1930), p. 187.

42 Louise Allison Cort, 'The Changing Fortunes of Three Archaic Japanese Textiles', in *Cloth and the Human Experience*, ed. Annette B. Weiner and Jane Schneider (Washington, DC, and London, 1989), pp. 378, 387.

43 Yanagida Kunio, comp. and ed., *Japanese Manners and Customs in the Meiji Era*, trans. Charles S. Terry (Tokyo, 1957), pp. 5, 16.

44 Sharon Takeda, 'Offertory Banners from Rural Japan: Echigo-Chijimi Weaving and Worship', in *Sacred and Ceremonial Textiles, Proceedings of the Fifth Biennial Symposium of The Textile Society of America* (Chicago, 1996), pp. 39–41.

45 Melissa M. Rinne, 'Preserving Echigo *Jōfu* and Nara *Sarashi*: Issues in Contemporary Bast Fiber Textile Production', in *Material Choices: Refashioning Bast and Leaf Fibers in Asia and the Pacific*, exh. cat., Fowler Museum at UCLA, Los Angeles (Los Angeles, 2007), pp. 142–6.

46 For detailed descriptions of garments in the John C. Weber Collection, see Terry Satsuki Milhaupt, 'Facets of the Kimono: Reflections of Japan's Modernity' and 'Meanings and Modes of Japanese Clothing', in *Arts of Japan: The John C. Weber Collection*, ed. Melanie Trede with Julia Meech, exh. cat., Museum of East Asian Art, National Museums in Berlin, Museum of Fine Arts, Boston, The Minneapolis Institute of Fine Arts (Berlin, 2006), pp. 195–225.

47 Keiichirō Nakagawa and Henry Rosovsky, 'The Case of the Dying Kimono: The Influence of Changing Fashions on the Development of the Japanese Woolen Industry', *Business History Review*, XXXVII/1–2 (Spring/Summer 1963), pp. 63–4.

48 D. T. Jenkins, 'The Response of the European Wool Textile Manufacturers to the Opening of the Japanese Market', *Textile History*, XIX/2 (1988), p. 255, 259–60.

49 On the origin of the *azumakōto*, see Domyō Mihoko, ed., *Sugu wakaru kimono no bi: kamikazari kara hakimono made* (The Beauty of the Kimono Quickly Understood: From Hair Ornaments to Footwear) (Tokyo, 2005), pp. 80–81.

50 Nakagawa and Rosovsky, 'Case of the Dying Kimono', p. 64.

51 Annie van Assche, 'Interweavings: Kimono Past and Present', in *Fashioning Kimono: Dress and Modernity in Early Twentieth Century Japan – The Montgomery Collection*, ed. Annie van Assche, exh. cat., Victoria & Albert Museum, London (Milan, 2005), p. 20.

52 Nakagawa and Rosovsky, 'Case of the Dying Kimono', pp. 64–5.

53 Ibid., pp. 73–4.

54 Sugiyama, 'Textile Marketing', pp. 290–91.

55 Nakagawa and Rosovsky, 'Case of the Dying Kimono', pp. 68–9.

56 Jenkins, 'Response of the European Wool Textile Manufacturers', pp. 269–70.

57 Morris-Suzuki, *Technological Transformation*, p. 83.

58 For specific examples of Japanese modifications of European technology, see Nakaoka

Tetsuro et al., 'The Textile History of Nishijin (Kyoto): East Meets West', *Textile History*, xix/2 (1988), pp. 117–39; Kiyokawa Yukihiko, 'The Transformation of Young Rural Women into Disciplined Labor under Competition-oriented Management: The Experience of the Silk-reeling Industry in Japan', in *The Textile Industry and the Rise of the Japanese Economy*, ed. Michael Smitka (New York and London, 1998), pp. 100–01; Furuta, 'Cultural Transformation', pp. 142–60.

59 On high-quality textiles produced by Kyoto-based makers for overseas markets, see Hiroko T. McDermott, 'Meiji Kyoto Textile Art and Takashimaya', *Monumenta Nipponica*, lxv/1 (Spring 2010), pp. 37–88.

60 Morris-Suzuki, *Technological Transformation*, p. 21.

61 Smith, *Native Sources*, pp. 29, 91.

62 Morris-Suzuki, *Technological Transformation*, p. 37.

63 Ibid., p. 95.

64 Smith, *Native Sources*, p. 44.

65 Morris-Suzuki, *Technological Transformation*, p. 92.

66 Yamanobe Tomoyuki and Fujii Kenzō, *Kyoto Modern Textiles: 1868–1940* (Kyoto, 1996), p. 4 and Nakaoka, et al., 'Textile History of Nishijin', pp. 126–30.

67 Los Angeles County Museum of Art et al., *Japan Goes to the World's Fairs: Japanese Art at the Great Expositions in Europe and the United States, 1867–1904*, exh. cat., Los Angeles County Museum of Art (Los Angeles, 2005), p. 28.

68 Viewed in the gallery of Nishijin Ori Kaikan (Nishijin Textile Centre) on 3 June 2005. The centre is located at Horikawa-Imadegawa, Kanigyō-ku, Kyoto.

69 Los Angeles County Museum of Art et al., *Japan Goes to the World's Fairs*, p. 26. Some scholars view the *teishitsu gigeiin* designation, established in 1890, as a precursor to the Living National Treasure system, discussed in chapter Five.

70 David G. Wittner, *Technology and the Culture of Progress in Meiji Japan*, Asian Studies Association of Australia East Asia Series (London and New York, 2008), pp. 36–7.

71 David. G. Wittner, 'The Mechanization of Japan's Silk Industry and the Quest for Progress and Civilization, 1870–1880', in *Building a Modern Japan: Science, Technology, and Medicine in the Meiji Era and Beyond*, ed. Morris Low (New York, 2005), pp. 142–3.

72 Chokki Toshiaki, 'Labor Management in the Cotton Spinning Industry', in *The Textile Industry and the Rise of the Japanese Economy*, ed. Michael Smitka (New York and London, 1998), pp. 1–4.

73 As Wittner persuasively argues, the logic that steered decisions on the design of the Tomioka mill was motivated less by technological and economic evaluations, and more by political grandstanding. Wittner, 'Mechanization of Japan's Silk Industry', pp. 135–59 and Wittner, *Technology and the Culture of Progress*, pp. 43–71.

74 Wigen, *Making of a Japanese Periphery*, pp. 173–4.

75 Morris-Suzuki, *Technological Transformation*, pp. 75–7.

76 Wigen, *Making of a Japanese Periphery*, pp. 172, 221.

77 Mariko Asano Tamanoi, *Under the Shadow of Nationalism: Politics and Poetics of Rural Japanese Women* (Honolulu, 1998), p. 102.

78 Morris-Suzuki, *Technological Transformation*, pp. 117–18. The Toyoda Company is the progenitor of the Toyota Motor Company established in 1937.

79 Yamanobe Tomoyuki, 'Japanese Kimono in the Meiji Period', in *Dressed in Splendor: Japanese Costume, 1700–1926*, ed. Merrily A. Peebles, exh. cat., Santa Barbara Museum of Art (Santa Barbara, CA, 1987), p. 13.

80 Fukatsu-Fukuoka Yuko, 'The Evolution of Yuzen-dyeing Techniques and Designs after the Meiji Restoration', *Appropriation, Acculturation, Transformation – Symposium Proceedings of the Textile Society of America, 9th Biennial Symposium, 2004* (Earlville, MD, 2005), p. 407.

81 Fujimoto Keiko, 'Yuzenzome no tenkai to Chisō' (Chisō and the development of the *yūzen* technique), in *Chisō korekushon: Kyō no yūga, kosode to byōbu* (The Elegance of Kyoto Style: *Kosode* and Folding Screens from the Chisō Collection), ed. Kyoto Bunka Hakubutsukan, exh. cat., Kyoto Bunka Hakubutsukan (Kyoto, 2005), pp. 197–202.

82 Otaki Mikio, 'Yūzen Tokyo-ha: sono shiren to kagayaki' (The Challenges and Splendor of Yuzen Dyeing in Tokyo), in *Yūzen: Tokyo-ha gojūnen no kiseki* (Yūzen Dyeing: Tracing a Fifty-year Tokyo Tradition), exh. cat., Bunka Gakuen Fukushoku Hakubutsukan, Tokyo (Tokyo, 1999), pp. 10–41.

83 See Yasuda Jōichi, *Kimono no rekishi* (History of the Kimono) (Tokyo, 1972), pp. 262–3.

84 Yamanobe and Fujii, *Kyoto Modern Textiles*, p. 204.

85 Reiko Mochinaga Brandon, *Bright and Daring: Japanese Kimonos in the Taisho Mode from the Oka Nobutaka Collection of the Suzaka Classic Museum*, exh. cat., Honolulu Academy of Arts (Honolulu, HI, 1996), pp. 11–15.

86 For detailed descriptions of how power looms were modified to accommodate narrower widths for Japan's domestic market, see Minami Ryoshin and Makino Fumio, 'Condition for Technological Diffusion: Case of Power Looms', in *The Textile Industry and the Rise of the Japanese Economy*, ed. Michael Smitka (New York and London, 1998), pp. 145, 147, 150–51.

87 Michael Smitka, ed., *The Textile Industry and the Rise of the Japanese Economy* (New York and London, 1998), p. xv.

88 These statistics are based on Uchida Hoshimi, 'Narrow Cotton Stripes and their Substitutes: Fashion, Technical Progress and Manufacturing Organization in Japanese Popular Clothing, 1850–1920', *Textile History*, XIX/2 (1988), pp. 159–70.

89 Ibid., pp. 166–7.

90 Nakagawa and Rosovsky credit Okajima Chiyozo as the inventor in 1881. Nakagawa and Rosovsky, 'Case of the Dying Kimono', p. 64. According to Yamanobe and Fujii, Horikawa Shinzaburo from Osaka invented the technique in 1879. Yamanobe and Fujii, *Kyoto Modern Textiles*, p. 7.

91 Yoshiko Iwamoto Wada, 'From Kitsch to Art Moderne: Popular Textiles for Women in the First Half of Twentieth-century Japan', *Creating Textiles: Makers, Methods, Markets – Proceedings of the Sixth Biennial Symposium of the Textile Society of America, Inc.* (Earleville, MD, 1999), p. 3.

92 Aoki Mihoko, 'Kikai nassen', in *Koko ni mo atta takumi no waza: Kikai nassen*, exh. cat., Kyoto Kōgei Sen'i Daigaku Bijutsu Kōgei Shiryōkan (Kyoto, 2010), pp. 1–14.

93 Yamanobe and Fujii, *Kyoto Modern Textiles*, p. 7.

94 Uchida, 'Narrow Cotton Stripes', pp. 167–8.

95 Yamanobe and Fujii, *Kyoto Modern Textiles*, pp. 201, 205, 211.

96 Van Assche, 'Interweavings', p. 20.

97 Yamanobe and Fujii, *Kyoto Modern Textiles*, p. 6.

98 Ibid., pp. 210, 227.

99 Ibid., p. 247.

100 Ibid., p. 256.

101 Morris-Suzuki, *Technological Transformation*, pp. 94–5.

102 Ibid., pp. 42–3.

103 Yamanobe and Fujii, *Kyoto Modern Textiles*, p. 214.

104 Kobayashi Keiko, 'The Effect of Western Textile Technology on Japanese *Kasuri*: Development, Innovation, and Competition', *The Textile Museum Journal*, XL–XLI (2001–02), p. 8.

105 Ibid., p. 3.

106 Ibid., pp. 13, 23, 25–6.

THREE: Shopping for Kimonos, Shaping Identities

1 Okakura Kakuzō, *The Awakening of Japan, Special Edition for Japan Society, Inc.* (New York, 1921, originally published in 1904), pp. 150–51.

2 Okakura Kakuzō, *The Ideals of the East: With Special Reference to the Art of Japan* (New York, Tokyo, Osaka, London, 2000, originally published in 1904), p. 1.

3 For an interesting case study of how prominent individuals, such as Charles Appleton Longfellow and Okakura Kakuzō, made 'use of the body and its coverings to articulate social and ethnic differences', see Christine M. E. Guth, 'Charles Longfellow and Okakura Kakuzō: Cultural Cross-dressing in the Colonial Context', *Positions East Asia Cultures Critique, Special Issue: Visual Cultures of Japanese Imperialism*, VIII/3 (Winter 2000), pp. 605–36.

4 Ibid., pp. 622–3.

5 Bert Winther-Tamaki, *Art in the Encounter of Nations: Japanese and American Artists in the Postwar Years* (Honolulu, HI, 2001), p. 14.

6 Leslie Pincus, *Authenticating Culture in Imperial Japan: Kuki Shūzō and the Rise of National Aesthetics* (Berkeley, CA, Los Angeles, London, 1996), p. 42.

7 Louise Young, 'Marketing the Modern: Department Stores, Consumer Culture, and the New Middle Class in Interwar Japan', *International Labor and Working-class History*, 55 (Spring 1999), pp. 52–5.

8 For an eyewitness description of business transactions conducted at the store in the 1890s, see Alice Mabel Bacon, *Japanese Girls and Women*, revised and enlarged edition with illustrations by Keishū Takenouchi (London, New York, Bahrain, 2001, originally published in 1891), pp. 221–2.

9 Brian Moeran, 'The Birth of the Japanese Department Store', in *Asian Department Stores*, ed. Kerrie L. MacPherson (Honolulu, HI, 1998), p. 148.

10 Claire Cuccio, 'Inside *Myōjō* (*Venus*, 1900–1908): Art for the Nation's Sake', PhD thesis, Stanford University, 2005, pp. 19–21. In the late Meiji climate of self-conscious nation building, Hayashida commented on the importance of the revival in classic design as a marker of the status the Japan of his day shared with the refined Genroku period.

11 Jinno Yuki, *Shumi no tanjō: Hyakkaten ga tsukatta teisuto* (Tokyo, 2000), pp. 124–8.

12 Ibid., pp. 79-80.

13 Ōmori Tetsuya, 'Gakatachi no egaita meisen bijin: Ashikaga meisen no senden posuta-kara', in *Meisen-Taishō Shōwa no oshare kimono, Bessatsu Taiyō*, ed. Fujii Kenzō (2004), pp. 108–13.

14 For a discussion of artists designing covers for the magazine 'Housewife's Companion' (*Shufu no tomo*), see Sarah Frederick, *Turning Pages: Reading and Writing Women's Magazines in Interwar Japan* (Honolulu, HI, 2006), pp. 101–10.

15 Aoki Mihoko, 'Taishō-Shōwa shokki no fuasshon', in *Wasō bijin kara yōsō bijin he: Taishō-Shōwa no joseizō*, exh. cat., Kyoto Furitsu Dōmoto Inshō Bijutsukan (Kyoto, 2009), pp. 119–20.

16 Matsuzakaya pamphlet dated Shōwa 12 (March 1937).

17 Yoshiko Iwamoto Wada, 'From Kitsch to Art Moderne: Popular Textiles for Women in the First Half of Twentieth-century Japan', *Creating Textiles: Makers, Methods, Markets – Proceedings of the Sixth Biennial Symposium of the Textile Society of America, Inc.* (Earleville, MD, 1999), p. 8

18 Moeran, 'The Birth of the Japanese', p. 148.

19 Maeda Ai, 'The Development of Popular Fiction in the Late Taishō Era: Increasing Readership of Women's Magazines', in *Text and the City: Essays on Japanese Modernity*, ed. James A. Fujii, trans. Rebecca Copeland (Durham and London, 2004), pp. 170–72.

20 Sharon L. Sievers, *Flowers in Salt: The Beginnings of Feminist Consciousness in Modern Japan* (Stanford, CA, 1983), p. 86.

21 The term *ryōsai kenbo* was coined by Nakamura Masanao in 1875. See ibid., p. 22.

22 The Cotsen Children's Library, Department of Rare Books and Special Collections, Princeton University Library.

23 Frederick, *Turning Pages*, p. 56.

24 Janet Hunter, *Women and the Labour Market in Japan's Industrialising Economy: The Textile Industry before the Pacific War* (London and New York, 2003), p. 5.

25 Sievers, *Flowers in Salt*, pp. 55–7.

26 E. Patricia Tsurumi, *Factory Girls: Women in the Thread Mills of Meiji Japan* (Princeton, NJ, 1990), p. 150.

27 Carol Gluck, *Japan's Modern Myths: Ideology in the Late Meiji Period* (Princeton, NJ, 1985), pp. 31–2.

28 Tsurumi, *Factory Girls*, p. 61.

29 Nakano Makiko, *Makiko's Diary: A Merchant Wife in 1910 Kyoto*, trans. Kazuko Smith (Stanford, CA, 1995), pp. 106–7, 147, 155, 172–3.

30 For a list of women's magazines published in the first quarter of the twentieth century, see Maeda, 'The Development of Popular Fiction', pp. 166–72.

31 Frederick, *Turning Pages*, p. 6.

32 Ibid., pp. 10–11.

33 Miriam Silverberg, 'Constructing the Japanese Ethnography of Meaning', *Journal of Asian Studies*, LI/1 (February 1992), p. 38. See also Andrew Gordon, *Fabricating Consumers: The Sewing Machine in Modern Japan* (Berkeley, CA, Los Angeles, London 2012), pp. 121–3.

34 Silverberg, 'Constructing the Japanese Ethnography', p. 39.

35 Ibid., p. 31.

36 Millie R. Creighton, 'The *Depāto*: Merchandising the West While Selling Japaneseness', in *Re-made in Japan: Everyday Life and Consumer Taste in a Changing Society*, ed. Joseph J. Tobin (New Haven, CT, and London, 1992), pp. 42–9, 52–6.

37 From 1908 to 1923, the women's magazine 'Ladies' Companion' (*Fujin no tomo*) experienced a fifteen-fold increase in circulation. See Louisa Daria Rubinfien, 'Commodity to National Brand: Manufacturers, Merchants, and the Development of the Consumer Market in Interwar Japan', PhD thesis, Harvard University, 1995, pp. 20–21. Kon Wajiro and Yoshida Kenkichi, 'Depaato fūzoku shakaigaku', in *Moderunorogio (Kōgengaku)* (Tokyo, 1986), pp. 206–7.

38 Ibid., p. 215.

39 As Barbara Sato notes, an article in a woman's magazine of 1927 entitled 'The Popularity of the Shawl' called it a symbol of today's modernism. See Barbara Sato, 'An Alternate Informant: Middle-class Women and Mass Magazines in 1920s Japan', in *Being Modern in Japan: Culture and Society from the 1910s to the 1920s*, ed. Elise K. Tipton and John Clark (Honolulu, HI, 2000), p. 147.

40 'Meiji, Taishō no senshoku' (Textiles of the Meiji and Taishō Periods), *Senshoku no bi*, 25 (Autumn 1983), p. 79.

41 Julia Sapin, 'Merchandising Art and Identity in Meiji Japan: Kyoto Nihonga Artists' Designs for Takashimaya Department Store, 1868–1912', *Journal of Design History*, XVII/4 (2004), p. 319.

42 'Meiji, Taishō no senshoku', p. 79.

43 P. F. Kornicki, 'Public Display and Changing Values: Early Meiji Exhibitions and Their Precursors', *Monumenta Nipponica*, XLIX/2 (Summer 1994), p. 167.

44 Julia Elizabeth Sapin, 'Liaisons between Painters and Department Stores: Merchandising Art and Identity in Meiji Japan, 1868–1912', PhD thesis, University of Washington, 2003, p. 57.

45 Eugene Soviak, 'On the Nature of Western Progress: The Journal of the Iwakura Embassy', in *Tradition and Modernization in Japanese Culture*, ed. Donald H. Shively (Princeton, NJ, 1976), p. 25.

46 Moeran, 'The Birth of the Japanese', pp. 143–4.

47 Edward Seidensticker, *Low City, High City – Tokyo from Edo to the Earthquake: How the Shogun's Ancient Capital Became a Great Modern City, 1867–1923* (Cambridge, MA, 1991), p. 115. Seidensticker goes on to note that 'no establishment has called itself a *kankōba* since the 1930s, but the *kankōba* must have been not unlike the shopping centers that are a threat to the Nihombashi store today'.

48 Kornicki, 'Public Display', pp. 189–90.

49 Ibid., p. 190. The writer Fukuzawa Yukichi, who had visited the International Exposition in London in 1862, used the term *hakurankai* to describe international expositions, 'a coinage that appears to date from the early 1860s and that, in its derivation from *hakuran* (Ch. *bolan*, "be widely read or experienced", clearly placed the emphasis on the viewer rather than the viewed).' Ibid., p. 169.

50 Based on her survey of seven Japanese department stores, Julia Sapin concludes that 'the stores that exhibited earliest and most frequently at the international expositions were also the stores that first started evolving into department stores'. Sapin, 'Liaisons', p. 60.

51 On the relationship between *hakurankai* and department stores see Jinno, *Shumi no tanjō*, pp. 47, 111–16.

52 Ibid., pp. 50–55.

53 Ibid., pp. 60–73.

54 Moeran, 'The Birth of the Japanese', pp. 152–3.

55 Jinno, *Shumi no tanjō*, pp. 70–71.

56 Ibid., pp. 67–8.

57 Julia Sapin, 'Department-Store Publicity Magazines in Early Twentieth-century Japan: Promoting Products, Producing New Cultural Perspectives', *Transactions of the International Conference of Eastern Studies*, 56 (2011), and Jinno, *Shumi no tanjō*, pp. 224–5, fn. 49.

58 Seidensticker, *Low City, High City*, pp. 46–7.

59 Moeran, 'The Birth of the Japanese', pp. 162–6.

60 Moeran notes that 'Mitsukoshi, for example, cultivated the merchant capitalist class and Kyoto aristocracy; Shirokiya former daimyo feudal lords and their families; Takashimaya members of the Imperial Household; and Matsuzakaya the Buddhist and Shintō clergy. Only Daimaru had customers from the lower and middle classes and so from its beginnings catered to a fairly general mass clientele.' Ibid., p. 151.

61 Jinno, *Shumi no tanjō*, pp. 72–6.

62 Ibid., p. 143.

63 Ibid., pp. 147–9.

64 Ibid., pp. 152–5.

65 Ibid., pp. 173–8.

66 Ibid., pp. 178–9, 191. The first Kōrin exhibition was held at Mitsukoshi in 1904 and patterns were solicited at that time.

67 Ibid., pp. 179–81.

68 Printing Museum, Tokyo, *Bijin no tsukurikata: sekiban kara hajimaru kōkoku posutaa ten* (Making Beauty: Early Japanese Lithographic Posters exhibition), exh. cat., Printing Museum, Tokyo (Tokyo, 2007), p. 90, fig. 88; p. 91, fig. 90; p. 94, fig. 91.

69 Ibid., p. 95.

70 Ibid., pp. 24–5, figs 14, 15.

71 Ibid., p. 89, fig. 81.

72 Yamanobe Tomoyuki and Fujii Kenzō, *Kyoto Modern Textiles: 1868–1940* (Kyoto, 1996), p. 219.

73 Mary Elizabeth Berry, *Japan in Print: Information and Nation in the Early Modern Period* (Berkeley, CA, Los Angeles, London, 2006), p. 157.

74 Constantine Nomikos Vaporis, *Breaking Barriers: Travel and the State in Early Modern Japan* (Cambridge, MA, and London, 1994), p. 224.

75 Berry, *Japan in Print*, p. 159

76 Makimura Yasuhiro, 'The Silk Road at Yokohama: A History of the Economic Relationships between Yokohama, the Kantō Region, and the World through the Japanese Silk Industry in the Nineteenth Century', PhD thesis, Columbia University, 2005, pp. 60–61.

77 *Kyō suzume ato-oi* ('More Traces of the Kyoto Sparrow') was published in 1678, and *Kyōto kaimono hitori annai* ('A Self-Guided Tour to Kyoto Shopping') was published in 1831. In the intervening years, shoppers' guides to Edo were also published. Berry, *Japan in Print*, pp. 166–7.

78 For a discussion of government promotion of '"famous regional products" (*meisanhin* or *meibutsu*)', see Kim Brandt, *Kingdom of Beauty: Mingei and the Politics of Folk Art in Imperial Japan* (Durham, NC, and London, 2007), p. 92.

79 As Kim Brandt states: 'The result was the increasing visibility of a redefined *mingei*, as it became a fashionable item of consumption among not only men but also women of taste. The changes in the production and consumption of *mingei* must be understood, however, in the context of larger changes in Japanese society and culture over the 1920s and 1930s. The economic troubles afflicting the countryside in particular during this period, the rise of nationalist ideology along with the international conflict of the 1930s, and the emergence of new roles and identities for educated, middle-class women underlay the new attention to native handicraft techniques and products.' Ibid., p. 84.

80 In relation to Taiwan, Barbara Molony notes how Japanese men in Western-style clothing documented 'backward Taiwanese' in their native dress; see Barbara Molony, 'Modernity, Gender and the Empire: Gender, Citizenship and Dress in Modernizing Japan', *IIAS Newsletter*, 46 (Winter 2008) p. 8. Harumi Befu notes that 'during its most expansive time, lasting from 1895 until 1945, "Japan" included Taiwan, the southern half of Sakhalin, the Kuriles, the Korean Peninsula and Micronesia. The "Japan" of that time was probably the most multi-ethnic and multicultural in Japanese history as it included numerous ethnic and racial groups in these territories.' Harumi Befu, 'Concepts of Japan, Japanese Culture, and the Japanese', in *The Cambridge Companion to Modern Japanese Culture*, ed. Yoshio Sugimoto (Melbourne, 2009), pp. 23–4.

81 Brandt, *Kingdom of Beauty*, p. 47.

82 Moeran, 'The Birth of the Japanese', pp. 159–60.

83 Brandt, *Kingdom of Beauty*, pp. 89–91.

84 Ibid., p. 143.

85 Frederick, *Turning Pages*, pp. 10–11.

86 Katherine Martin, *Highlights of Japanese Printmaking: Shin Hanga, Part Two* (New York, 2006), p. 34.

87 Andrew Gordon notes the emergence of 'a parallel linguistic divide between Japanese styles of sewing (*wasai*) and Western ones (*yōsai*)'. Gordon, *Fabricating Consumers*, p. 16.

88 The details of this complex relationship are described in Pincus, *Authenticating Culture*, pp. 27–9.

89 Kuki Shūzō, *Reflections on Japanese Taste: The Structure of Iki*, trans. John Clark, ed. Sakuko Matsui and John Clark (Sydney, 1997), pp. 37–46.

90 Yamanobe and Fujii, *Kyoto Modern Textiles*, p. 201.

91 Young, 'Marketing the Modern', p. 57.

92 Yamanobe and Fujii, *Kyoto Modern Textiles*, p. 209.

93 Ibid., pp. 223–4.

94 Jinno, *Shumi no tanjō*, pp. 7–14.

95 Margot Paul, 'A Creative Connoisseur: Nomura Shōjirō', in Amanda Mayer Stinchecum, *Kosode: 16th–19th Century Textiles from the Nomura Collection*, ed. Naomi

Noble Richard and Margot Paul, exh. cat., Japan Society, New York (New York and Tokyo, 1984), p. 16.

96 Fujimoto Keiko discusses the activities of the Bikōkai, a design cooperative composed of faculty, alumni and students of the Kyoto City Arts and Crafts School, kimono designers engaged in the retail trade, and industrialists. See Fujimoto Keiko, 'Kindai Kyōto no senshoku sangyō to zuan kenkyūkai', *Suzaku: Bulletin of The Museum of Kyoto*, 8 (1995), pp. 121–36.

97 The kimono with designs of irises and the bridge depicted in Okada's 1927 painting was clearly modelled after a kimono now in the Matsuzakaya collection. Nagoya-shi Hakubutsukan et al., eds, *Kosode: Edo no ōto kuchūru* (Kosode: Haute Couture Kimonos of the Edo Period), exh. cat. (Tokyo, 2008), p. 193.

98 Terry Satsuki Milhaupt, 'Flowers at the Crossroads: The Four-hundred-year Life of a Japanese Textile', PhD thesis, Washington University, 2002, pp. 200–03.

99 Pierre Bourdieu, *Distinction: A Social Critique of the Judgement of Taste*, trans. Richard Nice (Cambridge, MA, 1984), p. 56.

100 Yuniya Kawamura, *Fashion-ology: An Introduction to Fashion Studies* (Oxford and New York, 2005), p. 95.

101 Pincus, *Authenticating Culture*, p. 205.

102 Ibid., p. 206.

FOUR: The Kimono Ideal Migrates West

1 Kawakatsu Ken'ichi, *Kimono: Japanese Dress,* Tourist Library 3 (Tokyo, 1960, originally published in 1936), p. 7.

2 Roger Pineau, ed., *The Japan Expedition, 1852–1854: The Personal Journal of Commodore Matthew C. Perry* (Washington, DC, 1968), p. 181.

3 Ibid., p. 186.

4 Michael Cooper, ed., *They Came to Japan: An Anthology of European Reports on Japan, 1543–1640* (Berkeley, CA, Los Angeles, London, 1965), p. 205.

5 Nancy A. Corwin, 'The Kimono Mind: *Japonisme* and American Culture', in *The Kimono Inspiration: Art and Art-to-Wear in America*, exh. cat., The Textile Museum (Washington, DC, 1996), pp. 23–63.

6 On Marta Savigliano's concept of 'auto-exoticizing', see Dorinne Kondo, *About Face: Performing Race in Fashion and Theater* (New York and London, 1997), pp. 10–11.

7 Julia Meech-Pekarik, *The World of the Meiji Print: Impressions of a New Civilization* (New York and Tokyo, 1986), description on pp. 108–10.

8 Metropolitan Museum of Art acquisition number 1991.1073.105.

9 Allen Hockley, 'First Encounters – Emerging Stereotypes: Westerners and the Geisha in the Late Nineteenth Century', in *Geisha: Beyond the Painted Smile*, ed. Peabody Essex Museum, exh. cat., Peabody Essex Museum, Salem, MA and Asian Art Museum; Chong-Moon Lee Center for Asian Art and Culture, San Francisco (New York, 2004), pp. 60–61.

10 Osman Edwards, *Japanese Plays and Playfellows* (New York, 1901), pp. 102–03. For a more extensive quotation of Edwards's explication and an analysis of the geisha stereotype, see Hockley, 'First Encounters', pp. 51–65.

11 Lesley Downer, *Madame Sadayakko: The Geisha Who Bewitched the West* (New York, 2003), p. 25.

12 Barry Till, Michiko Warkentyne and Judith Patt, *The Kimono of the Geisha–Diva Ichimaru* (San Francisco, CA, 2006), p. 17.

13 Leslie Pincus, *Authenticating Culture in Imperial Japan: Kuki Shūzō and the Rise of National Aesthetics* (Berkeley, CA, Los Angeles, London, 1996), p. 201.

14 Takamura Itsue, 'Geisha to kifujinka', in *Takamura Itsue zenshū*, vol. v, *Josei no rekishi 2*, ed. Hashimota Kenzō (Tokyo, 1966), pp. 505–8. Among these government officials were Kido Takayoshi, Yamagata Aritomo and Itō Hirobumi.

15 Alice Mabel Bacon, *Japanese Girls and Women*, revised and enlarged edition with illustrations by Keishū Takenouchi (London, New York, Bahrain, 2001, originally published in 1891), p. 238.

16 Downer, *Madame Sadayakko*, p. 23.

17 Sharon L. Sievers, *Flowers in Salt: The Beginnings of Feminist Consciousness in Modern Japan* (Stanford, CA, 1983), p. 93.

18 Downer, *Madame Sadayakko*, p. 13.

19 Ibid., pp. 224–8.

20 Hockley, *First Encounters*, p. 61.

21 Ibid., p. 62 and Downer, *Madame Sadayakko*, p. 163.

22 Downer, *Madame Sadayakko*, pp. 188–9.

23 Ibid., pp. 264–5.

24 Ibid., pp. 266, 275.

25 Till et al., *The Kimono of the Geisha–Diva*, pp. 21–5.

26 See Michael Justin Wentworth, 'Tissot and Japonisme', in *Japonisme in Art: An International Symposium*, ed. Society for the Study of Japonisme (Japan, 1980), p. 128. A number of kimonos, as well as porcelains and other furnishings, were offered in the posthumous sale of Tissot's belongings in 1930.

27 Kanai Jun I., 'Japonism in Fashion: Overview', in *Japonism in Fashion: Tokyo*, exh. cat., Tokyo Fuasshon Taun Nishikan (Tokyo, 1996), p. 195.

28 Julia Meech, 'The Other Havemeyer Passion: Collecting Asian Art', in *Splendid Legacy: The Havemeyer Collection*, ed. Alice Cooney Frelinghuysen et al., exh. cat., Metropolitan Museum of Art (New York, 1993), pp. 129–30.

29 Louisine W. Havemeyer, *Sixteen to Sixty: Memoirs of a Collector*, privately printed for the family of Mrs H. O. Havemeyer and the Metropolitan Museum of Art, New York (New York, 1961), pp. 15–16.

30 Meech, 'The Other Havemeyer Passion', pp. 129–30.

31 Terry Satsuki Milhaupt, 'Second Hand Silk Kimono Migrating Across Borders', in *Old Clothes, New Looks: Second Hand Fashion*, ed. Alexandra Palmer and Hazel Clarik (Oxford and New York, 2005), pp. 72–5.

32 Bacon, *Japanese Girls and Women*, pp. 157–8.

33 Thomas Lawton, 'Yamanaka Sadajirō: Advocate for Asian Art', *Orientations*, XXVI/1 (January 1995), p. 81.

34 Ibid.

35 Margot Paul, 'A Creative Connoisseur: Nomura Shōjirō', in Amanda Mayer Stinchecum, *Kosode: 16th–19th Century Textiles from the Nomura Collection*, ed. Naomi Noble Richard and Margot Paul, exh. cat., Japan Society, New York, (New York and Tokyo, 1984), p. 13.

36 Adriana Proser, 'Abby Aldrich Rockefeller and Lucy Truman Aldrich: Sisters, Confidantes, and Collectors', *Orientations*, XXXVII/1 (January/February 2006), p. 36.

37 Ibid., p. 38.

38 Meech, 'The Other Havemeyer Passion', pp. 132–3.

39 Quoted in Ellen Conant, 'Introduction', *Challenging Past and Present: The Metamorphosis of Nineteenth-century Japanese Art*, ed. Ellen P. Conant (Honolulu, HI, 2006), p. 23, fn. 38.

40 I am grateful to Kristina Haughland, associate curator of costume and textiles, Philadelphia Museum of Art, for providing this information.

41 See 'Kimono Fabric 1860–1867', http://collections.vam.ac.uk., accessed 26 August 2013.

42 Hirota Takashi, 'Meiji-matsu Taishō shoki no yūshutsuyō kimono ni kansuru ikkōsatsu: Takashimaya Shiryōkan wo chūshin ni', *Fukushoku Bigaku*, XLII (2006), p. 22.

43 Susan Stewart, *On Longing: Narratives of the Miniature, the Gigantic, the Souvenir, the Collection* (Durham, NC, and London, 1993), p. 135.

44 Downer, *Madame Sadayakko*, p. 153, quoting Oscar Wilde's 'The Decay of Lying', originally published in *The Nineteenth Century*, January 1889.

45 Christopher Dresser, *Japan: Its Architecture, Art and Art Manufactures* (London, 1882).

46 Elizabeth Kramer, 'Master or Market? The Anglo–Japanese Textile Designs of Christopher Dresser', *Journal of Design History*, XIX/3 (2006), p. 201.

47 As quoted in Kramer, 'Master or Market?', p. 202.

48 Ibid., p. 207.

49 Dresser, *Japan*, p. 441.

50 Ibid., p. 446.

51 Thomas W. Cutler, *A Grammar of Japanese Ornament and Design* (London, 1880).

52 Ibid., p. v.

53 Ibid., pp. v–vi.

54 Ibid., p. 29.

55 The kimono is in the collection of the Marubeni Co., Kyoto. Kyoto Bunka Hakubutsukan, ed., *Kaiga to ishō: bi no meihinten – Marubeni korekushon* (Beauty of Pictures and Costumes: Masterpieces from the Marubeni Collection), exh. cat., Kyoto Bunka Hakubutsukan (Kyoto, 2007), p. 112, illus. 53.

56 Cutler, *A Grammar of Japanese Ornament*, p. 18.

57 Candace Wheeler, 'Decorative and Applied Art', in *Household Art*, ed. Candace Wheeler (New York, 1893), pp. 198–204.

58 For a detailed discussion of the intricacies of the business relationship among these four personalities, see Amelia Peck and Carol Irish, *Candace Wheeler: The Art and Enterprise of American Designs, 1875–1900*, exh. cat., Metropolitan Museum of Art (New Haven, CT, 2001), pp. 38–49.

59 Ibid., pp. 186–90, illus. 57.

60 Ibid., pp. 194–7, illus. 60–62.

61 Thomas C. Michie, 'Western Collecting of Japanese Stencils and their Impact in America', in *Carved Paper: The Art of the Japanese Stencil*, ed. Susan Shin-Tsu Tai, exh. cat., Santa Barbara Museum of Art; Museum of Art, Rhode Island School of Design; Mingei International Museum, San Diego (New York and Tokyo, 1998), p. 153.

62 William Hosley, *The Japan Idea: Art and Life in Victorian America*, exh. cat., Wadsworth Atheneum, Hartford (Hartford, CT, 1990), pp. 126–7.

63 See 'Water Jar with Design of Procession of Grasshoppers', Makuzu Kōzan, Accession Number 91.1.367a, b, www.metmuseum.org, accessed 26 August 2013.

64 Fukai Akiko, *Jyaponizumu in fuasshon* (Tokyo, 1994), p. 93.

65 Yamamori Yumiko, 'Japanese Arts in America, 1895–1920, and the A. A. Vantine and Yamanaka Companies', in *Studies in the Decorative Arts*, XV/2 (Spring/Summer 2008), p. 102.

66 Harold Koda and Andrew Bolton, 'Preface: The Prophet of Simplicity', in Harold Koda and Andrew Bolton, *Poiret*, exh. cat., Metropolitan Museum of Art (New Haven, CT, and London, 2007), pp. 13–14.

67 Ibid., pp. 59–61.

68 Okabe Masayuki, 'The Impact of the Kimono on Modern Fashion', *Journal of Japanese Trade and Industry* (November, 2002), n.p.

69 Ibid.

70 Downer, *Madame Sadayakko*, p. 171, quoting Ruth St Denis, *An Unfinished Life: An Autobiography (with portraits)* (New York and London, 1939), p. 40.

71 Corwin, 'The Kimono Mind', pp. 60–63.

72 Kim Brandt, *Kingdom of Beauty: Mingei and the Politics of Folk Art in Imperial Japan* (Durham, NC, and London, 2007), p. 133.

73 Ibid., pp. 132–3.

74 Bacon, *Japanese Girls and Women*, pp. 196–7.

75 Ibid., pp. 197–8.

76 Ibid., p. 198.

77 Ibid.

78 Okakura Kakuzō, *The Awakening of Japan, Special Edition for Japan Society, Inc.* (New York, 1921, originally published in 1904), pp. 197–9.

79 Donald A. Wood and Yuko Ikeda, eds, *Kamisaka Sekka: Rinpa no keishō kindai dezain no senkusha* (*Kamisaka Sekka: Rimpa Master-Pioneer of Modern Design*), exh. cat., National Museum of Modern Art, Kyoto; Sakura City Museum of Art; Los Angeles County Museum of Art; Birmingham Museum of Art (Kyoto and Birmingham, AL, 2003), p. 23.

80 Higa Akiko, 'Kamisaka Sekka's Design Collections', in *Kamisaka Sekka*, ed. Wood and Ikeda, pp. 307–08, 247, 249.

81 Ibid., p. 307. Sekka initially studied Shijō-style painting with Suzuki Zuigen and later shifted his allegiance to the Rinpa tradition after undertaking an apprenticeship with Kishi Kōkei.

82 Yamanobe Tomoyuki and Fujii Kenzō, *Kyoto Modern Textiles: 1868–1940* (Kyoto, 1996), entry number 168.

83 Kawakatsu, *Kimono*, p. vii.

84 Ibid., p. 90.

85 Ibid., p. 7.

FIVE: Kimono Designers

1 Kyoto Bunka Hakubutsukan, ed., *Kyō no yūga: Kosode to byōbu: Chisō korekushon* (The Elegance of Kyoto Style: Kosode Kimonos and Folding Screens from the Chiso Collection), exh. cat., Kyoto Bunka Hakubutsukan (Kyoto, 2005).

2 Julia Elizabeth Sapin, 'Liaisons between Painters and Department Stores: Merchandising Art and Identity in Meiji Japan, 1868–1912', PhD thesis, University of Washington, 2003, pp. 122–4.

3 Jinno Yuki, *Shumi no tanjō: Hyakkaten ga tsukatta teisuto* (The Birth of *Shumi*: Taste as Constructed by Department Stores) (Tokyo, 2000), p. 76.

4 Yokoya Kenichirō, 'Kimono Zuanchō in Kyoto', in *Zuanchō in Kyoto: Textile Design Books for the Kimono Trade*, exh. cat., Peterson Gallery and Munger Rotunda Green Library, Stanford University (Stanford, CA, 2008), p. 9.

5 Jinno, *Shumi no tanjō*, pp. 76–86.

6 For a comprehensive overview of Kōrin-style motifs and their relationship to textile design, see Oyama Yuzuruha, 'Kōrin moyō', *Nihon no bijutsu*, DXXIV (Tokyo, 2010).

7 Jinno, *Shumi no tanjō*, p. 78.

8 Fujii Kenzō, 'Biten no rekishi to sono ippin: bi wo umidasu chikara' (The History of *Biten* and Their Objects: Power that Gives Birth to Beauty), *Kosode kara kimono he, Bessatsu Taiyō*, LV (2005), pp. 58–86.

9 Kimura Uzan was designated a Living National Treasure in 1955.

10 Yamanobe Tomoyuki and Fujii Kenzō, *Kyoto Modern Textiles: 1868–1940* (Kyoto, 1996), p. 218.

11 Gennifer Weisenfeld, 'Japanese Modernism and Consumerism: Forging the New Artistic Field of *Shōgyō Bijutsu* (Commercial Art)', in *Being Modern in Japan: Culture and Society from the 1910s to the 1920s,* ed. Elise K. Tipton and John Clark (Honolulu, HI, 2000), p. 77.

12 Elise K. Tipton, *Modern Japan: A Social and Political History*, 2nd edn (London and New York, 2008), p. 131.

13 For a discussion of the problems of translating the term *mingei* as 'folk craft', see Amanda Mayer Stinchecum, 'Japanese Textiles and the Mingei Aesthetic', in Robert Moes, *Mingei: Japanese Folk Art from the Montgomery Collection* (Alexandria, VA, 1995), pp. 45–6.

14 Weisenfeld, 'Japanese Modernism', p. 78.

15 Kida Takuya, '"Traditional Art Crafts (*Dentō Kōgei*)" in Japan: From Reproductions to Original Works', *Journal of Modern Craft*, III/1 (March 2010), p. 20.

16 Richard Wilson, *The Potter's Brush: The Kenzan Style in Japanese Ceramics*, exh. cat., Freer Gallery of Art and Arthur M. Sackler Gallery, Smithsonian Institution (Washington, DC, 2001), p. 198.

17 Brian Moeran, 'The Art World of Contemporary Japanese Ceramics', *Journal of Japanese Studies*, XIII/1 (1987), pp. 27–50.

18 John W. Dower, *Embracing Defeat: Japan in the Wake of World War II* (New York, 1999), p. 95.

19 Midori Wakakuwa, 'War-promoting Kimono (1931–45)', in *Wearing Propaganda: Textiles on the Home Front in Japan, Britain, and the United States, 1931–1945*, ed. Jacqueline M. Atkin, exh. cat., The Bard Graduate Center for Studies in the Decorative Arts, Design, and Culture, New York (New Haven, CT, and London, 2005), pp. 185–6.

20 Bunka Gakuen Fukushoku Hakubutsukan, ed., *Yūzen: Tokyoha gojūnen no kiseki* (Yūzen Dyeing: Tracing a Fifty-year Tokyo Tradition), exh. cat., Bunka Gakuen Fukushoku Hakubutsukan, Tokyo (Tokyo, 1999), pp. 22–5.

21 On 'national dress' for men, 'standard dress' for women and the integration of *monpe* into clothing choices during the war years, see Andrew Gordon, *Fabricating Consumers: The Sewing Machine in Modern Japan* (Berkeley, CA, Los Angeles, London 2012), pp. 143–9.

22 Damaging clothing deemed inappropriate to the prevailing political climate also occurred in Japan-occupied Taiwan (then known as Formosa). See Dean Brink, 'Pygmalion Colonialism: How to Become a Japanese Woman in Late Occupied Taiwan', *Sungkyun Journal of East Asian Studies*, XII/1 (2012), p. 53.

23 As quoted in Kashiwagi Hiroshi, 'Design and War: Kimono as "Parlor Performance" Propaganda', in *Wearing Propaganda: Textiles on the Home Front in Japan, Britain, and the United States, 1931–1945*, ed. Jacqueline M. Atkin, exh. cat., The Bard Graduate Center for Studies in the Decorative Arts, Design, and Culture, New York (New Haven, CT, and London, 2005), pp. 179–80.

24 As quoted in Wakakuwa, 'War-Promoting Kimono', p. 186.

25 Christine M. E. Guth, 'Kokuhō: From Dynastic to Artistic Treasure', *Cahiers d'Extrême-Asie*, IX (1996–7), pp. 314–18; p. 318.

26 Satō Dōshin, *Modern Japanese Art and the Meiji State: The Politics of Beauty*, trans. Nara Hiroshi (Los Angeles, 2011), pp. 77–9.

27 As Satō Dōshin's research demonstrates, Imao Keinen's father was a *yūzen* fabric dyer, unlike many of his contemporaries, who traced their lineage to military ranks. Ibid., pp. 80–83.

28 For a discussion of 'the production of craft as artistic expression', see Kaneko Kenji, 'The Development of "Traditional Art Crafts" in Japan', in *Crafting Beauty in Modern Japan: Celebrating Fifty Years of the Japan Traditional Art Crafts Exhibition*, ed. Nicole Rousmaniere, exh. cat., British Museum (Seattle, WA, 2007), pp. 10–11. For a discussion of another government-sponsored programme known as the Law for the Promotion of Traditional Handcraft Industries (*densanhō*) see Louise Allison Cort, 'The Modern Shokunin', *Craft Horizons*, XXXVII/5 (August 1978), pp. 38–9.

29 Uchiyama Takeo, 'Japan Traditional Art Crafts Exhibitions: Its History and Spirit', in *Crafting Beauty in Modern Japan: Celebrating Fifty Years of the Japan Traditional Art*

Crafts Exhibition, ed. Nicole Rousmaniere, exh. cat., British Museum (Seattle, WA, 2007), p. 27.

30 *Shin shitei jūyō bunkazai: kōgei hin II* (Newly Designated Important Cultural Properties: Decorative and Applied Arts II) (Tokyo, 1983), p. 290.

31 Tani Shin'ichi, 'Ogata Kōrin: Artist to the Merchant Class', *Japan Quarterly*, V/4 (October–December 1958), p. 469.

32 Wilson, *The Potter's Brush*, pp. 183–5.

33 Harold P. Stern, *Rimpa: Masterworks of the Japanese Decorative School* (New York, 1971), p. 15.

34 Howard A. Link and Shimbo Toru, *Exquisite Visions: Rimpa Paintings from Japan*, exh. cat., Honolulu Academy of Arts (Honolulu, HI, 1980), pp. 138–9. A chronology of the Ogata family appears in Appendix II of this book.

35 Stern, *Rimpa*, p. 16.

36 Link and Shimbo, *Exquisite Visions*, p. 139.

37 Richard Wilson, 'Aspects of Rimpa Design', *Orientations*, XXI/12 (December 1990), p. 29.

38 Wilson, *The Potter's Brush*, p. 35.

39 Yokoya, 'Kimono Zuanchō', p. 17.

40 Nakaoka et al., 'The Textile History of Nishijin (Kyoto): East Meets West', *Textile History*, XIX/2 (1988), p. 135.

41 For examples of Kamisaka Sekka and Furuya Kōrin's designs and a discussion of their publications, see Fujii Kenzō, 'Meiji kōki no kōgei ishō to zuan zasshi', in Unsōdō, *Shin bijutsukai: Kamisaka Sekka, Furuya Kōrin* (The New World of Art: Kamisaka Sekka and Furuya Kōrin, Tokyo and Kyoto, 2006). For examples of Tsuda's designs and a biographical description of his career, see Fujii Kenzō, 'Tsuda Seifu no geijutsu to zuan' (Tsuda Seifu's Art and Design), in Unsōdō, *Tsuda Seifu no zuan: geijutsu to dezain* (Tsuda Seifu's Designs: Art and Design, Tokyo and Kyoto, 2008). On the history and current market for kimono pattern books, see Lisa Pevtzow, 'Kimono Design Books (Zuan-chō)', *Daruma*, XVIII (Winter 2011), pp. 34–52. See also Yokoya, 'Kimono Zuanchō', pp. 18–24.

42 Yokoya, 'Kimono Zuanchō', p. 27.

43 Kyoto Bunka Hakubutsukan, ed., *Kaiga to ishō: bi no meihinten – Marubeni korekushon* (Beauty of Pictures and Costumes: Masterpieces from the Marubeni Collection), exh. cat., Kyoto Bunka Hakubutsukan (Kyoto, 2007), pp. 161–84.

44 Yamanobe Tomoyuki, Tabata Kihachi and Kitamura Tetsurō, *Kosode* (Tokyo, 1963), pp. vi–viii.

45 Kirihata Ken, ed. *Kagayakeru kosode no bi: Tabata korekushon* (The Brilliant Beauty of Kosode: The Tabata Collection), exh. cat., Takashimaya, Kyoto; Matsuya Ginza, Tokyo; Takashimaya, Yokohama; Hakata Daimaru, Fukuoka; Umeda Hankyu, Osaka (Osaka, 1990).

46 Yamanobe et al., *Kosode*, p. vi.

47 Ibid.

48 Ibid., p. vii.

49 The technical term is *jūyō mukei bunkazai hojisha* (holder of an important intangible cultural property).

50 NHK Kinki medeia puran, ed., *Kyō yūzen no hana; Ningen kokuhō sandai Tabata Kihachi no bi* (Flowers of Kyō Yuzen: The Art of Tabata Kihachi, Third-generation Living National Treasure) exh. cat., Takashimaya, Kyoto; Takashimaya, Nanba (Kyoto, 2001), pp. 112–13.

51 Terry Satsuki Milhaupt, 'In the Guise of Tradition: Serizawa Keisuke and His Eclectic Designs', in *Serizawa: Master of Japanese Textile Design,* ed. Joe Earle, exh. cat., Japan Society, New York (New York, New Haven, CT, London, 2009), pp. 96–100.

52   Amanda Mayer Stinchecum, 'Serizawa Keisuke and Okinawa', in *Serizawa: Master of Japanese Textile Design,* ed. Joe Earle, exh. cat., Japan Society, New York (New York, New Haven, CT, London, 2009), pp. 106–11.

53   Indeed, Serizawa actively collected *munjado*, particularly from 1953, after much of his original collection was destroyed during the Second World War. See Shizuoka Shiritsu Serizawa Keisuke Bijutsukan, ed., *Serizawa Keisuke: Sono shōgai to sakuhin* (Serizawa Keisuke: His Life and Works) (Shizuoka City, Japan, 2008), pp. 24, 54.

54   Hamada Shukuko, 'The Art of Serizawa Keisuke', in *Serizawa: Master of Japanese Textile Design*, ed. Earle, pp. 117–18.

55   Elisabeth Frolet, 'Mingei: The Word and the Movement', in *Mingei: Masterpieces of Japanese Folkcraft*, ed. Japan Folk Crafts Museum (Tokyo, New York, London, 1991), p. 11.

56   Yanagi Sōetsu, 'Mingei to kojin sakka' (*Mingei* and the Individual Craftsperson), *Mingei*, LXXII (1958), pp. 4–7, and 'Saido mingei to sakka ni tsuite' (Another Look at the Relationship between *Mingei* and the Artist), *Mingei*, LXXIV (1959), pp. 4–11. As early as 1927 Yanagi philosophized about the role of the craftsperson in society, and in 1952 he lamented the rise of individualism, observing that 'the craftsman is essentially a communal worker; when individualism arises, the paths of "artist" and "craftsman" diverge'. Yanagi Sōetsu, adapted by Bernard Leach, *The Unknown Craftsman: A Japanese Insight into Beauty* (Tokyo, 1973), p. 116. For a more extensive discussion of Yanagi's views on 'craftsmanship' from 1927, see ibid., pp. 197–215.

57   Kim Brandt, 'Serizawa Keisuke and the Mingei Movement', in *Serizawa: Master of Japanese Textile Design*, ed. Earle, p. 110.

58   Uchiyama, 'Japan Traditional Art', p. 28.

59   One of the earliest illustrated examples of Serizawa's *iroha* syllabary is an eight-leaf screen produced in 1940. One of Serizawa's last works, produced in 1984, is a hanging scroll depicting the same characters: *i-ro-ha*. For a translation of the poem, see Donald Keene, *Seeds in the Heart: Japanese Literature from Earliest Times to the Late Sixteenth Century* (New York, 1993), p. 220.

60   Kim Brandt, *Kingdom of Beauty: Mingei and the Politics of Folk Art in Imperial Japan* (Durham, NC, and London, 2007), p. 109. See also Uchiyama, 'Japan Traditional Art', p. 26.

61   Yanagi Sōetsu, *Sakka no hinto mingeihin* (Works of the Artist and Mingei), trans. Mimura Kyoto [1961] in *Yanagi Sōetsu Zenshū* (Complete Words of Yanagi Sōetsu) (Tokyo, 1982), vol. XIV, pp. 55–60, and available from the Mingeikan website at http://web.archive.org/web/20120510171633, accessed 6 November 2013.

62   Yanagi, *The Unknown Craftsman*, p. 103.

63   The Japanese potter Hamada Shōji, another *mingei* proponent, once remarked to an inquiring journalist that 'we were as sick of the word *mingei* as we were of the opposed word *sakka*, meaning the current so-called individual or artist-craftsman'. Hamada said 'they had become, equally, misconceptions of Yanagi's intentions.' Ibid., p. 95.

64   Jan Fontein, ed., *Living National Treasures of Japan*, exh. cat., Museum of Fine Arts, Boston; Art Institute of Chicago; Japanese American Cultural and Community Center, Los Angeles (Boston, Chicago, Los Angeles, 1983), pp. 14–15.

65   Michele Bambling, 'Japan's Living National Treasures Program: The Paradox of Remembering', in *Perspectives on Social Memory in Japan*, ed. Tsu Yun Hui, Jan van Bremen and Eyal Ben-Ari (Folkestone, 2005), pp. 148–69.

66   Fontein, ed., *Living National Treasures*, pp. 22–3.

67   As Rupert Faulkner points out: 'Technically speaking, there is no difference between *kataezome* and other forms of *katazome*. The distinction is made on the basis of the perception that the *kataezome* artist's involvement in all stages of the making process

leads to the creation of more highly individualistic works than is possible under the system of division of labour traditionally associated with *katazome*.' Rupert Faulkner, *Japanese Studio Crafts: Tradition and the Avant-garde* (Philadelphia, PA, 1995), p. 132.

68 Serizawa may also have chosen to cut his own stencils so he would not be dependent upon stencil cutters whose specialized skills were no longer in great demand, resulting in fewer artisans engaged in this type of work.

69 As Kim Brandt points out: 'Of the thirty-seven individual craftspeople who had been chosen as living national treasures by 1975, five were closely associated with the early mingei movement. (A sixth, Kawai Kanjirō, declined the designation.)' Brandt, *Kingdom of Beauty*, pp. 225–6.

70 Yanagi, 'Works of the Artist', n.p.

71 In his 1954 discussion of the 'individual craftsman' and the 'folk craftsman' Yanagi stressed that 'the individual craftsman of today has the potentiality of shepherding craftsmanship towards a rebirth of true work . . . The great need of our time is for the artist–craftsman not only to produce his own good work but to ally himself closely with the artisan, so that eventually we may have beauty in common things again.' Yanagi, *The Unknown Craftsman*, pp. 105–6.

72 As a founding member of the Nihon Kōgei Kai, Serizawa must have been cognizant of shifting attitudes towards the concept of 'tradition'. In 1955, Nihon Kōgei Kai's first board director, Nishikawa Tekiho, expressed his hopes for the organization as follows: 'This association is not about being hidebound by the word "tradition", nor simply worshipping the culture of the past. Our foremost goal is to promote works that make the best of both Japanese traditions and elements learned from foreign countries.' Uchiyama, 'Japan Traditional Art', pp. 29–30. Uchiyama notes that as a result of struggles between old and new factions, 'in 1958, the word "tradition" was omitted from the exhibition title' but 'then, in the following year, 1959, for the sixth exhibition, the word "tradition" was put back in the title, which has remained unchanged ever since'. For the inherent paradox of 'how in trying to secure the art traditions, governmental measures often undermine the very institutions they set out to preserve', see Bambling, 'Japan's Living National Treasures', pp. 148–69.

73 Hamada, 'The Art of Serizawa', p. 119.

74 Rebecca Copeland, *The Sound of the Wind: The Life and Works of Chiyo Uno* (Boston, Rutland, VT, and Tokyo, 1993), p. vii.

75 Ibid., pp. 49–50.

76 Uno Chiyo, *Uno Chiyo kimono techō* (Uno Chiyo's Kimono Handbook) (Tokyo, 2004), pp. 22–4.

77 Copeland, *The Sound of the Wind*, pp. 20, 29, 34.

78 Elaine Gerbert, 'Space and Aesthetic Imagination in Some Taishō Writings', in *Japan's Competing Modernities: Issues in Culture and Democracy, 1900–1930*, ed. Sharon A. Minichiello (Honolulu, HI, 1998), p. 72. Uno also lived for a time in the Western-style Kikufuji Hotel in the Hongō district of Tokyo which was likened to 'la maison Vauguer', the boarding house in Balzac's novels, and included such personalities as the artist Takehisa Yumeji, the writer Tanizaki Jun'ichiro and the anarchist Ōsugi Sakae and his wife.

79 Copeland, *The Sound of the Wind*, pp. 55–62.

80 Uno, *Uno Chiyo kimono techō*, p. 7.

81 Ibid., pp. 26, 35.

82 Copeland, *The Sound of the Wind*, pp. 62–3.

83 Uno, *Uno Chiyo kimono techō*, p. 65.

84 Ibid., pp. 26–8, 46. Copeland, *The Sound of the Wind*, p. 63.

85 Copeland, *The Sound of the Wind*, p. 84.

86 The celebration took place on 3 November 1985. Ibid., p. 82.

87 Kubota Itchiku, *Lumiere Brodee: Itchiku Kubota*, exh. cat., Palais de Tokyo (Belgium, 1990), p. 18.

88 For a discussion of the etymology of the term *tsujigahana*, see Terry Satsuki Milhaupt, 'Flowers at the Crossroads: The Four-hundred-year Life of a Japanese Textile', PhD thesis, Washington University, 2002, pp. 3–10, 60–62.

89 Itō Toshiko's *Tsujigahanazome*, first published as a limited edition in Japanese in 1981, was translated into English as *Tsujigahana: The Flower of Japanese Textile Art* in the same year, also as a limited edition. The standard edition was published in 1985. Itō Toshiko, *Tsujigahana: The Flower of Japanese Textile Art*, trans. Monica Bethe (Tokyo, 1985).

90 Terry Satsuki Milhaupt, '*Tsujigahana* Textiles and their Fabrication', in *Turning Point: Oribe and the Arts of Sixteenth-century Japan*, ed. Miyeko Murase, exh. cat., Metropolitan Museum of Art (New York, New Haven, CT, London, 2003), pp. 319–23.

91 Susan-Marie Best, 'The Yuzen Kimono of Moriguchi Kunihiko', *Eastern Art Report*, III/2 (July/August 1991), p. 20.

92 Maruyama Tsuneo, 'Dentō ni tatsu futatsu no sōsaku: Moriguchi Kakō-Kunihiko ten ni yosete', in *Moriguchi Kakō, Kunihiko ten: fushi yūzen ningen kokuhō* (Moriguchi Kakō, Kunihiko Exhibition: Father-son Living National Treasures of Yūzen), exh. cat., Shiga Kenritsu Kindai Bijutsukan (Shiga, Japan, 2009), pp. 6–12.

93 Bambling, 'Japan's Living National Treasures', p. 158.

94 Ibid., p. 160.

95 Maruyama, 'Dentō ni tatsu futatsu no sōsaku', p. 7.

96 Ibid., p. 9.

97 Ibid., p. 10.

98 Judith Thurman, 'Letter from Japan: The Kimono Painter', *New Yorker* (17 October 2005), pp. 120–24.

99 Uchiyama, 'Japan Traditional Art', p. 32.

100 Thurman, 'Letter from Japan', p. 118.

101 Ibid., p. 120.

102 Ibid., p. 127.

103 Stephen Vlastos, 'Tradition: Past/Present Culture and Modern Japanese History', in *Mirror of Modernity: Invented Traditions in Modern Japan*, ed. Stephen Vlastos (Berkeley, CA, Los Angeles, London, 1998), p. 3.

104 See Ajioka Chiaki, 'When Craft Became Art: Modern Japanese Craft and the *Mingei Sakka*', in *Traditional Japanese Arts and Crafts in the 21st Century: Reconsidering the Future from an International Perspective*, ed. Inaga Shigemi and Patricia Fister (Kyoto, 2007), pp. 211–27.

six: Everyday and Extraordinary, Then and Now

1 Yohji Yamamoto, 'Special Contribution', in *Chisō kata yūzen dentō zuanshū: Yūzen gurafuikkusu 1: hana to kusaki hen* (Chisō Stencil-dyed *Yūzen* Traditional Design Collection: Yūzen Graphics 1: Foliage and Flora), ed. Ogasawara Sae (Tokyo, 2002), p. 5.

2 Ibid.

3 The Cotsen Children's Library, Department of Rare Books and Special Collections, Princeton University Library.

4 Miriam Silverberg, 'Constructing the Japanese Ethnography of Meaning', *Journal of Asian Studies*, LI/1 (February 1992), p. 38.

5 Inoue Masahito, *Nihonjin to yōfuku: Kokuminfuku to iu mōdo* (Japanese People and Western Clothing: The Fashion Known as 'National Dress') (Tokyo, 2001).

6   Yoshiko I. Wada, 'Changing Attitudes Toward the Kimono: A Personal Reflection', in *The Kimono Inspiration: Art and Art-to-Wear in America*, ed. Rebecca A. T. Stevens and Yoshiko Iwamoto Wada (Washington, DC, 1996), p. 170.

7   Kimura Taka and Watanabe Midori, *Michiko-sama no okimono: shashinshū* (Tokyo, 2009).

8   Yamanaka Norio, *The Book of Kimono* (Tokyo, New York, San Francisco, 1982), back cover of book.

9   Ibid.

10 Liza Dalby, *Kimono: Fashioning Culture* (New Haven, CT, and London, 1993), pp. 119–21.

11 See Sheldon Garon, 'Luxury Is the Enemy: Mobilizing Savings and Popularizing Thrift in Wartime Japan', *Journal of Japanese Studies*, XXVI/1 (2000), pp. 41–78.

12 Andrew Gordon, *Fabricating Consumers: The Sewing Machine in Modern Japan* (Berkeley, CA, Los Angeles, London, 2012), p. 85.

13 Ibid., pp. 138–41.

14 Ibid., pp. 193–4.

15 Kaat Debo and Paul Boudens, eds, *Yohji Yamamoto: An Exhibition Triptych* (Antwerp, 2006).

16 For a detailed discussion, see Dorinne Kondo, 'The Aesthetics and Politics of Japanese Identity in the Fashion Industry', in *Re-Made in Japan: Everyday Life and Consumer Taste in a Changing Society*, ed. Joseph J. Tobin (New Haven, CT, and London, 1992), p. 176.

17 Ibid.

18 Yuniya Kawamura, *The Japanese Revolution in Paris Fashion* (Oxford and New York, 2004), p. 96.

19 Guy Trebay, 'Mr Yamamoto's Blue Period', *New York Times Magazine* (13 March 2005), p. 71.

20 Patricia Mears, 'Formalism and Revolution: Rei Kawakubo and Yohji Yamamoto', in *Japan Fashion Now*, ed. Valerie Steele et al., exh. cat., Fashion Institute of Technology (New York, 2010), pp. 142–4.

21 Kondo, 'The Aesthetics and Politics', p. 177.

22 Millie R. Creighton, 'The *Depāto*: Merchandising the West While Selling Japaneseness', in *Re-made in Japan: Everyday Life and Consumer Taste in a Changing Society*, ed. Joseph J. Tobin (New Haven, CT, and London, 1992), p. 54.

23 Kerrie L. MacPherson, 'Introduction: Asia's Universal Providers', in *Asian Department Stores*, ed. Kerrie L. MacPherson (Honolulu, HI, 1998), p. 30. See also Millie Creighton, 'Consuming Rural Japan: The Marketing of Tradition and Nostalgia in the Japanese Travel Industry', *Ethnology*, XXXVI/3 (Summer 1997), pp. 239–54.

24 For her reflections on the experience of wearing kimonos, and thoughts on the future of the kimono, see Wada, 'Changing Attitudes', pp. 172–9. On the kimono as Japan's national dress, see Yoshiko I. Wada, 'The History of Kimono: Japan's National Dress', in *The Kimono Inspiration: Art and Art-to-wear in America*, ed. Rebecca A. T. Stevens and Yoshiko Iwamoto Wada (Washington, DC, 1996), pp. 131–60.

25 For a brief history of *yukata*, see Karen J. Mack, 'The *Naga-ita Chūgata Aizome* Dyeing Technique', *Atomi Gakuen Joshi Daigaku Bungakubu Kiyō*, XLV (September 2010), pp. 1–3.

26 'Genbei Yamaguchi', *Monocle Design* episode 7 (2008), at www.monocle.com; 'Master of the Robes', *Monocle*, II/13 (May 2008), pp. 154–5, at www.monocle.com.

27 Sasaki Sayo, 'All for the Love of Wearing Kimono: Young and Old Have Been Gathering in Ginza for Years to Promenade their Favorite Garb', *Japan Times* (31 December 2009).

BIBLIOGRAPHY

Aida Shōko, '*Kimono' shūgyō* (Tokyo, 2009)

Ajioka Chiaki, 'When Craft Became Art: Modern Japanese Craft and the *Mingei Sakka*', in *Traditional Japanese Arts and Crafts in the 21st Century: Reconsidering the Future from an International Perspective*, ed. Inaga Shigemi and Patricia Fister (Kyoto, 2007)

Aoki Mihoko, 'Kikai nassen', in *Koko ni mo atta takumi no waza: Kikai nassen*, exh. cat, Kyoto Kōgei Sen'i Daigaku Bijutsu Kōgei Shiryōkan (Kyoto, 2010), pp. 1–14

——, 'Taishō-Shōwa shokki no fuasshon', in *Wasō bijin kara yōsō bijin he: Taishō-Shōwa no joseizō,* exh. cat., Kyoto Furitsu Dōmoto Inshō Bijutsukan (Kyoto, 2009)

Bacon, Alice Mabel, *Japanese Girls and Women*, revised and enlarged edition with illustrations by Keishū Takenouchi (London, New York, Bahrain, 2001, originally published 1891)

Bambling, Michele, 'Japan's Living National Treasures Program: The Paradox of Remembering', in *Perspectives on Social Memory in Japan*, ed. Tsu Yun Hui, Jan van Bremen and Eyal Ben-Ari (Folkestone, 2005)

Beetham, Margaret, *A Magazine of Her Own? Domesticity and Desire in the Woman's Magazine, 1800–1914* (London and New York, 1996)

Befu, Harumi, 'Concepts of Japan, Japanese Culture, and the Japanese', in *The Cambridge Companion to Modern Japanese Culture*, ed. Yoshio Sugimoto (Melbourne, 2009)

Berry, Mary Elizabeth, *Japan in Print: Information and Nation in the Early Modern Period* (Berkeley, CA, Los Angeles, London, 2006)

Best, Susan-Marie, 'The Yuzen Kimono of Moriguchi Kunihiko', *Eastern Art Report*, III/2 (July/August 1991)

Bethe, Monica, 'Color: Dyes and Pigments', in Amanda Mayer Stinchecum, *Kosode: 16th–19th Century Textiles from the Nomura Collection*, ed. Naomi Noble Richard and Margot Paul, exh. cat., Japan Society, New York (New York and Tokyo, 1984)

Blaszczyk, Regina Lee, ed., *Producing Fashion: Commerce, Culture, and Consumers* (Philadelphia, PA, 2008)

Bourdieu, Pierre, *Distinction: A Social Critique of the Judgement of Taste*, trans. Richard Nice (Cambridge, MA, 1984)

Brandon, Reiko Mochinaga, *Bright and Daring: Japanese Kimonos in the Taisho Mode from the Oka Nobutaka Collection of the Suzaka Classic Museum*, exh. cat., Honolulu Academy of Arts (Honolulu, HI, 1996)

Brandt, Kim, 'Serizawa Keisuke and the Mingei Movement', in *Serizawa: Master of Japanese Textile Design*, ed. Joe Earle, exh. cat., Japan Society, New York (New York, New Haven, CT, and London, 2009)

——, *Kingdom of Beauty: Mingei and the Politics of Folk Art in Imperial Japan* (Durham, NC, and London, 2007)

Brink, Dean, 'Pygmalion Colonialism: How to Become a Japanese Woman in Late Occupied Taiwan', *Sungkyun Journal of East Asian Studies*, XII/1 (2012)

Bunka Gakuen Fukushoku Hakubutsukan, ed., *Yūzen: Tokyo-ha gojūnen no kiseki* (*Yūzen dyeing: Tracing a Fifty-year Tokyo Tradition*), exh. cat., Bunka Gakuen Fukushoku Hakubutsukan (Tokyo, 1999)

Chokki Toshiaki, 'Labor Management in the Cotton Spinning Industry', in *The Textile Industry and the Rise of the Japanese Economy*, ed. Michael Smitka (New York and London, 1998)

CLAMP Mokona, *CLAMP Mokona's Okimono Kimono* (Milwaukie, OR, 2010)

——, *CLAMP Mokona no okimono kimono* (Tokyo, 2007)

Clark, Timothy, 'Image and Style in the Floating World: The Origins and Development of Ukiyo-e', in *The Dawn of the Floating World 1650–1765: Early Ukiyo-e Treasures from the Museum of Fine Arts, Boston*, ed. Timothy Clark, Anne Nishimura Morse, Louise E. Virgin with Allen Hockley, exh. cat., Museum of Fine Arts, Boston (Boston, 2000–01)

——, *Ukiyo-e Paintings in the British Museum* (Washington, DC, 1992)

Conant, Ellen P., 'Introduction', in *Challenging Past and Present: The Metamorphosis of Nineteenth-century Japanese Art*, ed. Ellen P. Conant (Honolulu, HI, 2006)

Cooper, Michael, ed., *They Came to Japan: An Anthology of European Reports on Japan, 1543–1640* (Berkeley, CA, Los Angeles, London, 1965)

Copeland, Rebecca, *The Sound of the Wind: The Life and Works of Chiyo Uno* (Boston, Rutland, VT, and Tokyo, 1993)

Cort, Louise Allison, 'The Changing Fortunes of Three Archaic Japanese Textiles', in *Cloth and the Human Experience*, ed. Annette B. Weiner and Jane Schneider (Washington, DC, and London, 1989)

——, 'The Modern Shokunin', *Craft Horizons*, XXXVII/5 (August 1978)

Corwin, Nancy A., 'The Kimono Mind: *Japonisme* and American Culture', in *The Kimono Inspiration: Art and Art-to-wear in America*, exh. cat., Textile Museum (Washington, DC, 1996)

Creighton, Millie, 'Consuming Rural Japan: The Marketing of Tradition and Nostalgia in the Japanese Travel Industry', *Ethnology*, XXXVI/3 (Summer 1997)

——, 'The *Depāto*: Merchandising the West While Selling Japaneseness', in *Re-made in Japan: Everyday Life and Consumer Taste in a Changing Society*, ed. Joseph J. Tobin (New Haven, CT, and London, 1992)

Cuccio, Claire, 'Inside *Myōjō* (*Venus*, 1900–1908): Art for the Nation's Sake', PhD thesis, Stanford University, 2005

Cutler, T. W., *A Grammar of Japanese Ornament and Design* (London, 1880)

Dalby, Liza, *Kimono: Fashioning Culture* (New Haven, CT, and London, 1993)

Debo, Kaat, and Paul Boudens, eds, *Yohji Yamamoto: An Exhibition Triptych* (Antwerp, 2006)

Dōmyō Mihoko, *Sugu wakaru kimono no bi: kamikazari kara hakimono made* (Tokyo, 2005)

Dower, John W., *Embracing Defeat: Japan in the Wake of World War II* (New York, 1999)

Downer, Lesley, *Madame Sadayakko: The Geisha who Bewitched the West* (New York, 2003)

Dresser, Christopher, *Japan: Its Architecture, Art and Art Manufactures* (London, 1882)

Duus, Peter, 'Zaikabō: Japanese Cotton Mills in China, 1895–1937', in *The Textile Industry and the Rise of the Japanese Economy*, ed. Michael Smitka (New York and London, 1998)

Edwards, Osman, *Japanese Plays and Playfellows* (New York, 1901)

Faulkner, Rupert, *Japanese Studio Crafts: Tradition and the Avant-Garde* (Philadelphia, PA, 1995)

Finnane, Antonia, *Changing Clothes in China: Fashion, History, Nation* (New York, 2008)

Fontein, Jan, ed., *Living National Treasures of Japan*, exh. cat., Museum of Fine Arts, Boston; Art Institute of Chicago; Japanese American Cultural and Community Center, Los Angeles (Boston, Chicago, Los Angeles, 1983)

Forrer, Matthi, 'The Relationship Between Publishers and Print Formats in the Edo Period', in *The Commercial and Cultural Climate of Japanese Printmaking*, ed. Amy Reigle Newland (Amsterdam, 2004)

Francks, Penelope, *The Japanese Consumer: An Alternative Economic History of Modern Japan* (New York, 2009)

Frederick, Sarah, *Turning Pages: Reading and Writing Women's Magazines in Interwar Japan* (Honolulu, HI, 2006)

Frolet, Elisabeth, 'Mingei: The Word and the Movement', in *Mingei: Masterpieces of Japanese Folkcraft*, ed. Japan Folk Crafts Museum (Tokyo, New York, London, 1991)

Fujii Kenzō, 'Tsuda Seifū no geijutsu to zuan' (Tsuda Seifū's Art and Design), in *Tsuda Seifū no zuan: geijutsu to dezain* (Tsuda Seifū's Designs: Art and Design), ed. Unsōdō (Tokyo and Kyoto, 2008), pp. 78–85

——, 'Meiji kōki no kōgei ishō to zuan zasshi', in Unsōdō, *Shin bijutusukai: Kamisaka sekka, Furuya Kōrin* (The New World of Art: Kamisaka Sekka and Furuya Kōrin (Tokyo and Kyoto, 2006)

——, 'Biten no rekishi to sono ippin: bi wo umidasu chikara' (The History of *Biten* and Their Objects: Power that Gives Birth to Beauty), *Kosode kara kimono he, Bessatsu Taiyō*, LV (2005), pp. 58–86

Fujimoto Keiko, 'Yuzenzome no tenkai to Chisō' (Chisō and the Development of the *Yūzen* Technique), in *Chisō korekushon: Kyō no yūga, kosode to byōbu* (The Elegance of Kyoto Style: Kosode and Folding Screens from the Chisō Collection), ed. Kyoto Bunka Hakubutsukan, exh. cat., Kyoto Bunka Hakubutsukan (Kyoto, 2005)

——, 'Kindai Kyōto no senshoku sangyō to zuan kenkyūkai' (Research Group on Textile Design and Production in Modern Kyoto), *Suzaku: Bulletin of The Museum of Kyoto*, VIII (1995), pp. 121–36

Fujitani, T., *Splendid Monarchy: Power and Pageantry in Modern Japan* (Berkeley, CA, Los Angeles, London, 1996)

Fukai Akiko, *Jyaponizumu in fuasshon* (Tokyo, 1994)

Fukatsu-Fukuoka Yuko, 'The Evolution of Yuzen-dyeing Techniques and Designs after the Meiji Restoration', in *Appropriation, Acculturation, Transformation – Symposium Proceedings of the Textile Society of America, 9th Biennial Symposium* (2004)

Furuta Kazuko, 'Cultural Transformation in Japan's Industrialization: Local Adaptation to Foreign Silk Technology', in *The State and Cultural Transformation: Perspectives From East Asia*, ed. Hirano Ken'ichiro (Tokyo, New York, Paris, 1993)

Garon, Sheldon, 'Luxury is the Enemy: Mobilizing Savings and Popularizing Thrift in Wartime Japan', *Journal of Japanese Studies*, XXVI/1 (2000)

Gerbert, Elaine, 'Space and Aesthetic Imagination in Some Taishō Writings', in *Japan's Competing Modernities: Issues in Culture and Democracy, 1900–1930*, ed. Sharon A. Minichiello (Honolulu, HI, 1998)

Gerstle, C. Andrew, 'Flowers of Edo: Eighteenth-century Kabuki and Its Patrons', *Asian Theater Journal*, IV/1 (Spring 1987)

Gluck, Carol, *Japan's Modern Myths: Ideology in the Late Meiji Period* (Princeton, NJ, 1985)

Gordon, Andrew, *Fabricating Consumers: The Sewing Machine in Modern Japan* (Berkeley, CA, Los Angeles, London, 2012)

——, *A Modern History of Japan from Tokugawa Times to Present* (New York, Oxford, 2003)

Guth, Christine M. E., 'Charles Longfellow and Okakura Kakuzō: Cultural Cross-dressing in the Colonial Context', *Positions East Asia Cultures Critique, Special Issue: Visual Cultures of Japanese Imperialism*, VIII/3 (Winter 2000)

——, 'Kokuhō: From Dynastic to Artistic Treasure', *Cahiers d'Extrême-Asie*, IX (1996–7)

Hamada Shukuko, 'The Art of Serizawa Keisuke', in *Serizawa: Master of Japanese Textile Design*, ed. Joe Earle, exh. cat., Japan Society, New York (New York, New Haven, CT, and London, 2009)

Hanafusa Miki, 'Empress Tōfukumon'in and Empress Shōken', in *Amamonzeki – A Hidden Heritage: Treasures of the Japanese Imperial Convents*, ed. Medieval Japanese Studies Institute et al., exh. cat., University Art Museum, Tokyo University of the Arts (Osaka and Tokyo, 2009)

Hastings, Sally A., 'The Empress' New Clothes and Japanese Women, 1868–1912', *Historian*, XXXIII/4 (Summer 1993)

Hauser, William B., 'A New Society: Japan under Tokugawa Rule', in *When Art Became Fashion: Kosode in Edo-Period Japan*, ed. Dale Carolyn Gluckman and Sharon Sadako Takeda, exh. cat., Los Angeles County Museum of Art (Los Angeles, 1992)

——, *Economic Institutional Change in Tokugawa Japan: Ōsaka and the Kinai Cotton Trade* (London, 1974)

Havemeyer, Louisine W., *Sixteen to Sixty: Memoirs of a Collector*, privately printed for the Family of Mrs. H. O. Havemeyer and the Metropolitan Museum of Art, New York (New York, 1961)

Higa Akiko, 'Kamisaka Sekka's Design Collections', in *Kamisaka Sekka: Rinpa no keishō kindai dezain no senkusha* (*Kamisaka Sekka: Rimpa Master-Pioneer of Modern Design*), ed. Donald A. Wood and Yuko Ikeda, exh. cat., National Museum of Modern Art, Kyoto; Sakura City Museum of Art; Los Angeles County Museum of Art; Birmingham Museum of Art, Alabama (Kyoto and Birmingham, AL, 2003)

Hillier, Jack, *The Art of the Japanese Book*, 2 vols (New York, 1987)

Hirano Eriko, *Kimono, Kiyō, yo!* (Tokyo, 2008)

Hirano, Ken'ichiro, 'The Westernization of Clothes and the State in Meiji Japan', in *The State and Cultural Transformation: Perspectives From East Asia*, ed. Hirano Ken'ichiro (Tokyo, New York, Paris, 1993)

Hirota Takashi, 'Meiji-matsu Taishō shoki no yūshutsuyō kimono ni kansuru ikkōsatsu: Takashimaya Shiryōkan wo chūshin ni' (Thoughts on Late Meiji and Early Taishō Period Export Kimono: The Takashimaya Archive), *Fukushoku Bigaku*, XLII (2006), pp. 19–35

Hockley, Allen, 'First Encounters – Emerging Stereotypes: Westerners and the Geisha in the Late Nineteenth Century', in *Geisha: Beyond the Painted Smile*, ed. Peabody Essex Museum, exh. cat., Peabody Essex Museum, Salem, MA, and Asian Art Museum; Chong-Moon Lee Center for Asian Art and Culture, San Francisco (New York, 2004)

——, *The Prints of Isoda Koryūsai: Floating World Culture and its Consumers in Eighteenth-century Japan* (Seattle, WA, 2003)

Hosley, William, *The Japan Idea: Art and Life in Victorian America*, exh. cat., Wadsworth Atheneum, Hartford (Hartford, CT, 1990)

Houchins, Chang-su, *Artifacts of Diplomacy: Smithsonian Collections from Commodore Matthew Perry's Japan Exhibition (1853–1854)* (Washington, DC, 1995)

Hunter, Janet, *Women and the Labour Market in Japan's Industrialising Economy: The Textile Industry before the Pacific War* (London and New York, 2003)

Huyssen, Andreas, 'Geographies of Modernism in a Globalizing World', in *Geographies of Modernism*, ed. Peter Brooker and Andrew Thacker (London, 2005)

Ichida Hiromi, 'A Brief History of Kimono', *Chanoyū Quarterly*, XXI (1978)

Ikegami, Eiko, *Bonds of Civility: Aesthetic Networks and the Political Origins of Japanese Culture* (New York, 2005)

Inoue Masahito, *Nihonjin to yōfuku: Kokuminfuku to iu mōdo* (*Japanese People and Western Clothing: The Fashion Known as 'National Dress'*) (Tokyo, 2001)

Itakura Toshirō, Nomura Kihachi, Motoi Chikara, Yoshikawa Seibei and Yoshida Mitsukuni, eds, *Genshoku senshoku daijiten* (Illustrated Textile Dictionary) (Kyoto, 1977)

Itō Toshiko, *Tsujigahanazome* (Tokyo, 1981)

Jenkins, D. T., 'The Response of the European Wool Textile Manufacturers to the Opening of the Japanese Market', *Textile History*, XIX/2 (1998)

Jinno Yuki, *Shumi no tanjō: Hyakkaten ga tsukatta teisuto* (*The Birth of 'Shumi': Taste as Constructed by Department Stores*) (Tokyo, 2000)

Kanai Jun I., 'Japonism in Fashion: Overview', in *Japonism in Fashion: Tokyo*, exh. cat., Tokyo Fuasshon Taun Nishikan (Tokyo, 1996)

Kaneko Kenji, 'The Development of "Traditional Art Crafts" in Japan', in *Crafting Beauty in Modern Japan: Celebrating Fifty Years of the Japan Traditional Art Crafts Exhibition*, ed. Nicole Rousmaniere, exh. cat., British Museum (Seattle, WA, 2007)

Kashiwagi Hiroshi, 'Design and War: Kimono as "Parlor Performance" Propaganda', in *Wearing Propaganda: Textiles on the Home Front in Japan, Britain, and the United States, 1931–1945*, ed. Jacqueline M. Atkin, exh. cat., The Bard Graduate Center for Studies in the Decorative Arts, Design, and Culture, New York (New Haven, CT, and London, 2005)

Kawakatsu Ken'ichi, *Kimono: Japanese Dress,* Tourist Library 3 (Tokyo, 1960, first edition 1936)

Kawamura, Yuniya, *Fashion-ology: An Introduction to Fashion Studies* (Oxford and New York, 2005)

——, *The Japanese Revolution in Paris Fashion* (Oxford and New York, 2004)

Keene, Donald, *Seeds in the Heart: Japanese Literature from Earliest Times to the Late Sixteenth Century* (New York, 1993)

Kennedy, Alan, *Japanese Costume: History and Tradition* (Paris, 1990)

Kida Takuya, '"Traditional Art Crafts (*Dentō Kōgei*)" in Japan: From Reproductions to Original Works', *Journal of Modern Craft*, III/1 (March 2010)

Kimura Taka and Watanabe Midori, *Michiko-sama no okimono: shashinshū* (Tokyo, 2009)

Kirihata Ken, ed., *Kagayakeru kosode no bi: Tabata korekushon*, exh. cat., Takashimaya, Kyoto; Matsuya Ginza, Tokyo; Takashimaya, Yokohama; Hakata Daimaru, Fukuoka; Umeda Hankyu, Osaka (Osaka, 1990)

Kiyokawa Yukihiko, 'The Transformation of Young Rural Women into Disciplined Labor under Competition-oriented Management: The Experience of the Silk-reeling Industry in Japan', in *The Textile Industry and the Rise of the Japanese Economy*, ed. Michael Smitka (New York and London, 1998)

Kobayashi Keiko, 'The Effect of Western Textile Technology on Japanese *Kasuri*: Development, Innovation, and Competition', *Textile Museum Journal*, XL–XLI (2001–2)

Koda, Harold, and Andrew Bolton, 'Preface: The Prophet of Simplicity', in *Poiret*, ed. Harold Koda and Andrew Bolton, exh. cat., Metropolitan Museum of Art (New Haven, CT, and London, 2007)

Kon Wajiro and Yoshida Kenkichi, 'Depaato fūzoku shakaigaku' (Sociology of Department Store Manners), in *Moderunorogio (Kōgengaku)* (Tokyo, 1986)

Kondo, Dorinne, *About Face: Performing Race in Fashion and Theater* (New York and London, 1997)

——, 'The Aesthetics and Politics of Japanese Identity in the Fashion Industry', in *Re-made in Japan: Everyday Life and Consumer Taste in a Changing Society*, ed. Joseph J. Tobin (New Haven, CT, and London, 1992)

Kornicki, P. F., 'Public Display and Changing Values: Early Meiji Exhibitions and Their Precursors', *Monumenta Nipponica*, XLIX/2 (Summer 1994)

Kramer, Elizabeth, 'Master or Market? The Anglo–Japanese Textile Designs of Christopher Dresser', *Journal of Design History*, XIX/3 (2006)

Kubota Itchiku, *Lumiere Brodee: Itchiku Kubota*, exh. cat., Palais de Tokyo (Belgium, 1990)

Kuki Shūzō, *Reflections on Japanese Taste: The Structure of Iki*, trans. John Clark, ed. Sakuko Matsui and John Clark (Sydney, 1997)

Kyoto Bunka Hakubutsukan, ed., *Kaiga to ishō: bi no meihinten – Marubeni korekushon* (*Beauty of Pictures and Costumes: Masterpieces from the Marubeni Collection*), exh. cat. Kyoto Bunka Hakubutsukan (Kyoto, 2007)

——, *Kyō no yūga: Kosode to byōbu: Chisō korekushon* (*The Elegance of Kyoto Style: Kosode Kimonos and Folding Screens from the Chisō Collection*), exh. cat., Kyoto Bunka Hakubutsukan (Kyoto, 2005)

Lawton, Thomas, 'Yamanaka Sadajirō: Advocate for Asian Art', *Orientations*, XXVI/1 (January 1995)

Liddell, Jill, *The Story of the Kimono* (New York, 1989)

Link, Howard A., and Shimbo Toru, *Exquisite Visions: Rimpa Paintings from Japan,* exh. cat., Honolulu Academy of Arts (Honolulu, HI, 1980)

Los Angeles County Museum of Art et al., *Japan Goes to the World's Fairs: Japanese Art at the Great Expositions in Europe and the United States, 1867–1904,* exh. cat., Los Angeles County Museum of Art (Los Angeles, 2005)

Ma, Debin, 'The Modern Silk Road: The Global Raw-silk Market, 1850–1930', *Journal of Economic History*, LVI/2 (1996)

McDermott, Hiroko T., 'Meiji Kyoto Textile Art and Takashimaya', *Monumenta Nipponica*, LXV/1 (Spring 2010)

Mack, Karen J., 'The *Naga-ita Chūgata Aizome* Dyeing Technique', *Atomi Gakuen Joshi Daigaku Bungakubu Kiyō* (Journal of the Atomi Women's University Faculty of Letters), XLV (September 2010), pp. 1–9.

MacPherson, Kerrie L., 'Introduction: Asia's Universal Providers', in *Asian Department Stores,* ed. Kerrie L. MacPherson (Honolulu, HI, 1998)

Maeda Ai, 'The Development of Popular Fiction in the Late Taishō Era: Increasing Readership of Women's Magazines', in *Text and the City: Essays on Japanese Modernity*, trans. Rebecca Copeland, ed. James A. Fujii (Durham, NC, and London, 2004)

Makimura Yasuhiro, 'The Silk Road at Yokohama: A History of the Economic Relationships between Yokohama, the Kantō Region, and the World through the Japanese Silk Industry in the Nineteenth Century', PhD thesis, Columbia University, 2005

Maniglier Maïa, *Parijiennu no kimono hajime* (Tokyo, 2005)

Martin, Katherine, *Highlights of Japanese Printmaking: Shin Hanga, Part Two* (New York, 2006)

Maruyama Nobuhiko, *Edo mōdo no tanjō: monyō no ryūkō to sutaa-eshi* (Tokyo, 2008)

——, 'Kosode hinagatabon kenkyū joshō: kinsei no ryūkō ni okeru shuppan no yakuwari o chūshin ni' (A Preliminary Study of Kosode Miniature Pattern Books: The Role of Publishing in Early Modern Fashion Trends), in *Nihon bijutsushi no suimyaku* (*Currents in Japanese Art History*), ed. Hashimoto Aiki (Tokyo, 1993)

——, 'Fashion and the Floating World: The *Kosode* in Art', in *When Art Became Fashion: Kosode in Edo-period Japan*, ed. Dale Carolyn Gluckman and Sharon Sadako Takeda, exh. cat., Los Angeles County Museum of Art (Los Angeles, 1992)

Maruyama Nobuhiko, ed., *Edo no kimono to iseikatsu: Nihon bizuaru seikatsushi* (Tokyo, 2007)

Maruyama Tsuneo, 'Dentō ni tatsu futatsu no sōsaku: Moriguchi Kakō-Kunihiko ten ni yosete', in *Moriguchi Kakō, Kunihiko ten: fushi yūzen ningen kokuhō*, exh. cat., Shiga Kenritsu Kindai Bijutsukan (Shiga, Japan, 2009)

Mears, Patricia, 'Formalism and Revolution: Rei Kawakubo and Yohji Yamamoto', in *Japan Fashion Now*, ed. Valerie Steele et al., exh. cat., Fashion Institute of Technology (New York, 2010)

Meech, Julia, 'For the Good of the Nation', *Asian Art*, VI/1 (Winter 1993)

——, 'The Other Havemeyer Passion: Collecting Asian Art', in *Splendid Legacy: The Havemeyer Collection*, ed. Alice Cooney Frelinghuysen et al., exh. cat., Metropolitan Museum of Art (New York, 1993)

Meech-Pekarik, Julia, *The World of the Meiji Print: Impressions of a New Civilization* (New York and Tokyo, 1986)

'Meiji, Taishō no senshoku' (Textiles of the Meiji and Taishō Periods), *Senshoku no bi*, 25 (Autumn 1983)

Michie, Thomas C., 'Western Collecting of Japanese Stencils and their Impact in America', in *Carved Paper: The Art of the Japanese Stencil*, ed. Susan Shin-Tsu Tai, exh. cat., Santa Barbara Museum of Art; Museum of Art, Rhode Island School of Design; Mingei International Museum, San Diego (New York and Tokyo, 1998)

Milhaupt, Terry Satsuki, 'In the Guise of Tradition: Serizawa Keisuke and His Eclectic Designs', in *Serizawa: Master of Japanese Textile Design,* ed. Joe Earle, exh. cat., Japan Society, New York (New York, New Haven, CT, and London, 2009)

——, 'Facets of the Kimono: Reflections of Japan's Modernity', in *Arts of Japan: The John C. Weber Collection*, ed. Melanie Trede with Julia Meech, exh. cat., Museum of East Asian Art, National Museums in Berlin, Museum of Fine Arts, Boston, Minneapolis Institute of Fine Arts (Berlin, 2006)

——, 'Meanings and Modes of Japanese Clothing', in *Arts of Japan: The John C. Weber Collection,* ed. Melanie Trede with Julia Meech, exh. cat., Museum of East Asian Art, National Museums in Berlin, Museum of Fine Arts, Boston, Minneapolis Institute of Fine Arts (Berlin, 2006)

——, 'Second Hand Silk Kimono Migrating Across Borders', in *Old Clothes, New Looks: Second Hand Fashion*, ed. Alexandra Palmer and Hazel Clarik (Oxford and New York, 2005)

——, '*Tsujigahana* Textiles and their Fabrication', in *Turning Point: Oribe and the Arts of Sixteenth-century Japan*, ed. Miyeko Murase, exh. cat., Metropolitan Museum of Art (New York, New Haven, CT, and London, 2003)

——, 'Flowers at the Crossroads: The Four-hundred-year Life of a Japanese Textile', PhD thesis, Washington University, 2002

Minami Ryoshin and Makino Fumio, 'Condition for Technological Diffusion: Case of Power Looms', in *The Textile Industry and the Rise of the Japanese Economy*, ed. Michael Smitka (New York and London, 1998)

Minnich, Helen Benton, in collaboration with Nomura Shōjirō, *Japanese Costume and the Makers of its Elegant Tradition* (Rutland, VT, and Tokyo, Japan, 1963)

Miyoshi Masao, *As We Saw Them: The First Japanese Embassy to the United States* (New York, Tokyo, London, 1979, reprinted in 1994)

Moeran, Brian, 'The Birth of the Japanese Department Store', in *Asian Department Stores*, ed. Kerrie L. MacPherson (Honolulu, HI, 1998)

——, 'The Art World of Contemporary Japanese Ceramics', *Journal of Japanese Studies*, XIII/1 (1987)

Molony, Barbara, 'Modernity, Gender and the Empire: Gender, Citizenship and Dress in Modernizing Japan', *IIAS Newsletter*, 46 (Winter 2008)

Momi: Kimono kimawashi kōdinēto bukku, vol. II (Fukuoka, 2009)

Mori Rie, 'Kimono and Colony: From Testimonies and Literatures', *Voices from Japan*, XXV (March 2011)

——, 'Perceptions of Kimono in Literature, Film, and Other Forms of Visual Media During Japan's Colonization of Korea', *Journal of the International Association of Costume*, XXXVIII (2010)

——, 'Kimono no joseika, fuasshonka to minzoku ishōka', in *Tokimeku fuasshon: Komachi musume kara modan ga-ru made*, ed. Ehimeken Rekishi Bunka Hakubutsukan, exh. cat., Ehimeken Rekishi Bunka Hakubutsukan (Ehime, Japan, 2007)

Morris-Suzuki, Tessa, *The Technological Transformation of Japan from the Seventeenth to the Twenty-first Century* (Cambridge, New York, Melbourne, 1994)

Nagasaki Iwao, 'Kosode kara kimono he', *Nihon no bijutsu*, CDXXXV (Tokyo, 2002)

——, 'Designs for a Thousand Ages: Printed Pattern Books and *Kosode*', in *When Art Became Fashion: Kosode in Edo-period Japan*, ed. Dale Carolyn Gluckman and Sharon Sadako Takeda, exh. cat., Los Angeles County Museum of Art (Los Angeles, 1992)

Nagoya-shi Hakubutsukan, ed., *Kosode: Edo no ōto kuchūru* (*Kosode: Haute Couture Kimonos of the Edo Period*), exh. cat. (Tokyo, 2008)

Nakagawa Keiichirō and Henry Rosovsky, 'The Case of the Dying Kimono: The Influence of Changing Fashions on the Development of the Japanese Woolen Industry', *Business History Review*, XXXVII/1–2 (Spring/Summer 1963)

Nakano Makiko, *Makiko's Diary: A Merchant Wife in 1910 Kyoto*, trans. Kazuko Smith (Stanford, CA, 1995)

Nakaoka Tetsuro, Aikawa Kayoko, Miyajima Hayao, Yoshii Takao and Nishizawa Tamotsu, 'The Textile History of Nishijin (Kyoto): East Meets West', *Textile History*, XIX/2 (1988), pp. 117–39

NHK Kinki medeia puran, ed., *Kyō yūzen no hana; Ningen kokuhō sandai Tabata Kihachi no bi*, exh. cat., Takashimaya, Kyoto; Takashimaya, Nanba (Kyoto, 2001)

Nishikawa Sukenobu shū jōken, vol. 1 (Osaka, 1999)

Okabe Masayuki, 'The Impact of the Kimono on Modern Fashion', *Journal of Japanese Trade and Industry* (November, 2002)

Okakura Kakuzō, *The Awakening of Japan, Special Edition for Japan Society, Inc.* (New York, 1921, originally published in 1904)

——, *The Ideals of the East: With Special Reference to the Art of Japan* (New York, Tokyo, Osaka, London, 2000, originally published in 1904)

Ōmori Tetsuya, 'Gakatachi no egaita meisen bijin: Ashikaga meisen no senden posutaa-kara', in *Meisen-Taishō Shōwa no oshare kimono, Bessatsu Taiyō*, ed. Fujii Kenzō (2004), pp. 108–13

Otaki Mikio, 'Yūzen Tokyo-ha: sono shiren to kagayaki' (The Challenges and Splendor of Yuzen Dyeing in Tokyo), in *Yūzen: Tokyo-ha gojūnen no kiseki* (*Yūzen Dyeing: Tracing a Fifty-year Tokyo Tradition*), exh. cat., Bunka Gakuen Fukushoku Hakubutsukan, Tokyo (Tokyo, 1999)

Oyama Yuzuruha, 'Kōrin moyō', *Nihon no bijutsu*, DXXIV (Tokyo, 2010)

Paul, Margot, 'A Creative Connoisseur: Nomura Shōjirō', in Amanda Mayer Stinchecum, *Kosode: 16th–19th Century Textiles from the Nomura Collection*, ed. Naomi Noble Richard and Margot Paul, exh. cat., Japan Society, New York (New York and Tokyo, 1984)

Peck, Amelia, and Carol Irish, *Candace Wheeler: The Art and Enterprise of American Designs, 1875–1900*, exh. cat., Metropolitan Museum of Art (New Haven, CT, 2001)

Pevtzow, Lisa, 'Kimono Design Books (Zuan-chō)', *Daruma*, XVIII/1 (Winter 2011), pp. 34–52

Pincus, Leslie, *Authenticating Culture in Imperial Japan: Kuki Shūzō and the Rise of National Aesthetics* (Berkeley, CA, Los Angeles, London, 1996)

Pineau, Roger, ed., *The Japan Expedition, 1852–1854: The Personal Journal of Commodore Matthew C. Perry* (Washington, DC, 1968)

Pollack, David, 'Designed for Pleasure: Ukiyo-e as Material Culture', in *Designed for Pleasure: The World of Edo Japan in Prints and Paintings, 1680–1860*, ed. Julia Meech and Jane Oliver, exh. cat., Asia Society, New York (Seattle, WA, and London, 2008)

——, 'Marketing Desire: Advertising and Sexuality in Edo Literature, Drama, and Art', in *Gender and Power in the Japanese Visual Field*, ed. Joshua S. Mostow, Norman Bryson and Maribeth Graybill (Honolulu, HI, 2003)

Printing Museum, Tokyo, *Bijin no tsukurikata: sekiban kara hajimaru kōkoku posutaa ten* (*Making Beauty: Early Japanese Lithographic Posters Exhibition*), exh. cat., Printing Museum, Tokyo (Tokyo, 2007)

Proser, Adriana, 'Abby Aldrich Rockefeller and Lucy Truman Aldrich: Sisters, Confidantes, and Collectors', *Orientations*, XXXVII/1 (January/February 2006)

Rinne, Melissa M., 'Preserving Echigo *Jōfu* and Nara *Sarashi*: Issues in Contemporary Bast Fiber Textile Production', in *Material Choices: Refashioning Bast and Leaf*

Fibers in Asia and the Pacific, exh. cat., Fowler Museum at UCLA, Los Angeles (Los Angeles, 2007)

Rubinfien, Louisa Daria, 'Commodity to National Brand: Manufacturers, Merchants, and the Development of the Consumer Market in Interwar Japan', PhD thesis, Harvard University, 1995

Sapin, Julia, 'Department-store Publicity Magazines in Early Twentieth-century Japan: Promoting Products, Producing New Cultural Perspectives', *Transactions of the International Conference of Eastern Studies*, 56 (2011)

——, 'Merchandising Art and Identity in Meiji Japan: Kyoto Nihonga Artists' Designs for Takashimaya Department Store, 1868–1912', *Journal of Design History*, XVII/4 (2004)

——, 'Liaisons between Painters and Department Stores: Merchandising Art and Identity in Meiji Japan, 1868–1912', PhD thesis, University of Washington, 2003

Sasaki Sayo, 'All for the Love of Wearing Kimono: Young and Old Have Been Gathering in Ginza for Years to Promenade their Favorite Garb', *Japan Times* (31 December 2009)

Sato, Barbara, 'An Alternate Informant: Middle-class Women and Mass Magazines in 1920s Japan', in *Being Modern in Japan: Culture and Society from the 1910s to the 1920s*, ed. Elise K. Tipton and John Clark (Honolulu, HI, 2000)

Satō Dōshin, *Modern Japanese Art and the Meiji State: The Politics of Beauty*, trans. Nara Hiroshi (Los Angeles, 2011)

Seidensticker, Edward, *Low City, High City – Tokyo from Edo to the Earthquake: How the Shogun's Ancient Capital Became a Great Modern City, 1867–1923* (Cambridge, MA, 1991)

Shadan Hōjin Zen Nihon Kimono Shinkōkai, ed., *Kimono no kihon – Kimono bunka kentei kōshiki kyōbon I* (Tokyo, 2006)

Shin shitei jūyō bunkazai: Kōgei hin II (Tokyo, 1983)

Shively, Donald H., 'Sumptuary Regulation and Status in Early Tokugawa Japan', *Harvard Journal of Asiatic Studies,* XXV (1964–5)

Shizuoka Shiritsu Serizawa Keisuke Bijutsukan, ed. *Serizawa Keisuke: Sono shōgai to sakuhin* (Shizuoka City, Japan, 2008)

Sievers, Sharon L., *Flowers in Salt: The Beginnings of Feminist Consciousness in Modern Japan* (Stanford, CA, 1983)

Silverberg, Miriam, 'Constructing the Japanese Ethnography of Meaning', *Journal of Asian Studies*, LI/1 (February 1992)

Slade, Toby, *Japanese Fashion: A Cultural History* (Oxford, New York, 2009)

Smith, Henry D. II, 'The Floating World in Its Edo Locale, 1750–1850', in *The Floating World Revisited*, ed. Donald Jenkins, exh. cat., Portland Art Museum (Portland, OR, and Honolulu, HI, 1993)

Smith, Thomas C., *Native Sources of Japanese Industrialization, 1750–1920* (Berkeley, CA, Los Angeles, London, 1988)

Smitka, Michael, ed., *The Textile Industry and the Rise of the Japanese Economy* (New York and London, 1998)

Soviak, Eugene, 'On the Nature of Western Progress: The Journal of the Iwakura Embassy', in *Tradition and Modernization in Japanese Culture*, ed. Donald H. Shively (Princeton, NJ, 1976)

St Denis, Ruth, *An Unfinished Life: An Autobiography (with portraits)* (New York and London, 1939)

Stern, Harold P., *Rimpa: Masterworks of the Japanese Decorative School* (New York, 1971)

Stewart, Susan, *On Longing: Narratives of the Miniature, the Gigantic, the Souvenir, the Collection* (Durham and London, 1993)

Stinchecum, Amanda Mayer, 'Serizawa Keisuke and Okinawa', in *Serizawa: Master of Japanese Textile Design*, ed. Joe Earle, exh. cat., Japan Society, New York (New York, New Haven, CT, and London, 2009)

——, 'Japanese Textiles and the Mingei Aesthetic', in *Mingei: Japanese Folk Art from the Montgomery Collection*, ed. Robert Moes (Alexandria, VA, 1995)

Sugiyama Shinya, 'Textile Marketing in East Asia, 1860–1914', *Textile History*, XIX/2 (1988), pp. 287–9

Svendsen, Lars, *Fashion: A Philosophy*, trans. John Irons (London, 1996)

Takamura Itsue, 'Geisha to kifujinka', in Takamura Itsue, *Takamura Itsue zenshū*, vol. V, *Josei no rekishi 2*, ed. Hashimoto Kenzō (Tokyo, 1966)

Takeda Sharon, 'Offertory Banners from Rural Japan: Echigo-Chijimi Weaving and Worship', in *Sacred and Ceremonial Textiles, Proceedings of the Fifth Biennial Symposium of The Textile Society of America* (Chicago, 1996)

Tamanoi, Mariko Asano, *Under the Shadow of Nationalism: Politics and Poetics of Rural Japanese Women* (Honolulu, HI, 1998)

Tani Shin'ichi, 'Ogata Kōrin: Artist to the Merchant Class', *Japan Quarterly*, V/4 (October–December 1958)

Taylor, Lou, 'De-coding the Hierarchy of Fashion Textiles', in *Disentangling Textiles: Techniques for the Study of Designed Objects*, ed. Mary Schoeser and Christine Boydell (London, 2002)

Thurman, Judith, 'Letter from Japan: The Kimono Painter', *New Yorker* (17 October 2005)

Till, Barry, Michiko Warkentyne and Judith Patt, *The Kimono of the Geisha–Diva Ichimaru* (San Francisco, CA, 2006)

Tipton, Elise K., *Modern Japan: A Social and Political History*, 2nd edn (London and New York, 2008)

Tomii, Reiko, '"International Contemporaneity" in the 1960s: Discoursing on Japan and Beyond', *Japan Review*, XXI (2009), pp. 123–47

Trebay, Guy, 'Mr Yamamoto's Blue Period', *New York Times Magazine* (13 March 2005)

Tsurumi, E. Patricia, *Factory Girls: Women in the Thread Mills of Meiji Japan* (Princeton, NJ, 1990)

Uchida Hoshimi, 'Narrow Cotton Stripes and their Substitutes: Fashion, Technical Progress and Manufacturing Organization in Japanese Popular Clothing, 1850–1920', *Textile History*, XIX/2 (1988)

Uchiyama Takeo, 'Japan Traditional Art Crafts Exhibitions: Its History and Spirit', in *Crafting Beauty in Modern Japan: Celebrating Fifty Years of the Japan Traditional Art Crafts Exhibition*, ed. Nicole Rousmaniere, exh. cat., British Museum (Seattle, WA, 2007)

Uhlenbeck, Chris, 'Production Constraints in the World of Ukiyo-e: An Introduction to the Commercial Climate of Japanese Printmaking', in *The Commercial and Cultural Climate of Japanese Printmaking*, ed. Amy Reigle Newland (Amsterdam, 2004)

Uno Chiyo, *Uno Chiyo kimono techō* (Tokyo, 2004)

van Assche, Annie, 'Interweavings: Kimono Past and Present', in *Fashioning Kimono: Dress and Modernity in Early Twentieth Century Japan – The Montgomery Collection*, ed. Annie van Assche, exh. cat., Victoria & Albert Museum, London (Milan, 2005)

Vaporis, Constantine Nomikos, *Breaking Barriers: Travel and the State in Early Modern Japan* (Cambridge, MA, and London, 1994)

Vlastos, Stephen, 'Tradition: Past/Present Culture and Modern Japanese History', in *Mirror of Modernity: Invented Traditions in Modern Japan*, ed. Stephen Vlastos (Berkeley, CA, Los Angeles, London, 1998)

Volker, T., *Ukiyo-e Quartet: Publisher, Designer, Engraver and Printer* (Leiden, 1949)

Wada, Yoshiko Iwamoto, 'From Kitsch to Art Moderne: Popular Textiles for Women in the First Half of Twentieth-century Japan', in *Creating Textiles: Makers, Methods, Markets – Proceedings of the Sixth Biennial Symposium of the Textile Society of America, Inc.* (Earleville, MD, 1999)

——, 'Changing Attitudes Toward the Kimono: A Personal Reflection', in *The Kimono Inspiration: Art and Art-to-Wear in America*, ed. Rebecca A. T. Stevens and Yoshiko Iwamoto Wada (Washington, DC, 1996)

——, 'The History of Kimono: Japan's National Dress', in *The Kimono Inspiration: Art and Art-to-wear in America*, ed. Rebecca A. T. Stevens and Yoshiko Iwamoto Wada (Washington, DC, 1996)

Wakakuwa, Midori, 'War-promoting Kimono (1931–45)', in *Wearing Propaganda: Textiles on the Home Front in Japan, Britain, and the United States, 1931–1945*, ed. Jacqueline M. Atkins, exh. cat., The Bard Graduate Center for Studies in the Decorative Arts, Design, and Culture, New York (New Haven, CT, and London, 2005)

Waterhouse, David, 'Hishikawa Moronobu: Tracking Down an Elusive Master', in *Designed for Pleasure: The World of Edo Japan in Prints and Paintings, 1680–1860*, ed. Julia Meech and Jane Oliver, exh. cat., Asia Society, New York (Seattle, WA, and London, 2008)

——, 'The Cultural Milieu of Suzuki Harunobu', in *The Commercial and Cultural Climate of Japanese Printmaking*, ed. Amy Reigle Newland (Amsterdam, 2004)

Weisenfeld, Gennifer, 'Japanese Modernism and Consumerism: Forging the New Artistic Field of *Shōgyō Bijutsu* (Commercial Art)', in *Being Modern in Japan: Culture and Society from the 1910s to the 1920s*, ed. Elise K. Tipton and John Clark (Honolulu, HI, 2000)

Wentworth, Michael Justin, 'Tissot and Japonisme', in *Japonisme in Art: An International Symposium*, ed. Society for the Study of Japonisme (Japan, 1980)

Wheeler, Candace, 'Decorative and Applied Art', in *Household Art*, ed. Candace Wheeler (New York, 1893)

Wigen, Kären, *The Making of a Japanese Periphery* (Berkeley, CA, Los Angeles, London, 1995)

Wilson, Richard, *The Potter's Brush: The Kenzan Style in Japanese Ceramics*, exh. cat., Freer Gallery of Art and Arthur M. Sackler Gallery, Smithsonian Institution (Washington, DC, 2001)

——, 'Motifs and Meanings', in *Carved Paper: The Art of the Japanese Stencil*, ed. Susan Shin-Tsu-Tai, exh. cat., Santa Barbara Museum of Art; Museum of Art, Rhode Island School of Design; Mingei International Museum, San Diego (New York and Tokyo, 1998)

——, 'Aspects of Rimpa Design', *Orientations*, XXI/12 (December 1990)

Winther-Tamaki, Bert, *Art in the Encounter of Nations: Japanese and American Artists in the Postwar Years* (Honolulu, HI, 2001)

Wittner, David. G., *Technology and the Culture of Progress in Meiji Japan* (London and New York, 2008)

——, 'The Mechanization of Japan's Silk Industry and the Quest for Progress and Civilization, 1870–1880', in *Building a Modern Japan: Science, Technology, and Medicine in the Meiji Era and Beyond*, ed. Morris Low (New York, 2005)

Wood, Donald A., and Yuko Ikeda, eds, *Kamisaka Sekka: Rinpa no keishō kindai dezain no senkusha* (*Kamisaka Sekka: Rimpa Master-Pioneer of Modern Design*), exh. cat., National Museum of Modern Art, Kyoto; Sakura City Museum of Art; Los Angeles County Museum of Art; Birmingham Museum of Art, Alabama (Kyoto and Birmingham, AL, 2003)

Yamakawa Kikue, *Women of the Mito Domain: Recollections of Samurai Family Life*, trans. Kate Wildman Nakai (Stanford, CA, 2001)

Yamamori Yumiko, 'Japanese Arts in America, 1895–1920, and the A. A. Vantine and Yamanaka Companies', in *Studies in the Decorative Arts*, XV/2 (Spring/Summer 2008)

Yamamoto Yohji, 'Special Contribution', in *Chisō kata yūzen dentō zuanshū: Yuzen gurafuikkusu 1: hana to kusaki hen* (*Chisō stencil-dyed yūzen traditional design collection: Yūzen Graphics 1: Foliage and Flora*), ed. Ogasawara Sae (Tokyo, 2002)

Yamanaka Norio, *The Book of Kimono* (Tokyo, New York, San Francisco, 1982)

Yamanobe Tomoyuki, 'Japanese Kimono in the Meiji Period', in *Dressed in Splendor: Japanese Costume, 1700–1926*, ed. Merrily A. Peebles, exh. cat., Santa Barbara Museum of Art (Santa Barbara, CA, 1987)

Yamanobe Tomoyuki and Fujii Kenzō, *Kyoto Modern Textiles: 1868–1940* (Kyoto, 1996)

Yamanobe Tomoyuki and Ueno Saeko, *Kosode moyō hinagata bon shūsei* (*Compendium of 'Kosode' Pattern Books*), 4 vols (Tokyo, 1974)

Yamanobe Tomoyuki, Tabata Kihachi and Kitamura Tetsurō, *Kosode* (Tokyo, 1963)

Yanagi Sōetsu, 'Sakka no hin to mingeihin' (Works of the Artist and Mingei) [1961], in *Yanagi Sōetsu Zenshū* (Tokyo, 1982), vol. XIV

——, *The Unknown Craftsman: A Japanese Insight into Beauty*, adapted by Bernard Leach (Tokyo, 1973)

——, 'Saido mingei to sakka ni tsuite' (Another Look at the Relationship between Mingei and the Artist), *Mingei*, LXXIV (1959)

——, 'Mingei to kojin sakka' (Mingei and the Individual Craftsperson), *Mingei*, LXXII (1958)

Yanagida Kunio, comp. and ed., *Japanese Manners and Customs in the Meiji Era*, trans. Charles S. Terry (Tokyo, 1957)

Yasuda Jōichi, *Kimono no rekishi* (*History of Kimono*) (Tokyo, 1972)

Yokoya Kenichirō, 'Kimono Zuanchō in Kyoto', in *Zuanchō in Kyoto: Textile Design Books for the Kimono Trade*, exh. cat., Peterson Gallery and Munger Rotunda Green Library, Stanford University (Stanford, CA, 2008)

Yoshioka Sachio, *Nihon no iro jiten* (Dictionary of the Colours of Japan) (Kyoto, 2000)

Young, Louise, 'Marketing the Modern: Department Stores, Consumer Culture, and the New Middle Class in Interwar Japan', *International Labor and Working-class History*, 55 (Spring 1999)

Zielenziger, Michael, *Shutting Out the Sun: How Japan Created its Own Lost Generation* (New York, 2007)

ACKNOWLEDGEMENTS

This book highlights not only extant kimono, but also the constellation of objects related to the production, consumption, and marketing of kimono fashion, such as silk, pattern books and department store posters, to name a few. In order to contextualize these objects, I draw on existing research from diverse areas of study (textiles and art, as well as business, economic and cultural history) and build on foundations laid by scholars from many disciplines whose findings appeared in books, specialist journals and limited edition exhibition catalogues. By incorporating both a specific selection of kimono-related objects from museums, libraries and private collections and the synthesized findings of Japanese and non-Japanese scholars working in varied disciplines related to Japanese clothing and textile history, this book presents a broad perspective on what I call the 'modern kimono fashion system', and its intertwined relationship with other fashion systems.

My hope is that the ideas and information contained within these pages will stimulate the reader to reflect deeply and broadly on what the kimono has meant at various points in its long history and possibly to motivate others to pursue further research, as much about this aspect of Japanese cultural history remains to be uncovered and understood.

As a result of the broad perspective I have taken on the subject and the wide range of material on which I have drawn, the book has been influenced by conversations with colleagues from academia, museums and the field of textile design too numerous to mention individually. Nonetheless, I would be remiss in not listing by name the many people and institutions that were instrumental to my research: the John C. Weber Collection and assistant Lori van Houten; Elizabeth Semmelhack for introducing me to Reaktion Books and my editor there, Vivian Constantinopoulos; Claire Cuccio; Margot Landman; Soyoung Lee; Sara Oka and Darius Homay at the Honolulu Museum of Art; Sharon Takeda at the Los Angeles Country Museum of Art; Janice Katz, the volunteers Jeanne Cohen and Keiko Okuizumi, collections manager Mary Albert, and textile collection manager Ryan Paveza, all of the Art Institute of Chicago; Fujii Kenzō; Keiko Suzuki, Masaaki Kidachi and Takaaki Okamoto at the Art Research Center; Masako Yoshida; Yamakawa Aki of the Kyoto National Museum; Izumi Yōjirō of Chisō; Ueda Aya, for the introduction to her grandfather's collection at the Kyoto Institute of Technology (KIT); Namiki Seishi, the director of KIT; Moriguchi Kunihiko; Izukura Akihiko and the staff at Hinaya; Hirota Hajime and Kawakami Kazuo at Takashimaya Shiryōkan; Hirota Takashi of Kyoto Women's University; Marubeni; Kawakami Shigeki at Kwansei University; Nagasaki Iwao of Kyoritsu Women's University; Murayama Nobuhiko of Musashi University; Sawada Kazuto at the National Museum of Japanese History; Okunishi Michiko and Makoto; the Tanaka Yoku Collection; Akemi Narita; Oyama Yuzuruha at the Tokyo National Museum; Julia Bell, Marcela Gulati, Grace Unemori, Joyce Unemori, Karen Matsushima and Wendy Shiira.

My research was supported by several generous grants. The North East Asia Council of the Association for Asian Studies (with financial assistance from the Japan-United States Friendship Commission) provided funding to study pattern books. The Costume Society of America supported research on the kimono collections at the Honolulu Museum of Art and the Los Angeles County Museum of Art. A Japan Foundation Short-Term Research Grant provided funding for a research trip to Kyoto and Tokyo.

AFTERWORD

This book represents the professional capstone of my wife Terry's all-too-brief life. It reflects the years of expertise accumulated in her work on her PhD dissertation, in researching far-flung kimono collections, and in preparing for lectures and speaking engagements in the United States, Japan and Europe. Terry's professional path to an internationally recognized textile scholar was motivated by her abiding fascination with the significance of objects *to people*. I believe Terry's love of textiles, and clothing in particular, was ultimately rooted in their closeness to people's lives and to the important role clothing plays in the identity and social lives of individuals everywhere. Indeed, Terry's interest in kimono was initially sparked at a young age by viewing one of her grandmother's kimono, and learning of its significance to her grandmother's life as a Japanese immigrant to Hawaii early in the twentieth century. A wedding photograph of Terry's parents, her mother dressed in formal kimono regalia, appears in chapter Six. The central narrative of Terry's book is the evolving role that kimono have played, both as garments and as art, in the lives of the Japanese people, as well as in the conception of 'Japan' by others. As her book demonstrates so vividly, the kimono is indelibly linked to the self-identity and modern social history of an entire nation.

Terry was nearly finished with the manuscript for *Kimono: A Modern History*, when she died on 21 November 2012. Together with Terry's editor at Reaktion, Vivian Constantinopoulos, I took up the remaining work of readying the manuscript for publication. While minor stylistic changes were made and various technical issues were clarified in the editorial process with the help of Terry's many colleagues and dear friends in the fields of art history and textiles, this is Terry's book through and through. Of course, the work of publishing a book – however close to completion – without the author's input on the myriad issues that arise in the final stages of the process inevitably requires that some judgement calls be made. In consultation with others, I have made these decisions to the best of my ability, with an overriding concern for factual accuracy and maintaining Terry's narrative voice. To the extent that shortcomings remain, I take full responsibility and ask for the reader's understanding of the far-from-ideal circumstances under which the book was finished. Many people provided generous and invaluable assistance to me in completing Terry's project. I thank Monika Bincsik, Chris Brady, John Carpenter, Julie Davis, Alice Izumo, Martha Jay, Kentaro Matsubara, Matthew McKelway, Conrad Milhaupt, Joanne Sandstrom, Keiko Suzuki and John Vollmer. Sharon Takeda of the Los Angeles County Museum of Art deserves special thanks; her expertise was crucial in organizing the illustrations and answering queries on the manuscript. My deepest thanks go to Vivian and everyone at Reaktion Books who stuck with this project despite the difficult circumstances.

On the theme of gratitude, the Acknowledgements that appear just prior to this Afterword is based on a draft I found on Terry's computer. I edited the draft slightly and confirmed the accuracy of the names and affiliations she listed. But this was obviously an early draft, and one only thinks of *all* the people who helped in the writing of a book when it is truly finished. I have no doubt that Terry would have added other names to the Acknowledgements as she returned to her draft when the last sentence of the manuscript had been revised to her satisfaction. To all who assisted Terry on this project over the years, I trust that her warmth, compassion, and enthusiasm were ample reward for your generous assistance. On behalf of my son Conrad and Terry's entire family, I extend my heartfelt gratitude to you. Words cannot convey the emotion we feel in holding this book in our hands.

I hope that readers have not only enjoyed and learned from the book, but also taken inspiration from Terry's treatment of her subject, viewing the kimono not simply as an 'object to be worn' or even as an object of art – but through the many stories it tells, and the many lives, including Terry's, which are woven deeply into the remarkable history of this distinctive garment.

Curtis J. Milhaupt

LIST OF ILLUSTRATIONS

1 Cover of *Utsukushii Kimono* (Spring 2003). © Hachette Fujin Gahō. Used with permission.

2 Cover of *Kimono Hime* (April 2003). © Shotensha. Used with permission.

3 Cover of *An An* (May 2009). © Magazine House. Used with permission.

4 Woman's summer kimono (*hitoe*) with design of crickets and cricket cages, late 19th–early 20th century, resist-dyeing, hand painting and silk embroidery on gauze silk ground, 165.1 × 127 cm. The Metropolitan Museum of Art, Gift of Abby Aldrich Rockefeller, 1937 (37.92.13). Image © The Metropolitan Museum of Art.

5 Page with design of cricket cages, from *On-Hiinagata* ('Kosode Pattern Book', 1667), vol. 1, woodblock-printed book, ink on paper, 17.8 × 12.7 cm. The Metropolitan Museum of Art, lent by Paul T. and Betty M. Nomura. Image © The Metropolitan Museum of Art.

6 Page from 'Collection of Shōun's Patterns' (*Shōun moyō shū*), a book of modern kimono designs (1901), polychrome woodblock-printed book, embossing, ink, colour and metallic paint on paper, 39 × 29 cm. The Metropolitan Museum of Art, Thomas J. Watson Library. Image © The Metropolitan Museum of Art.

7 Woman's long-sleeved kimono (*furisode*) with design of hydrangeas and cherry blossoms, late 19th–early 20th century, resist-dyeing and hand painting on satin silk ground, 165.1 × 129.5 cm, The Metropolitan Museum of Art, Purchase, Roy R. and Marie S. Neuberger Foundation Inc. and several members of The Chairman's Council Gifts, 2000 Benefit Fund, and funds from various donors, 2001 (2001.428.51). Image © The Metropolitan Museum of Art.

8 Woman's wedding overrobe (*uchikake*) with design of cartwheels floating amid a stream of cherry blossoms, 1897, resist-dyeing with gold and silver-leaf painting and embroidery on patterned silk, 164.5 × 133 cm. Marubeni Corporation.

9, 10 Garment with small-sleeve openings (*kosode*) with design of shells and sea grasses, early 17th century, silk embroidery and gold leaf imprinting patterned with warp floats on plain-weave silk ground, 153.7 × 124.5 cm. The Metropolitan Museum of Art, Gift of Mr and Mrs Paul T. Nomura, in memory of Mr and Mrs S. Morris Nomura, 1992 (1992.253). Image © The Metropolitan Museum of Art.

11 Utagawa Hiroshige III, 'Cherry Blossom Viewing in Ueno Park' (from the 'Famous Places of Tokyo' series), 1881, triptych of polychrome woodblock prints, ink and colour on paper, 34.9 × 71.4 cm. The Metropolitan Museum of Art, Gift of Lincoln Kirstein, 1959 (JP3259). Image © The Metropolitan Museum of Art.

12 Utagawa Kuniyasu, 'Mirror of High Officials of the Empire' (*Kokoku kōkan kagami*), 1887, triptych of polychrome woodblock prints, ink and colour on paper, 37 × 75 cm. The British Museum (1906, 1220, 0.1839.1-3). Image © Trustees of the British Museum.

13 Woman's long-sleeved kimono (*furisode*) with design of yachts in a landscape setting, 1920s–30s, paste-resist dyeing on silk crepe ground, 158 × 124 cm. Private collection, Tokyo.

14 Woman's kimono with design of pines, plum and bamboo, second quarter of the 20th century, ink and gold, silk embroidery on figured silk ground, 157.5 × 132.1 cm. The Metropolitan Museum of Art, Gift of Sue Cassidy Clark, in memory of Terry Satsuki Milhaupt, 2013 (2013. 510.4). Image © The Metropolitan Museum of Art.

15 Woman's garment with small-sleeve openings (*kosode*) with design of fishing net and characters (warbler, '*uguisu*'), probably 1660s, silk, metallic threads, silk embroidery, tied resist-dyeing (*shibori*), 153.4 × 127.6 cm. The Metropolitan Museum of Art, Purchase, Harris Brisbane Dick Fund, Mary and James G. Wallach Foundation and Parnassus Foundation/Jane and Raphael Bernstein Gifts, and funds from various donors, 2011 (2011.155). Image © The Metropolitan Museum of Art.

16, 17 Farmer's jacket, first half of 20th century, recycled strips of woven cotton for wefts and wisteria for warps, 120.7 × 129.6 cm. John C. Weber Collection. Photo Lori van Houten.

18 Isoda Koryūsai, 'Courtesan Takamura of the Komatsuya with her Two Young Attendants', from the series 'Pattern Book of the Year's First Designs, Fresh as Spring Herbs' (*Hinagata wakana no hatsumoyō*), *c*. 1775, polychrome woodblock print, ink and colour on paper, 38.3 × 25.1 cm. The British Museum (1906, 1220, 0.94). Image © Trustees of the British Museum.

19 Kitagawa Utamaro, 'Suited to Tie-dyed Fabrics Stocked by Matsuzakaya' (*Matsuzakaya shi-ire no shibori muki*), from the series 'Contemporary Beauties in Summer Garments' (*Natsu ishō tōsei bijin*), *c*. 1804–06, polychrome woodblock print, ink and colour on paper, 38.7 × 25.9 cm. Museum of Fine Arts, Boston, William S. and John T. Spaulding Collection (21.6514).

20, 21 Woman's garment with small-sleeve openings (*kosode*) with design of willow tree and Chinese characters, 18th century, paste-resist dyeing and stencil dyeing with silk embroidery and couched gold thread on silk, 152 × 117 cm. John C. Weber Collection. Photo John Bigelow Taylor.

22 Woman's wedding overrobe (*uchikake*) with design of auspicious imagery, early 19th century, shaped-resist dyeing with silk embroidery and couched gold thread on silk, 162 × 130 cm. John C. Weber Collection. Photo John Bigelow Taylor.

23, 24 Woman's summer garment (*hitoe*) with design of cormorant fishing and Tokugawa crest, early 19th century, paste-resist dyeing with silk embroidery and couched gold thread on silk, 179.5 × 121 cm. John C. Weber Collection. Photo John Bigelow Taylor.

25 Woman's summer kimono (*hitoe*) with design of cormorant fishing, second quarter of the 20th century, paste-resist dyeing and hand painting with silk embroidery and supplementary weft lacquered threads on silk, 152 × 129 cm. John C. Weber Collection. Photo John Bigelow Taylor.

37 Yōshū (Toyohara) Chikanobu, sewing of Western clothes for high-ranking ladies (Empress Shōken promoting Western modes of dress), 1887, triptych of polychrome woodblock prints, ink and colour on paper, 36.4 × 75.4 cm. The Metropolitan Museum of Art, Gift of Lincoln Kirstein, 1959 (JP3340). Image © The Metropolitan Museum of Art.

38, 39 Empress Shōken's ceremonial dress, late 19th–early 20th century, roses woven and embroidered with various grades of wrapped gold thread and sequins on silk satin. Daishōji, Kyoto.

40 Nakajima Ishimatsu, 'Likenesses of their Imperial Highnesses' (*Teikoku shison no on-kage*), 1896, colour lithograph, ink and colour with gold on paper, 63.2 × 47.2 cm. The British Museum (1991, 0810, 0.2). Image © Trustees of the British Museum.

41 Woman's long-sleeved kimono (*furisode*) with flowing water and Western autumn flowers and plants design, previously owned by Mieko, second daughter of Prince Takehito Arisugawa, *c.* 1908, paste-resist dyeing on silk, 164 × 103.5 cm. National Museum of Japanese History (H-36-8).

42 Yōshū Chikanobu, 'Illustration of the Ladies' Charity Bazaar at the Rokumeikan' (*Rokumeikan ni oite kifujin jizenkai no zu*), 1887, triptych of polychrome woodblock prints; ink and colour on paper, 37.1 × 72.7 cm. Museum of Fine Arts, Boston, Jean S. and Frederic A. Sharf Collection (2000.495a–c).

43 Yōshū Chikanobu, 'Ceremony of the Issuance of the Constitution', 1889, triptych of polychrome woodblock prints, ink and colour on paper, 36.8 × 75.2 cm. The Metropolitan Museum of Art, Gift of Lincoln Kirstein, 1959 (JP3240). Image © The Metropolitan Museum of Art.

44, 45 Man's informal garment or under-kimono (*nagajuban*) with design of the Thirty-six Immortal Poets, early 20th century, stencilled paste-resist dyeing on silk, 128 × 126 cm. John C. Weber Collection. Photo John Bigelow Taylor.

46 Yōshū Chikanobu, beautiful woman with a towel, calendar print for April 1910 targeted at export market, 1909, polychrome woodblock print, ink and colour on paper, 36.3 × 25.5 cm. Museum of Fine Arts, Boston, Jean S. and Frederic A. Sharf Collection (2000.298).

47 Pouch with design of birds and flowers, 18th century, printed colours and gold on cotton, 6 × 7 cm. The Metropolitan Museum of Art, H. O. Havemeyer Collection, Bequest of Mrs H. O. Haveymeyer, 1929 (29.100.812). Image © The Metropolitan Museum of Art.

48 Girl's under-kimono with designs related to early Meiji period Yokohama, 1870s–80s, paste-resist dyeing on imported wool muslin, 106 × 102 cm. Collection of Michiko and Makoto Okunishi. Photo Artec262/Nakagawa Tadaaki.

49, 50 Woman's summer robe (*katabira*) with design of plovers above sandbars and flowering plants, 18th century, paste-resist dyeing on ramie, 150 × 113 cm. John C. Weber Collection. Photo John Bigelow Taylor.

51 Kimono fabric exhibited at the Paris International Exhibition of 1867 and purchased by the Victoria & Albert Museum (red bamboo and plum blossom design), *c.* 1860–67, stencilled paste-resist dyeing on silk crepe, 1800 × 47 cm. Victoria & Albert Museum (842–1869). Photo © Victoria & Albert Museum, London.

52 Utagawa Yoshitora, imported silk spinning machine at Tsukiji in Tokyo, *c.* 1876, triptych of polychrome woodblock prints, ink and colour on paper, 36.8 × 73 cm. The Metropolitan Museum of Art, Gift of Lincoln Kirstein, 1959 (JP3346). Image © The Metropolitan Museum of Art.

53, 54 Design (*zuan*) for kimono with fans and poem cards, 1902, ink and colour on paper. The back lists 34 different colours that were used in the production. Art Research Center Collection, Ritsumeikan University, Kyoto. Photo Art Research Center, Ritsumeikan University.

55 Masuyama Ryūhō, woman's kimono with 'Evening by the Sumida River' design, *c.* 1919, stencilled paste-resist dyeing (*yūzen*) on silk, 153.5 cm. Tokyo National Museum (I-). Photo Tokyo National Museum Image Archives.

56, 57 Woman's kimono with design of weeping cherry trees, bundles of brushwood, and stylized snow roundels, late 19th century, minute stencil-dyed patterns of pine needles and chrysanthemums in white with fine paste-resist dyed and embroidered designs against a black, plain-weave silk ground, 153.5 × 118 cm. Private collection, Tokyo.

58, 59 Woman's kimono with design of castles and maple leaves, 1930s, stencilled paste-resist dyeing on raw silk, 143 × 124 cm. Collection of Michiko and Makoto Okunishi. Photo Artec262/Nakagawa Tadaaki.

60 Woman's under-kimono (*juban*) with design of modern paintings, late 1920s–early 1930s, stencilled paste-resist dyeing on wool muslin, 125 × 120 cm. Tanaka Yoku Collection. Photo Artec262/Nakagawa Tadaaki.

61, 62 Woman's long-sleeved kimono (*furisode*) with design of phoenixes amid paulownia and roses, first quarter of 20th century, paste-resist dyeing on silk crepe ground, 151.5 × 121 cm. Private collection, Tokyo.

63 Length of fabric with design of trains and bridges, *c.* 1918, stencilled paste-resist dyeing on silk crepe, 272 × 39 cm. Collection of Michiko and Makoto Okunishi. Photo Artec262/Nakagawa Tadaaki.

64 Length of fabric with design of steam train, *c.* 1870s, thread-resist dyeing (*Kurume gasuri*) on cotton ground, 36 × 33.5 cm. Collection of Michiko and Makoto Okunishi. Photo Artec262/Nakagawa Tadaaki.

65 Utagawa Hiroshige III, scenic view of Tokyo enlightenment, the Ginza from Kyōbashi, December 1874, triptych of polychrome woodblock prints, ink and colour on paper, 37 × 75 cm. Kanagawa Prefectural Museum of Cultural History.

66 Kitagawa Utamaro, 'Suited to Crepes Stocked by Echigoya', from the series 'Contemporary Beauties in Summer Garments' (*Natsu ishō tōsei bijin*), *c.* 1804–06, polychrome woodblock print, ink and colour on paper, 39 × 26 cm. Museum of Fine Arts, Boston, William S. and John T. Spaulding Collection (21.6515).

67 Hashiguchi Goyō, Mitsukoshi department store poster, 1911, colour lithograph. Mitsukoshi Isetan Holdings.

68 Sugiura Hisui, Mitsukoshi department store poster, 1914, colour lithograph. Mitsukoshi Isetan Holdings.

69 Pamphlet for Matsuzakaya department store, March 1937, 37 × 52 cm. Collection of Michiko and Makoto Okunishi. Photo Artec262/Nakagawa Tadaaki.

70 Poster for Ashikaga Honmeisen with actress Tanaka Kinuyō as model, 1932, colour lithograph, 54.4 × 22.8 cm. The Kyoto Institute of Technology Museum and Archives (AN.5377–08).

71 Mitsukoshi department store poster with Shinbashi geisha dressed in the 'Genroku style', 1907, ink and colour on paper. Mitsukoshi Isetan Holdings.

72 Sugiura Hisui, 'New Game of Fashions for the Family' (*Shin-an katei ishō awase*), supplement to *Mitsukoshi Times* magazine, VIII/1 (January 1910), 53 × 40 cm. Princeton University Library.

73 Sugiura Hisui, poster for the Shinjuku branch of the Mitsukoshi department store, 1925, colour lithograph. Mitsukoshi Isetan Holdings.

74 Woman's kimono with design of open books and spools of thread, first half of the 20th century, stencilled paste-resist dyeing and silver threads on silk, 144.8 × 119.4 cm. John C. Weber Collection. Photo John Bigelow Taylor.

75 Kon Wajirō, 'Index' of Japanese- and Western-style fashion, *1925 Survey of Customs in Tokyo Ginza in Early Summer*, 1925, published in *Fujin Kōron* magazine. Kōgakuin University Library.

76 Watanabe Ikuharu, 'Comparison of Shōwa Beauties: December, Snow, Sky' (*Shōwa bijo sugata kurabe-harumachizuki, yukizora*), *c.* 1920s–30s, polychrome woodblock print, ink and colour on paper, 42.0 × 26.9 cm. Scholten Japanese Art, New York. Photo Scholten Japanese Art, New York.

77 Utagawa Hiroshige, 'View of Suruga-chō' (showing the Echigoya fabric and kimono shop), from 'Series of Famous Places in the Eastern Capital', *c.* 1844, polychrome woodblock print, ink and colour on paper, 24.3 × 36.8 cm. The Metropolitan Museum of Art, Purchase, Joseph Pulitzer Bequest, 1918 (JP601). Photo © The Metropolitan Museum of Art.

78 Kitano Tsunetomi, poster for Ashikaga Honmeisen, 1927, colour lithograph, 101 × 60.4 cm. The Kyoto Institute of Technology Museum and Archives (AN.2694-10).

79 Okada Saburōsuke, Chiyoko, the wife of Mitsukoshi's director, in a poster for the Mitsukoshi department store, 1909, ink and colour on paper, 75.1 × 61.4 cm. The Kyoto Institute of Technology Museum and Archives (AN.5203–01).

80 Actress Mizutani Yaeko modelling a Chichibu Meisen kimono, 1930s, postcard, 14 × 9 cm. Collection of Saburou Ishiguro. Photo Artec262/Nakagawa Tadaaki.

81 Utagawa Hiroshige, 'Narumi: Shop with Famous Arimatsu Tie-dyed Cloth' (*Narumi meisan Arimatsu shibori mise*), from the series 'Famous Sights of the Fifty-three Stations' (*Gojūsan tsugi meisho zue*), 1855, polychrome woodblock print, ink and colour on paper, 34.9 × 23.5 cm. The Metropolitan Museum of Art, Joseph Pulitzer Bequest, 1918 (JP637). Image © The Metropolitan Museum of Art.

82 Itō Shinsui, from the series 'Twelve Figures of Modern Beauties: Woman from Oshima Island' (*Shin bijin jūni sugata: shima no onna*), 1922, polychrome woodblock print, ink and colour on paper, 43 × 26 cm. Scholten Japanese Art, New York. Photo Scholten Japanese Art, New York.

83 'Custom of Oshima Peoples' [*sic*], 1930s, postcard, 13.5 × 8.8 cm. Collection of Saburou Ishiguro. Photo Artec262/Nakagawa Tadaaki.

84 Design no. 21 with plovers over waves, page from pattern book *Shin hinagata chitose sode* (1800), woodblock-printed book, ink on paper. From *Kosode moyō hinagatabon shūsei* (reproduction), ed. Saeko Ueno, Tomoyuki Yamanobe, Gakushū kenkyū sha (1974), vol. IV.

85, 86 Kimono with design of plovers over waves, late 19th–early 20th century, 158 cm. Tokyo National Museum (I-). Photo Tokyo National Museum Image Archives.

87, 88, 89 Woman's three-piece kimono ensemble with design of plovers over waves, early 20th century, woven with supplementary gold metallic threads, hand painted with dyes, inks and pigment, brushed shaded dyeing, silk embroidery with seed pearls and coral beads on silk crepe, 161.9 × 159.4 cm. Gift of Mr and Mrs Carl Archibald Bilicke, Los Angeles County Museum of Art (M.79.27.1-). Digital Image © 2011 Museum Associates/LACMA. Licensed by Art Resource, NY.

90 'The fragrance of Waseda' (*Waseda no kaori*), design with orchids, postcard advertisement for the Mitsukoshi store, inscribed 1909, colour lithograph, 8.8 × 13.8 cm. Museum of Fine Arts, Boston, Leonard A. Lauder Collection of Japanese Postcards (2002.10994).

91, 92 Woman's summer kimono (*hitoe*) with design of plovers in flight over stylized waves, 1900–1925, silk embroidery and metallic thread on silk ground, 154.9 × 127 cm. The Metropolitan Museum of Art, Gift of Atsuko Irie, in honor of Suga Irie, 1998 (1998.487.5). Image © The Metropolitan Museum of Art.

93 Postcard of Shōjirō Nomura, manufacturer of silk embroideries, no. 25 Shinmonzen, Kyoto, late 19th to early 20th century, collotype, 8.8 × 13.8 cm. Museum of Fine Arts, Boston, Leonard A. Lauder Collection of Japanese Postcards (2002.6354).

94 Frontispiece to Ken'ichi Kawakatsu, *Kimono: Japanese Dress* (1936), published by the Board of Tourist Industry, Japanese Government Railways.

95 Woman's over-robe (*uchikake*) with design of pine, plum and bamboo (purportedly given to a member of Commodore Perry's crew on the second expedition to Japan, *c.* 1854), *c.* 1825–50, gold-wrapped threads couched on silk satin. Gift of Dr and Mrs W. Glenn Marders, 1981. Photo University of Hawaii Historic Costume Collection.

96 James Tissot, *La Japonaise au bain*, 1864, oil on canvas, 208 × 124 cm. Musée des Beaux-Arts, Dijon. Photo François Jay.

97 Pierre-Auguste Renoir, *Madame Hériot*, 1882, oil on canvas, 65 × 54 cm. Hamburger Kunsthalle, Hamburg, Germany. Photo Bildarch Preussischer Kulturbesitz/Art Resource, NY.

98 Utagawa Kunisada III, fold-out frontispiece from 'Japanese Biography of Mr Grant' (*Gurandoshi den Yamato bunsho*) – visit of General Ulysses Grant and his wife to Japan in

1879 (July 1879), polychrome woodblock-printed book, ink and colour on paper. Property of Mary Griggs Burke. Photo Otto E. Nelson.

99 Alfredo Müller, poster of Sada Yacco, 1899–1900, colour lithograph, 219 × 76.5 cm. The Kyoto Institute of Technology Museum and Archives (AN.2679-31).

100 Buddhist vestment (*kesa*) with design of maple leaves and fans, 1750–1850, paste-resist dyeing, silk and metallic thread embroidery and shaped-resist dyeing on crepe silk, 108.6 × 170.8 cm. The Metropolitan Museum of Art, Gift of Edward G. Kennedy, 1932 (32.65.25). Image © The Metropolitan Museum of Art.

101 Buddhist vestment (*kesa*) with design of autumn grasses and butterflies (made from a Noh costume), 1750–1850, silk and metallic threads in supplementary weft-patterned twill-weave silk, 118.1 × 202.6 cm. The Metropolitan Museum of Art, Joseph Pulitzer Bequest, 1919 (19.93.10). Image © The Metropolitan Museum of Art.

102 Interior of the Buddha Room, the Eyrie, Seal Harbor, Maine (the Rockefeller summer home in Mount Desert Island), 1960, colour photograph. Rockefeller Archive Center. Photo Ezra Stoller © Esto. All rights reserved.

103, 104 Takashimaya department store, woman's kimono gown for the Western market with design of clouds silhouetted with cherry blossoms, and detail of label, late 19th century, paste-resist stencil-dyeing on silk crepe, 147.3 × 146.1 cm. Gift of Mrs Hamish McLaurin, Los Angeles County Museum of Art (47.45.2b). Digital image © 2011 Museum Associates/ LACMA. Licensed by Art Resource, NY.

105 Exterior view of the Takashimaya store in Kyoto, 1893, photograph. Courtesy of Takashimaya Shiryōkan (Takashimaya Archives).

106 Kimono design for foreigners (*Gaijin muke kimono zuan*), 1909–16, underdrawing, ink and colour on paper. Courtesy of Takashimaya Shiryōkan (Takashimaya Archives).

107 Woman's kimono gown and sash for the Western market with design of maple leaves, early 20th century, silk embroidery and knotted silk fringe on plain weave silk, 135.9 × 144.8 cm. Purchased with funds provided by Suzanne A. Saperstein and Michael and Ellen Michelson, with additional funding from the Costume Council, the Edgerton Foundation, Gail and Gerald Oppenheimer, Maureen H. Shapiro, Grace Tsao and Lenore and Richard Wayne, Los Angeles County Museum of Art (M.2007.211.783a-b). Digital Image © 2011 Museum Associates/LACMA. Licensed by Art Resource, NY.

108 Kobayashi Gyokunen, 'Pattern Sketches' (*Moyō-e*), 1901, polychrome woodblock-printed book, ink and colour on paper. Gift of Martin A. Ryerson, The Art Institute of Chicago (15534). Photo © The Art Institute of Chicago.

109 Illustration (plate 20) from Thomas W. Cutler, *A Grammar of Japanese Ornament and Design* (1880), published by W. Batsford, London.

110, 111 Woman's summer garment (*hitoe*) with design of insect procession, 1850–1900, paste-resist dyeing and embroidery on silk, 153 × 124 cm. Marubeni Corporation.

112 Woman's kimono with design of swirling water, bamboo and birds, 1850–1900, paste-resist dyeing and embroidery in silk and metallic thread on silk, purchased by the Victoria &

127, 128 Obi with design of warplanes and bombs, 1930s, silk with metallic threads, 330.5 × 31 cm. Tanaka Yoku Collection. Photo courtesy of Bard Graduate Center: Decorative Arts, Design History, Material Culture. Photo Artec262/Nakagawa Tadaaki.

129 Adult's under-kimono (*nagajuban*) with design of the Great Wall and aeroplanes, *c.* 1941, printed on fabric of cotton mixed with bark and wood pulp fibre known as *sufu*, 126 × 114.5 cm. Collection of Michiko and Makoto Okunishi. Photo courtesy of Bard Graduate Center: Decorative Arts, Design History, Material Culture. Photo Artec262/Nakagawa Tadaaki.

130 Invitation to special clients of Matsuzakaya Department Store, March 1940, gold, silver foil and pigments on paper, 26.5 × 19 cm. Collection of Michiko and Makoto Okunishi. Photo Artec262/Nakagawa Tadaaki.

131 Imao Kazuo, woman's long-sleeved kimono (*furisode*) with design of boats in a Western-style landscape, 1936, pigment infused resist-dyeing and embroidery on silk, 174 × 128 cm. Marubeni Corporation.

132 Woman's kimono (*tomesode*) with design of stylized pine trees and gold mist, first half of the 20th century, paste-resist dyeing and painted gold accents on silk crepe ground, 165.1 × 121.9 cm. The Metropolitan Museum of Art, Gift of Sue Cassidy Clark in memory of Terry Satsuki Milhaupt, 2013 (2013.510.6). Image © The Metropolitan Museum of Art.

133, 134 Sakai Hōitsu, woman's garment with small-sleeve opening (*kosode*) with design of flowering plum tree and detail of Sakai Hōitsu's seal, early 19th century, painting in ink and pigments on silk, 149 × 115 cm. National Museum of Japanese History.

135 Tsuda Seifū, design of butterflies and stylized flowers, illustrated in *Kamonfu* (1900), published by Honda Ichijirō (Kyoto), polychrome woodblock-printed book, ink, colour and silver paint on paper, 18.5 × 25.5 cm. Lisa Pevtzow Collection, Chicago.

136 Design (*zuan*) for kimono with flowers and butterflies amid clouds, awarded first prize in Mie prefecture, 1909, underdrawing, ink and colour on paper. Art Research Center Collection, Ritsumeikan University, Kyoto. Photo Art Research Center, Ritsumeikan University.

137 Tabata Kihachi, woman's long-sleeved kimono (*furisode*) of 'Cranes in a Pine Grove', May 1955, paste-resist dyeing and silk embroidery on silk, 169 × 132 cm. Tabata Kohei.

138 Tabata Kihachi, 'Cranes in a Pine Grove' design for woman's long-sleeved kimono (*furisode*), 1954, underdrawing, ink and colour on paper, 68.6 × 65.5 cm. Tabata Kohei.

139 Serizawa Keisuke, length of fabric with design of Japanese *iroha* syllabary, *c.* 1960s, stencil dyeing on raw silk, 65.5 × 35 cm. John C. Weber Collection. Photo John Bigelow Taylor.

140 'Kimono suits even foreigners quite well', double-page spread in *Kimono dokuhon* magazine (December 1952), ed. Uno Chiyo, published by 'Style'.

141 Itchiku Kubota, *Symphony of Light*, displayed in 2009 at the Canton Museum of Art, Ohio, for the *Kimono As Art: The Landscape of Itchiku Kubota* exhibition. Itchiku Tsujigahana Co., Ltd.

INDEX